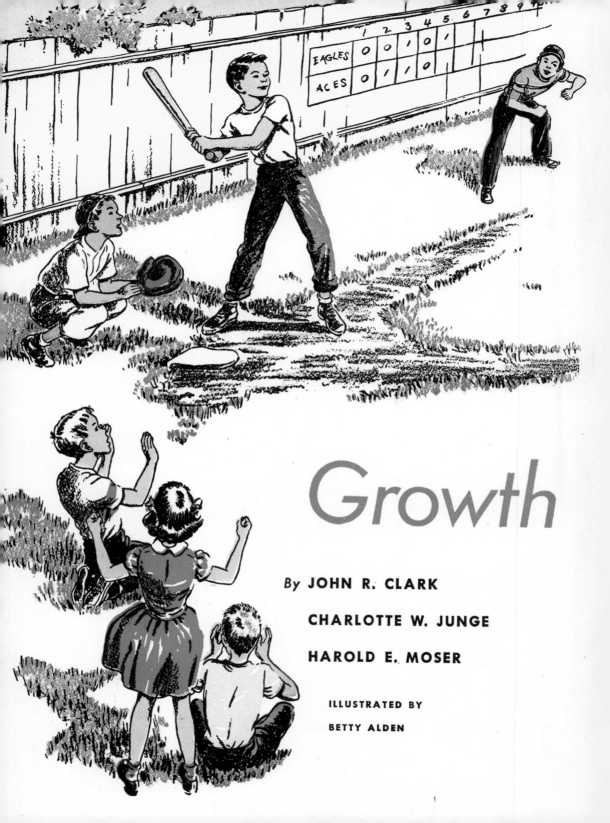

Growth

By **JOHN R. CLARK**

CHARLOTTE W. JUNGE

HAROLD E. MOSER

ILLUSTRATED BY

BETTY ALDEN

in Arithmetic

GRADE FOUR

World Book Company

YONKERS · ON · HUDSON · NEW YORK

Contents

UNIT	UNIT TOPICS	PAGE

Using arithmetic
Review and extension
of time telling

UNIT
1

Thinking about time

1. Look at the picture. When is the Green County Fair this year?

2. Children's Day at the fair is on what day of September?

3. At what time do the fair-grounds open? What two letters tell that they open *in the morning?*

4. At what time is each special event for Children's Day?

5. Show how a toy clock looks when it is time for each event.

6. What two letters tell which events are *in the afternoon?*

Twelve o'clock at night is called *midnight.* Twelve o'clock in the day is called *noon.*
A.M. means before noon.
P.M. means after noon.

7. What are you usually doing at 2:15 A.M.?

Tell some things you might do at: 7:30 A.M. 1:30 A.M.
        7:30 P.M. 1:30 P.M.

8. Bring schedules of radio and television programs to school.

Show how the toy clock looks when it is time to tune in on your favorite programs.

9. Bring a bus schedule and a train timetable to school. Learn how to use them.

10. Do you have a program for your classes in school?

At what time does arithmetic class begin? lunch period?

11. When does your school open in the morning? close for the day?

Time telling

1. Move the hands of a toy clock to show 1 o'clock; 2 o'clock; and so on up to 12 o'clock.

2. Make your clock say half past one; half past two; and so on up to half past twelve.

3. Make your clock say quarter after one; quarter after two; and so on.

4. Make the clock say quarter of one; quarter of two; and so on.

5. Tell what time it is for every five minutes from three o'clock until four o'clock. Show how the clock looks at each of these times.

6. Make your clock say:

4:10	6:30	6:35	6:40	6:45
6:50	6:55	7:00	3:15	7:05
7:10	7:15	7:20	7:25	7:30

7. Make your clock say:

3:30	4:45	5:35	7:40	1:50
8:00	5:50	2:55	2:10	8:05
3:10	4:35	5:55	7:45	8:50

Which clock below (A, B, C, or D) shows each of these times?

8. Half past nine
9. Nine fifteen
10. 10 minutes of 10
11. Nine thirty-five

12. Nine fifty
13. Nine thirty
14. Quarter past nine
15. 25 minutes of 10

16. 9:30
17. 9:50
18. 9:15
19. 9:35

  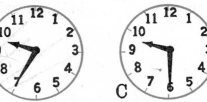 

A B C D

20. Read the time shown by each of the clocks above in as many different ways as you can.

21. The 8:30 bus did not come until 8:40 this morning. It was _?_ minutes late.

22. The school bell rang at 8:55 instead of at 9:00. It rang _?_ minutes early.

23. The bus leaves Market St. at 8:30 A.M. It arrives at Hillside Park at 8:45. It takes the bus _?_ minutes to make the trip.

Time-telling problems

Use a toy clock to help you find the answers to these time-telling problems. You will not need a pencil.

1. Barbara was going next door to Ellen's house to play. Barbara's mother said, "You may stay an hour."

Barbara looked at the clock. It was 20 minutes of 4. She could stay until _?_ minutes of _?_ .

2. A bus for Wilton leaves the town square every 20 minutes.

The last bus left at 10 minutes after 2. The next leaves at _?_ past _?_ .

3. Alice began to practice her music lesson at 20 minutes after 4. She must practice for a half hour.

She will finish practicing at _?_ minutes of _?_ .

4. Jenny is baking biscuits. She put them in the oven at 20 minutes of 6. They should bake for 15 minutes. When should she take them out of the oven?

5. Marie and her father went to the station to take the 9:10 train to Chester.

A trainman told them the train would be 15 minutes late. That meant the train would not leave until _?_ minutes after _?_ .

6. At the bus station Ellen asked, "When does the next bus leave for Westfield?" The ticket agent said, "At one twenty."

Ellen looked at the clock. It was ten minutes after one. How long did she have to wait?

7. Andrew went to see Uncle Bill about making a bow and arrow. Uncle Bill said, "I'm very busy now, Andrew. Come back in fifteen minutes."

Andrew looked at the clock. It was 20 minutes after 3. At what time should he have gone back to talk with Uncle Bill?

8. Miss Beck's class swims in the school pool from 3:45 P.M. to 4:15 P.M. every Wednesday. How long is swimming class?

9. Paul said, "Band practice will be over at 4:45. It takes me 10 minutes to walk home. I'll be home at _?_ minutes of _?_ ."

10. George heard a radio announcer say, "The time is now eight twenty." George's watch read quarter after 8. Was his watch fast or slow? How much?

3

1. How long will Joe have to wait for the store to open?

2. At 5 o'clock the long hand (minute hand) points to 12. What time will it be the next time the minute hand points to 12?

3. How long does it take the long hand to go from 12 around to 12?

4. Use a clock to prove there are 60 minutes in an hour. Count the minute marks by 5's.

5. From 5 o'clock to 6 o'clock is how many hours? minutes?

6. How many hours does it take the short hand (hour hand) to go from 5 around to 5? Count on the clock if you need to: From 5 to 6 is 1 hour, and so on.

7. How many hours are there between 5 A.M. today and 5 P.M. today? between 5 A.M. today and 5 A.M. tomorrow?

8. Joe says there are 24 hours from any time today to that same time tomorrow. Is he right?

This example teaches that there are *24 hours in a day.*

9. Watch a clock while someone takes 60 steps. Does it take him about a minute? If so, he takes about *one second* to make each step.

10. Tell a short way of writing second; minute; hour; day.

11. How long does it take you to go to school each morning?

12. What time-telling problems have you had at home?

> LEARN
> THIS

60 seconds (sec.) = 1 minute (min.)
60 minutes (min.) = 1 hour (hr.)
24 hours (hr.) = 1 day (da.)

4

Picturing numbers

The pictures below show many facts about numbers. Explain how the box of eggs teaches the following facts:

1. 4 and 4 and 4 are 12
2. 3 and 3 and 3 and 3 are 12
3. 8 and 4 are 12
4. 4 and 8 are 12
5. 6 and 6 are 12
6. 9 and 3 are 12
7. 3 and 9 are 12
8. 3 from 12 is 9
9. 6 from 12 is 6
10. 9 from 12 is 3

11. 3 fours are 12
12. 4 threes are 12
13. In 12 there are 3 fours
14. In 12 there are 4 threes
15. $\frac{1}{3}$ of 12 is 4
16. Half of 12 is 6
17. $\frac{1}{4}$ of 12 is 3
18. 2 sixes are 12
19. 6 twos are 12
20. In 12 there are 2 sixes

21. What number facts can you see in each of the other pictures below?

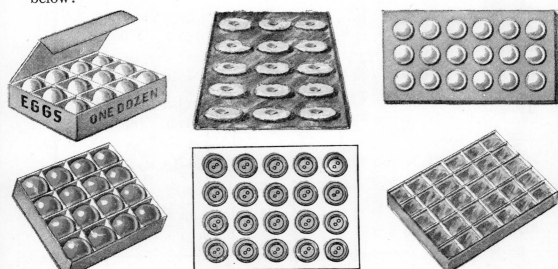

Draw a picture to show that:

22. $\frac{1}{3}$ of 15 = 5, and in 15 there are 5 threes.

23. $\frac{1}{4}$ of 8 = 2, and in 8 there are 4 twos.

Thinking about numbers

1. Explain Ray's thinking. ⟶

   $10 + 7 = 17$
   so
   $9 + 7 = 16$

2. $10 + 8 = 18$, so $9 + 8 = $ _?_
3. $10 + 5 = 15$, so $9 + 5 = $ _?_
4. $10 + 3 = 13$, so $9 + 3 = $ _?_
5. $10 + 6 = 16$, so $9 + 6 = $ _?_
6. $10 + 4 = 14$, so $9 + 4 = $ _?_

7. $10 + 9 = 19$, so $9 + 9 = $ _?_
8. Make up a rule that Exs. 2 to 7 teach you. Illustrate.

---

9. $6 + 4 = 10$, so $4 + 6 = $ _?_
10. $9 + 8 = 17$, so $8 + 9 = $ _?_
11. $5 + 8 = 13$, so $8 + 5 = $ _?_
12. $9 + 7 = 16$, so $7 + 9 = $ _?_

13. $4 + 9 = 13$, so $9 + 4 = $ _?_
14. $6 + 8 = 14$, so $8 + 6 = $ _?_
15. Make up a rule that Exs. 9 to 14 teach you. Illustrate.

---

16. $9 + 8 = 17$, so $17 - 9 = $ _?_
17. $6 + 9 = 15$, so $15 - 9 = $ _?_
18. $7 + 5 = 12$, so $12 - 5 = $ _?_
19. $8 + 8 = 16$, so $16 - 8 = $ _?_

20. $6 + 7 = 13$, so $13 - 6 = $ _?_
21. $9 + 5 = 14$, so $14 - 5 = $ _?_
22. Make up a rule that Exs. 16 to 21 teach you. Illustrate.

---

23. $8 + 8 = 16$, so two 8's are _?_
24. $7 + 7 = 14$, so two 7's are _?_
25. $6 + 6 = 12$, so two 6's are _?_

26. $9 + 9 = 18$, so two 9's are _?_
27. Make up a rule that Exs. 23 to 26 teach you. Illustrate.

---

28. $3 \times 8 = 24$, so $8 \times 3 = $ _?_
29. $6 \times 4 = 24$, so $4 \times 6 = $ _?_
30. $4 \times 7 = 28$, so $7 \times 4 = $ _?_
31. $9 \times 5 = 45$, so $5 \times 9 = $ _?_

32. $6 \times 3 = 18$, so $3 \times 6 = $ _?_
33. $9 \times 3 = 27$, so $3 \times 9 = $ _?_
34. Make up a rule that Exs. 28 to 33 teach you. Illustrate.

---

35. $4 + 4 + 4 + 4 + 4 = 20$ shows that _?_ fours are _?_.
36. $8 + 8 + 8 = 24$ shows that _?_ eights are _?_.
37. $7 + 7 + 7 = 21$ shows that _?_ sevens are _?_.
38. $5 + 5 + 5 + 5 + 5 = 25$ shows that _?_ fives are _?_.

Thinking about tens

1. Count by 10's from 10 to 300.

2. How many dimes does it take to make $1.00? $1.20? $2.00?

3. How many 10's does it take to make 100? 120? 200?

4. $13¢$ = ___?___ dime and ___?___ cents
   13 = ___?___ ten and ___?___ ones

5. $35¢$ = ___?___ dimes and ___?___ cents
   35 = ___?___ tens and ___?___ ones

6. 1 dime and 7 cents = ___?___ cents
   1 ten and 7 ones = ___?___ ones

7. 14 dimes = ___?___ dollar and ___?___ dimes
   14 tens = ___?___ hundred and ___?___ tens

8. 27 dimes = ___?___ dollars and ___?___ dimes
   27 tens = ___?___ hundreds and ___?___ tens

9. _1_ dollar and _6_ dimes = ___?___ dimes
   _1_ hundred and _6_ tens = ___?___ tens

10. $3 + 2 = 5$	3 tens + 2 tens = ___?___ tens	$30 + 20 =$ ___?___
11. $4 + 3 = 7$	4 tens + 3 tens = ___?___ tens	$40 + 30 =$ ___?___
12. $6 + 4 = 10$	6 tens + 4 tens = ___?___ tens	$60 + 40 =$ ___?___
13. $6 + 6 = 12$	6 tens + 6 tens = ___?___ tens	$60 + 60 =$ ___?___
14. $6 + 7 = 13$	6 tens + 7 tens = ___?___ tens	$60 + 70 =$ ___?___
15. $9 + 5 = 14$	9 tens + 5 tens = ___?___ tens	$90 + 50 =$ ___?___
16. $8 + 6 = 14$	8 tens + 6 tens = ___?___ tens	$80 + 60 =$ ___?___
17. $7 + 8 = 15$	7 tens + 8 tens = ___?___ tens	$70 + 80 =$ ___?___

18. Make up a rule that Exs. 10 to 17 teach you. Illustrate.

19. $7 - 4 = 3$	7 tens − 4 tens = ___?___ tens	$70 - 40 =$ ___?___
20. $9 - 3 = 6$	9 tens − 3 tens = ___?___ tens	$90 - 30 =$ ___?___
21. $13 - 6 = 7$	13 tens − 6 tens = ___?___ tens	$130 - 60 =$ ___?___
22. $17 - 9 = 8$	17 tens − 9 tens = ___?___ tens	$170 - 90 =$ ___?___
23. $15 - 6 = 9$	15 tens − 6 tens = ___?___ tens	$150 - 60 =$ ___?___

24. Make up a rule that Exs. 19 to 23 teach you. Illustrate.

Magic numbers

1. Jack and his friends are watching a television show called "Magic Numbers."

The magician is showing them a magic square that is partly filled in. They are to copy it and fill in the missing numbers.

When they add the numbers in each row, in each column, and along each arrow, they should get 15. See if you can do it.

In the finished square each number from 1 to 9 is used only once.

These number riddles were on the show. Try to answer all of them.

2. If you take half of me, you have 4. What number am I?

3. If you put 9 more with me, you have 18. What number am I?

4. If you put 9 more with me, you have 9. What number am I?

5. If you take 4 away from me, you have 8 left. What number am I?

6. If you divide me into 3 equal parts, there are 2 in each part. What number am I?

7. If you divide me into 4 equal parts, you have none in each part. What number am I?

8. I am the largest number you can write with 2 figures. What number am I?

9. I am the smallest number you can write with 3 figures. What number am I?

Making sure of addition
Review of meaning, facts,
adding by endings, column
additions

UNIT
3

Using addition

Paul and Tom went fishing. Paul caught 3 fish. Tom caught 4 fish.

▶ How many fish did *both* boys catch?

▶ How many fish did the boys catch *all together?*

▶ How many fish did they catch *in all?*

▶ How many fish did the *two* boys catch?

▶ What was the *total* number of fish they caught?

To find the answer to each question above, you put 3 fish and 4 fish together. You *add* 3 and 4. You do an *addition* example.

One of these problems ***cannot*** *be done by addition. Which one is it? Tell all the answers.*

1. Ned bought two 5-cent tops. How much did he spend for both?

2. Burt ate 6 cookies. David ate 7 cookies. How many cookies did the two boys eat?

3. Janet got 9 votes for president of her club. Molly got 10 votes. How many votes did they get in all?

4. Nancy paid 20¢ for a doll. She paid 30¢ for a ball. How much did she pay all together for the toys?

5. Mark made 5 airplanes. Dick made 4 airplanes. How many airplanes did the two boys make in all?

6. Sam caught 7 fish. Dan caught 3 fish. How many more fish did Sam catch than Dan?

7. Tell the total number of fish Sam and Dan caught (Ex. 6).

9

Addition helps

1. The answer to an addition example is called the *sum*. The sum of 13 and 5 is __?__.

$$\begin{array}{r} 13 \\ + 5 \\ \hline 18 \end{array}$$

2. $9 + 3 = 12$ is read "9 plus 3 equals __?__."

You remember the **+** sign in addition. It is called the *plus sign*. It tells you to __?__.

The sign $=$ is called the *equal sign*. What does it mean?

3. Tell the missing numbers:

The sum of 4 and 8 is __?__.

7 plus 9 is __?__.

The sum of 7 and 4 equals the sum of 9 and __?__.

14 is the sum of 7 and __?__.

4. How many different answers can you find for these examples?

10 is the sum of __?__ and __?__.

12 is the sum of __?__ and __?__.

13 is the sum of __?__ and __?__.

Here are some hints that help in learning addition facts:

5. You know that $8 + 7 = 15$, so you know that $7 + 8 = $ __?__.

6. What other facts does each of these facts teach you?

$3 + 4 = 7$ $5 + 9 = 14$

$8 + 6 = 14$ $8 + 9 = 17$

7. $6 + 6 = 12$, so $6 + 7 = $ __?__

$6 + 6 = 12$, so $6 + 5 = $ __?__

$4 + 4 = 8$, so $4 + 5 = $ __?__

8. What other facts can you learn from each of these?

$5 + 5 = 10$ $7 + 7 = 14$ $8 + 8 = 16$

9. Counting from 1 to 10 teaches you what addition facts?

10. Counting by 2's to 10 teaches you what addition facts?

11. Finish this counting: 1, 3, 5, __?__, __?__, 11. What addition facts does it teach you?

12. When you find the sum of a number and zero, is the sum the same as the number?

Make up a rule about adding zero to a number. Illustrate.

13. $7 + 10 = 17$, so $7 + 9 = $ __?__

$8 + 10 = 18$, so $8 + 9 = $ __?__

$6 + 10 = 16$, so $6 + 9 = $ __?__

$5 + 10 = 15$, so $5 + 9 = $ __?__

Make up a rule about adding 9 to any number from 1 to 9.

Joe said, "When I add 9 to a number, I just add 10, then back up 1." Explain what he meant.

14. Can you give the class any other hints that help in learning the facts on the next page?

Test on addition facts

Say the answers to these addition facts. Then try to write the answers on folded paper in 5 min. See page 305.

Make and study Help-Yourself Cards for any facts you do not know. See pages 305–306. Practice taking the test until you can write every answer in 5 minutes.

1. 2 2	1 7	5 4	1 8	1 1	5 5	1 3	2 1
2. 1 5	4 3	3 2	2 8	6 1	3 1	4 4	2 5
3. 7 1	4 1	9 1	6 4	4 5	2 4	1 4	4 6
4. 3 6	6 2	8 1	1 9	7 2	5 1	5 3	1 2
5. 5 2	2 7	7 3	3 5	2 3	3 4	2 6	3 7
6. 8 8	9 2	8 3	6 6	2 9	8 7	9 9	7 6
7. 9 8	9 3	7 7	6 5	3 8	3 9	8 4	4 8
8. 9 4	6 7	9 5	4 9	7 5	4 7	8 6	8 9
9. 8 5	9 6	7 8	5 7	6 9	6 8	9 7	5 8
10. 3 3	8 2	4 2	6 3	7 4	5 6	5 9	7 9

1	2	3	4	5	6	7	8	9	10
11	12	13	14	15	16	17	18	19	20
21	22	23	24	25	26	27	28	29	30
31	32	33	34	35	36	37	38	39	40
41	42	43	44	45	46	47	48	49	50

Using key facts in addition

As you do Exs. 1–3, point to 7 on the number chart. Then point to 17; to 27; to 37; to 47.

1. $7 + 2$ **2.** $7 + 3$ **3.** $7 + 4$
$17 + 2$ $17 + 3$ $17 + 4$
$27 + 2$ $27 + 3$ $27 + 4$
$37 + 2$ $37 + 3$ $37 + 4$
$47 + 2$ $47 + 3$ $47 + 4$

Find these sums. The chart will help you.

4. $15 + 3$ **5.** $3 + 4$ **6.** $7 + 6$
$15 + 4$ $13 + 4$ $17 + 6$
$15 + 5$ $23 + 4$ $27 + 6$
$15 + 6$ $33 + 4$ $37 + 6$
$15 + 7$ $43 + 4$

7. When Jane finds the sum of 27 and 6, she says her *key fact* is $7 + 6$. What does she mean?

Tell the key fact in each of these additions. Then add.

8.

16	27	33	44	28
7	5	6	8	3

9.

6	9	9	7	8
7	6	8	8	5
4	3	6	6	7

10.

9	5	6	5	7
3	7	8	9	7
6	8	8	7	7

11. Find the cost of a 25-cent game and an 8-cent balloon.

12. Find the cost of a 26-cent toy and a 6-cent candy bar.

13. George has 27 pennies and a nickel. All together, he has ___?___ cents.

Solving addition problems

Each of these addition problems is solved in two ways. Explain both ways. Which way is quicker and easier to write?

---

1. John had 20¢. He earned 30¢. How much did he have then?

Long Way: 20¢ = 2 dimes

30¢ = 3 dimes

5 dimes = 50¢

Short Way: 20¢

+ 30¢

50¢

---

2. Peter had 15 marbles. Tom gave him 14 more. How many marbles did he have then?

Long Way: 15 = 1 ten and 5 ones

14 = 1 ten and 4 ones

2 tens and 9 ones = 29

Short Way: 15

+ 14

29

---

3. Jane had 37¢. She found 25¢. How much did she have then?

Long Way: 37¢ = 3 dimes and 7 cents

25¢ = 2 dimes and 5 cents

5 dimes and 12 cents

Short Way: 37¢

+ 25¢

62¢

Change the 12 cents to 1 dime and 2 cents.

Then you have 6 dimes and 2 cents, or __?__ ¢.

---

4. Betty paid $4.65 for shoes and 69¢ for socks. How much did she spend in all?

Long Way:

$4.65 = 4 dollars 6 dimes   5 cents

$ .69 =   6 dimes   9 cents

4 dollars 12 dimes 14 cents

Short Way:

$4.65

+ .69

$5.34

- Change the 14 cents to 1 dime and 4 cents.
  Then you have 4 dollars, 13 dimes, and 4 cents.
- Change the 13 dimes to 1 dollar and 3 dimes.
  Then you have 5 dollars, 3 dimes, and 4 cents, or __?__ .

Addition practice

Add down. Check by adding up. If you get the same answer both times, your sum is probably right.

	a	b	c	d	e	f	g	h
1.	70	70	80	80	90	90	140	150
	20	23	40	45	10	12	230	220
2.	75	35	38	47	48	36	246	370
	52	26	23	28	67	97	127	350
3.	83	92	56	37	46	29	325	381
	17	18	34	59	79	98	68	472
4.	94	86	78	90	75	78	876	684
	78	47	67	83	67	45	89	269

5. Tom added 73 and 50 in his head by thinking, "70 and 50 are 120, and 3 more are __?__."

$$\begin{array}{r} 73 \\ + 50 \\ \hline \end{array}$$

When Tom adds mentally, he begins *at the left*. But when he does written addition, he begins *at the right*. Explain.

6. Now go back and do Ex. 1 mentally.

Copy, add, and check:

7.	87	68	97	49
	78	81	10	20
	12	21	23	82

8.	91	72	68	7
	9	29	74	80
	82	8	9	75

9. Now go back and see if each answer in Exs. 7 and 8 is sensible. That is, *estimate* each answer.
In the first one think:
87 is about 9 tens
78 is about 8 tens
12 is about 1 ten
Sum is about 18 tens, or 180

10. If a book costs 59¢ and a ruler 19¢, would you estimate the cost of both to be about 60¢, or 70¢, or 80¢? Why?

11. Would you estimate the cost of a 79-cent knife and a 31-cent whistle to be about $1.00, $1.10, or $1.20?

12. Estimate the cost of a 69-cent ball and a 50-cent bat.

Written addition practice

Do not copy examples 1–4; use folded paper. Add down. Check each example by adding up to see if you get the same answer you got when you added down.

	a	b	c	d	e	f	g	h
1.	54 33	87 52	68 51	75 64	96 56	83 46	32 73	51 67
2.	48 37	56 39	86 76	97 46	35 85	59 73	65 49	84 93
3.	4 9 3 4	6 0 6 5	4 7 9 8	7 6 3 7	5 4 7 6	8 7 6 4	6 8 7 5	8 2 3 9
4.	32 40 5	43 2 64	82 30 4	83 21 5	83 26 34	76 87 72	92 63 56	74 81 6

Copy, add, and check:

	a	b	c	d	e	f
5.	$.27 .32 .04	$8.05 .07 3.29	$6.20 3.49 8.75	$.89 .47 .06	$4.25 .76 6.38	$3.75 5.50 .21

6. $4.05 + $2.26 + $1.60

7. $7.29 + $.48 + $3.25

8. $9.50 + $2.28 + $5.49

9. $5.60 + $5 + $2.84

10. $.85 + $1.74 + $3

11. $10 + $2.85 + $3.65

12. $3 + $6 + $.34

13. $.25 + $.69 + $5

14. James has $6.75 in Savings Stamps and $9.38 in the bank. How much money has he in all?

15. Find the total cost of cowboy boots at $4.98, frontier pants at $5.19, and a cowboy hat at $2.65.

Addition tryout

Copy the examples. Add and check. If you make more than one error on Test I, do Practice Set I on the next page. Do the same for the other tests.

▶ TEST I

1. 25	2. 23	3. 64	4. 56	5. 73	6. 37	7. 95
+43	64	35	62	46	82	54

▶ TEST II

1. 69	2. 85	3. 98	4. 37	5. 73	6. 84	7. 99
76	76	57	95	98	97	94

▶ TEST III

1. 56	2. 87	3. 97	4. 77	5. 38	6. 46	7. 76
83	96	68	60	59	83	85
75	63	35	57	46	92	43

▶ TEST IV

1. 685	2. 746	3. 876	4. 965	5. 368
974	839	398	76	975
308	59	421	897	803

▶ TEST V

1. $5.63	2. $5.75	3. $4.25	4. $7.89
8.24	2.80	.20	3.46
3.00	.75	9.60	2.85

▶ TEST VI

1. $2.75 + $3.28   4. $.45 + $.98   7. $.87 + $.69 + $.75

2. $4.35 + $6.00   5. $3.75 + $5 + $2.75   8. $3 + $.75 + $1.54

3. $9.25 + $.75   6. $6.34 + $.06 + $6   9. $6 + $.25 + $.69

If you need to try again

If you made more than one error on Test I on page 16, do Practice Set I below. Add and check each example. Then take Test I on page 16 again; and so on.

▶ **PRACTICE SET I**

1. 35	2. 43	3. 23	4. 72	5. 97	6. 74	7. 82
24	46	45	46	42	65	37

▶ **PRACTICE SET II**

1. 86	2. 89	3. 78	4. 37	5. 94	6. 75	7. 86
87	65	95	98	87	58	99

▶ **PRACTICE SET III**

1. 63	2. 76	3. 87	4. 98	5. 49	6. 74	7. 64
95	88	97	30	67	85	87
57	64	45	68	58	62	53

▶ **PRACTICE SET IV**

1. 278	2. 407	3. 984	4. 684	5. 764
346	836	79	395	803
975	542	863	98	975

▶ **PRACTICE SET V**

1. $3.45	2. $5.60	3. $4.36	4. $8.96
.20	3.90	9.53	2.39
8.40	.85	5.00	3.85

▶ **PRACTICE SET VI**

1. $3.45 + $4.57
2. $5.75 + $8.00
3. $6.25 + $.65
4. $.65 + $.89
5. $4.65 + $5 + $3.65
6. $7.42 + $.07 + $3
7. $.49 + $.37 + $.65
8. $4 + $.85 + $1.32
9. $7 + $.85 + $.69

17

UNIT

4

*Making sure of subtraction
Review of meaning, facts, and
subtraction with and without borrowing*

Subtraction problem helps

1. Patsy has 7 Merry-Go-Round tickets. If she gives away 4, how many will she have left?

> When you know how many things there were at first and how many were taken away, to find how many are left, you subtract.

Make up some problems to illustrate the rule above.

2. A club president wants to award an honor badge to each of 6 boys. He has only 4 badges. How many more badges does he need?

> To find how many more things you need, you subtract.

Make up some problems to illustrate.

3. Peter is 68 inches tall. Pat is 60 inches tall. How much taller is Peter than Pat?

> To find how much larger or smaller one number is than another, you subtract. You subtract to find the difference between the numbers.

Make up some problems to illustrate.

4. Jack has 6 ping-pong balls. He can find only 4. How many must he hunt for?

> When you know how many there were at first and how many there are now, to find how many were taken away, you subtract.

Make up some problems to illustrate.

5. Jenny knows that 7 children came to band practice. She knows that 3 of them were girls. How many boys came?

> When you know how many there are in a whole group and how many of one kind there are, to find how many of the other kind there are, you subtract.

Make up some problems that will illustrate the rule above.

Two of these problems are not *subtraction problems. Which ones are they? Write the work you do to find each answer.*

6. In a show, 9 boys need to wear firemen's helmets. They have 6 helmets. How many more do they need?

7. Jim had 16 tadpoles in a jar. Nine turned into frogs. How many tadpoles were left?

8. Sam has 19 goldfish. Donald has 13. How many more goldfish has Sam than Donald?

9. Dan gave Joe 4 pigeons. Dan has 5 pigeons left. How many did Dan have at first?

10. Joan bought 12 chocolate bars. She has 3 left. She ate the others. How many did she eat?

11. George has 24 rabbits. 12 of them are white. The others are brown. How many are brown?

12. Ted has 15¢. If he buys an ice-cream cone for 6¢, how much will he have left?

13. Diana bought a dozen eggs. She dropped the box. All but 5 eggs broke. How many broke?

14. There are 19 pupils in Miss Green's class. 10 are boys. How many are girls?

15. John spent 9¢. He has 16¢ left. How much did he have at first?

16. Joan has 18¢. She wants to buy a 30-cent movie ticket. How much more money does she need?

17. Billy and Tom collect match folders. Billy has 36. Tom has 33. How many more has Billy than Tom?

Subtraction helps

1. This subtraction shows that when you take 5 from 18, _?_ are left.

$$\begin{array}{r} 18 \\ -\ 5 \\ \hline 13 \end{array}$$

The answer to a subtraction example is called the *difference* or *remainder*.

The difference, or remainder, in this subtraction is _?_ .

2. You remember the sign — in subtraction. It is called a *minus sign*. It tells you to _?_ .

$13 - 4 = 9$ may be read in any of these ways:

- 13 minus 4 equals 9
- 13 take away 4 is 9
- 4 from 13 is 9

3. Read these subtractions in several ways:

$12 - 6 = 6$ $17 - 8 = 9$
$16 - 9 = 7$ $13 - 7 = 6$

4. Counting backward by 1's from 10 teaches 10 subtraction facts. What are they?

5. What 5 subtraction facts does counting backward by 2's from 10 teach you?

In Exs. 6–9, use counters to prove that you are right.

6. $14 - 5 = 9$, so $14 - 9 =$ _?_
$15 - 7 = 8$, so $15 - 8 =$ _?_

7. $16 - 7 = 9$, so $16 - 9 =$ _?_
$13 - 7 = 6$, so $13 - 6 =$ _?_

8. $9 + 6 = 15$, so $15 - 9 =$ _?_
and $15 - 6 =$ _?_

9. $8 + 5 = 13$, so $13 - 8 =$ _?_
and $13 - 5 =$ _?_

10. The 4 facts below are called a Number Family. Why?

$8 + 3 = 11$ $11 - 8 = 3$
$3 + 8 = 11$ $11 - 3 = 8$

11. Tell the 3 other members in the Number Family of each of these facts.

$5 + 4 = 9$ $11 - 4 = 7$
$16 - 7 = 9$ $17 - 9 = 8$

12. $18 - 10 = 8$, so $18 - 9 =$ _?_

13. $17 - 10 = 7$, so $17 - 9 =$ _?_

14. $16 - 10 = 6$, so $16 - 9 =$ _?_

15. Jane says that Exs. 12–14 teach her how to find the answers to the subtractions below. Explain what she means.

$15 - 9$ $12 - 9$ $14 - 9$

16. When you subtract zero from a number, is the remainder the same as the number?

Make up a rule about subtracting zero from a number. Illustrate.

Test on subtraction facts

Practice saying the answers to these subtraction facts. Try to write all the answers on folded paper in 5 minutes.

Make and study Help-Yourself Cards for any facts you do not know. See pages 305 and 307. Practice taking the test until you can write every answer in 6 minutes.

1.	5 1	4 2	7 7	8 1	6 6	5 4	1 1	3 2	3 3
2.	9 9	6 5	7 1	8 4	9 8	4 3	5 5	9 1	4 4
3.	5 3	8 7	2 1	4 1	6 3	3 1	5 2	6 1	7 5
4.	2 2	8 6	7 2	8 3	9 7	7 4	9 5	7 6	6 2
5.	8 2	9 3	8 8	7 3	9 4	9 6	10 2	12 6	10 1
6.	11 2	10 7	8 5	9 2	6 4	11 6	16 8	11 9	18 9
7.	11 7	10 4	12 9	10 5	11 4	10 6	10 9	14 7	12 4
8.	10 8	12 8	13 6	15 8	11 5	11 8	10 3	14 6	11 3
9.	13 8	13 7	16 7	12 5	12 7	14 8	15 6	12 3	17 9
10.	14 5	16 9	13 4	14 9	13 5	13 9	17 8	15 7	15 9

Subtracting mentally

1. Explain John's thinking. →

2. Use John's method to subtract:

12 from 50	22 from 70
14 from 60	32 from 80
13 from 70	12 from 100
15 from 80	23 from 100
11 from 90	34 from 100

3. Can you think of an easy way to do these subtractions?

20 from 63	40 from 122
30 from 72	50 from 163
40 from 81	100 from 125
20 from 104	100 from 256
30 from 108	120 from 240

4. John wanted to subtract 23 from 72. First, he subtracted 20 from 72, leaving __?__. Then he subtracted 3 from __?__.
So 72 − 23 = __?__.

5. Use the method of Ex. 4 to subtract:

24 from 72	32 from 100
23 from 61	43 from 100
34 from 82	37 from 74
42 from 91	73 from 92
21 from 50	82 from 120

6. To subtract 39 from 100, John first subtracted 40 from 100, leaving 60. Then he added 1 to 60. Why? So 100 − 39 = __?__.

7. Use John's method in Ex. 6 to subtract:

39 from 60	27 from 100
28 from 50	39 from 72
47 from 100	48 from 84
68 from 100	57 from 92
79 from 100	49 from 81

8. Is 89 − 38 about 40 or 50?

9. Is 100 − 48 about 60 or 50?

Do not use a pencil to find these answers:

10. Peter has 63¢. How much will he have left if he spends 20¢? 21¢? 22¢?

11. Mildred had 40 subtraction examples to do. She has done 19. How many more does she have to do?

12. Joan weighs 73 lb. Kathy weighs 68 lb. How much more does Joan weigh than Kathy?

13. Dave has 63 marbles. Ed has 49. How many more must Ed get to catch up with Dave?

22

Using subtraction

1. Fred has 89¢. If he spends 25¢ for fishhooks, how much will he have left?

Use toy coins (dimes and pennies) to explain these two ways to solve this problem. Which way is quicker? Which way is easier to write?

Long Way		Short Way		CHECK
He had	89¢ = 8 dimes 9 cents	He has	89¢	64¢
He spends 25¢ = 2 dimes 5 cents		He spends	− 25¢	+ 25¢
He has left	6 dimes 4 cents = 64¢	He has left	64¢	89¢

2. Use toy coins (dimes and pennies) to prove that this rule for checking subtraction works in Ex. 1:

> To check a subtraction, add the difference to the number you subtract. The sum should equal the number you subtracted from.

3. Copy, subtract, and check:

95¢	87¢	68¢	77¢	98¢	79¢	86¢	95¢
23¢	45¢	33¢	54¢	63¢	18¢	24¢	52¢

4. Jane needs 75 cereal-box tops to get a ring. She already has 52 box tops. How many more must she get?

Explain these two ways to solve the problem. Which way is quicker? Which way is easier to write?

Long Way		Short Way		CHECK
No. she needs	75 = 7 tens 5 ones	No. she needs	75	23
No. she has	52 = 5 tens 2 ones	No. she has	− 52	+ 52
No. she must get	2 tens 3 ones = 23	No. she must get	23	75

5. Copy, subtract, and check:

69	78	93	87	89	78	96	89
42	32	43	54	36	24	66	64

Using subtraction

1. John has 72¢. If he buys a ball for 49¢, how much will he have left?

Use toy coins (dimes and pennies) to explain these two ways of doing this subtraction. Check the answer.

Long Way	Short Way
John has 72¢ = 7 dimes 12 cents	John has 6 12 7 2¢
John spends 49¢ = 4 dimes 9 cents	John spends − 4 9¢
John has left 2 dimes 3 cents = 23¢	John has left 2 3¢

Copy, subtract, and check:

2.
82¢	91¢	82¢	94¢	$.83	$.85	$.72
64¢	63¢	18¢	55¢	.26	.37	.37

3.
93	82	93	85	73	94	87
38	46	89	78	26	18	69

4. Use toy money (dollars, dimes, and pennies) to explain these two ways of taking $1.75 from $4.39:

Long Way	Short Way	CHECK
$4.39 = 4 dollars 3 dimes 9 cents	3 13 $4 .3 9	$2.64
$1.75 = 1 dollar 7 dimes 5 cents	− 1 .7 5	+ 1.75
2 dollars 6 dimes 4 cents = $2.64	$2 .6 4	$4.39

5. Use toy money to show how to take $2.87 from $5.41. Then write the subtraction the long way; the short way.

6. Does $3.28 = 2 dollars, 12 dimes, 8 cents?

7. Does $5.00 = 4 dollars, 9 dimes, 10 cents?

Copy, subtract, and check:

8.
$4.68	$5.74	$7.35	$9.23	$7.00	$9.00	$8.00
1.83	2.28	1.78	6.87	6.20	2.06	1.75

Problems and practice

1. Jim has $3.25. He wants to buy skates that cost $4.39. How much more money does he need?

2. Peter has 39¢. If he spends a quarter, how much will be left?

3. There are 31 children in the fourth grade. 17 are boys. How many are girls?

4. Diana had $1.35 in her pocket. Now she has only $1.10. She said, "Oh! I lost a _?_."

5. Harry earned $2.85. John earned $3.15. How much more did John earn than Harry?

6. Joe has a wallet worth 65¢. Dan has a key ring worth 25¢. The boys want to trade.

What must Dan do to make an even trade of ring for wallet?

7. John got 549 for the answer to a subtraction. The answer should have been 639. His answer was _?_ too small.

8. Carl had 75 magazines to sell. He has sold all but 17. He has sold _?_ magazines.

9. There are 324 pages in Marie's reader. She has read 198 pages. She has _?_ more to read.

Subtract and check. Use folded paper.

	a	b	c	d	e	f
10.	74 43	76 50	148 68	175 98	864 241	$6.75 3.05
11.	62 36	74 56	187 99	134 97	596 378	$5.63 3.54
12.	725 664	656 383	817 748	852 575	408 359	$4.00 2.83

Copy, subtract, and check:

	a	b	c	d
13.	75 − 38	807 − 134	500 − 284	$9.72 − $6.24
14.	84 − 78	563 − 287	780 − 357	$8.50 − $2.79
15.	90 − 39	974 − 456	800 − 499	$9.00 − $3.94

Subtraction tryout

Copy, subtract, and check. If you make more than one error in Test I, do Practice Set I on the next page. Do the same for the other tests.

▶ **TEST I**

1. 95	2. 86	3. 79	4. 69	5. 147	6. 129
72	43	54	36	74	65

▶ **TEST II**

1. 26	2. 75	3. 63	4. 154	5. 172	6. 158
18	58	39	77	87	69

▶ **TEST III**

1. 80	2. 50	3. 60	4. 70	5. 90	6. 60
26	35	34	28	37	43

▶ **TEST IV**

1. 785	2. 863	3. 987	4. 574	5. 684	6. 593
324	453	643	372	652	493

▶ **TEST V**

1. 426	2. 539	3. 648	4. 765	5. 647	6. 768
374	275	376	493	379	664

▶ **TEST VI**

1. 463	2. 249	3. 633	4. 806	5. 507	6. 200
87	75	74	278	438	79

▶ **TEST VII**

1. $4.72 − $3.41   2. $7.95 − $6.78   3. $5.00 − $.75

4. $5.75 − $2.95   5. $7 − $.56   6. $8 − $3.20

26

If you need to try again

If you made more than one error in Test I on page 26, do Practice Set I below. Work and check each example. Then take Test I on page 26 again; and so on.

▶ PRACTICE SET I

1. 87
  63

2. 48
  24

3. 97
  32

4. 86
  52

5. 168
   82

6. 187
   93

▶ PRACTICE SET II

1. 37
  28

2. 84
  65

3. 75
  48

4. 176
   88

5. 152
   75

6. 184
   87

▶ PRACTICE SET III

1. 90
  36

2. 60
  23

3. 50
  14

4. 80
  35

5. 60
  48

6. 70
  27

▶ PRACTICE SET IV

1. 689
  234

2. 796
  386

3. 869
  233

4. 587
  282

5. 798
  765

6. 872
  672

▶ PRACTICE SET V

1. 529
  234

2. 647
  393

3. 756
  272

4. 867
  594

5. 632
  489

6. 976
  873

▶ PRACTICE SET VI

1. 742
   87

2. 469
   73

3. 544
   95

4. 605
  288

5. 403
  289

6. 400
   96

▶ PRACTICE SET VII

1. $5.93 − $2.21

2. $9.86 − $4.29

3. $7.00 − $.83

4. $6.35 − $2.75

5. $9 − $.43

6. $5 − $1.30

UNIT
5

Large numbers. Review
and extension through
5-place numbers

Up to a thousand

The State Forester asked the Scouts to help plant trees. He sent them the number of trees shown at the bottom of the page.

1. Look at the first box of trees. How many trees are in each row? How many rows are there? How many trees are there in the box?

2. How many boxes of trees are shown? Count the trees by 100's. *Ten hundred* is *one thousand* trees. One thousand is written: 1,000.

3. Write the numbers from 100 to 1,000, counting by 100's.

4. Tom set out 3 rows of 10 trees and 8 trees more. That was _?_ trees. 3 tens and 8 are _?_ .

5. Bill, Jim, and Dick set out 2 whole boxes of trees, 4 rows of ten trees, and 6 more trees. They set out _?_ trees in all.

6. David said, "In the number 123 the 1 is in the hundreds place, the 2 is in the tens place, and the 3 is in the ones place.

"The 1 stands for 100; the 2 stands for 20; and the 3 stands for just 3." Was David right?

7. In the number 321 the 3 stands for _?_ ; the 2 stands for _?_ ; and the 1 stands for _?_ .

So 321 means 300 + 20 + 1 and is read "3 hundred 21."

8. In the number 507 there are _?_ hundreds, _?_ tens, _?_ ones.

507 means 500 + _?_ and is read "5 hundred _?_ ."

9. Write the number that means 6 hundreds, 5 tens, 8 ones.

10. Which number is larger?
753 or 537   687 or 876
320 or 230

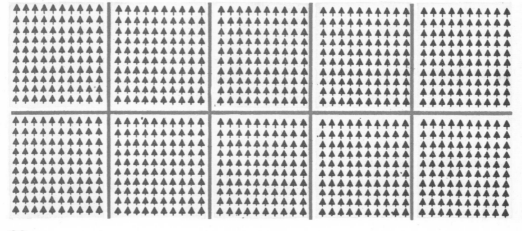

11. Jane says 395 means all these things. Does it?
- 395 means 300 + 90 + 5.
- 395 means 3 hundreds, 9 tens, 5 ones.
- 395 means 39 tens and 5 ones.
- 395 means 395 ones.
- 395 is *almost* 400.

12. Tell what these numbers mean in as many ways as you can:

756	204	350	473
609	960	506	98

13. In the number 900 there are _?_ hundreds, _?_ tens, and _?_ ones.

14. In the number 506 there are _?_ hundreds, _?_ tens, and _?_ ones. Add 500 and 6.

15. Tell the sum of 700 + 80 + 4 without writing the numbers.

16. If you put together 500 and 50 and 5, you get _?_.

Tell the missing numbers:

17. 796, 797, 798, _?_, _?_, _?_, 802, _?_, _?_, 805, _?_.

18. 888, 892, 896, _?_, _?_, 908, 912, _?_, _?_, 924, _?_.

19. 485, 490, _?_, _?_, _?_, 510, _?_, _?_, 525, _?_, _?_.

20. 550, 560, 570, _?_, _?_, _?_, 610, _?_, 630, _?_, 650.

21. 600, 625, 650, _?_, _?_, 725, _?_, 775, _?_, _?_, 850.

22. 450, 500, _?_, 600, _?_, _?_, 750, _?_, _?_, _?_, _?_.

23. 440, 430, 420, _?_, _?_, _?_, 380, _?_, _?_, _?_, _?_.

24. 510, 508, 506, _?_, _?_, _?_, _?_, 496, _?_, _?_, _?_.

25. 875, 850, 825, _?_, _?_, _?_, 725, _?_, _?_, _?_, _?_.

26. 950, 900, 850, _?_, _?_, _?_, 650, _?_, _?_, _?_, _?_.

27. Martha has 3 dollar bills, 4 dimes, and 2 cents. She says her money is worth 342 cents. Is it?

28. Write the numbers from 42 to 142 by 10's.

29. Write the numbers from 67 to 167 by 10's.

30. Write the numbers from 50 to 1,000 by 50's; from 75 to 325 by 25's.

Up to ten thousand

One Saturday the Scouts and the Firemen planted trees at Bear Creek. They set out 10 boxes of 100 trees. That was *ten hundred* trees.

The men and the boys drove out on the fire truck to plant the trees. Dan and Tom sat with the driver. When they started, the speedometer showed that the truck had gone 999 miles. After they had driven 1 mile, the speedometer changed to look like this:———

Dan said, "999 miles plus 1 mile equals 1,000 miles." Add 1 to 999 and prove that Dan was right.

1. How did the speedometer look after the truck had gone another mile? Look at the third number in the picture.

2. Read the numbers that show how the speedometer changed on the way to Bear Creek.

3. Count from 1,000 to 1,020 by ones. Write the numbers.

4. Count from 1,000 to 10,000 by thousands. Write the numbers.

5. Count from 5,000 to 6,000 by hundreds. Write the numbers.

6. How many trees are shown on page 28? If 2 children open their books to page 28 and hold them up, how many trees can you see? How many trees can you see if 3 children do this? 6? 9? 10?

999
1000
1001
1002
1003
1004
1005
1006
1007
1008
1009
1010
1011
1012

7. 1,000 trees were set out at Bear Creek, 800 at Stony Run, and 75 near the covered bridge.

How many trees were planted in the three places?

$1{,}000 + 800 + 75 = \underline{\ ?\ }.$

8. 2,000 trees were set out at Eagle Rock, 90 at Cedar Grove, and 8 at Lost Mine.

How many trees were planted in the three places?

$2{,}000 + 90 + 8 = \underline{\ ?\ }.$

9. 8,642 means ___?___ thousands, ___?___ hundreds, ___?___ tens, and ___?___ ones

10. 7,031 means ___?___ thousands, ___?___ hundreds, ___?___ tens, and ___?___ one.

Read these numbers:

	a	b	c	d	e	f
11.	8,643	7,689	4,326	2,876	4,789	2,806
12.	7,076	4,404	6,450	7,500	8,008	6,007
13.	9,473	7,054	5,060	1,050	5,870	3,870

14. Write the numbers in Exs. 11–13 as your teacher dictates them. When she says thousand, write a comma. There must be *three* figures after the comma.

15. These numbers are *2-figure* or *2-place* numbers. What is the largest 2-place number? the smallest?

| 10 |
| 35 |
| 99 |

16. How many tens are there in each number in Ex. 15? How many ones?

17. These are *3-figure* or *3-place* numbers. What is the largest 3-place number? the smallest?

| 100 |
| 407 |
| 999 |

18. How many hundreds are there in each number in Ex. 17? How many tens? How many ones?

19. These are *4-figure* or *4-place* numbers. What is the largest 4-place number? the smallest?

| 1,000 |
| 1,523 |
| 9,999 |

20. How many thousands are there in each number in Ex. 19? How many hundreds? How many tens? How many ones?

21. The smallest 2-place number has one zero. How many zeros has the smallest 3-place number? the smallest 4-place number?

22. Tell what the zeros mean.

101	110	1,020
1,001	1,010	1,000
1,100	2,002	1,001

Without copying the numbers, tell the sums; write the sums.

23. $4,000 + 500 + 40 + 6$

24. $7,000 + 600 + 30 + 5$

25. $8,000 + 800 + 80 + 8$

26. $3,000 + 40 + 3$

27. $4,000 + 500 + 7$

28. $5,000 + 400 + 9$

TREES PLANTED IN GREEN COUNTY

1st week in Oct.	9,000
2nd week in Oct.	16,000
3rd week in Oct.	32,000
4th week in Oct.	42,000
Total	99,000

Tens of thousands

1. The State Forester sent the Scouts this report. Read it.

How many more trees did they plant the 2nd week than the 1st?

Did they plant twice as many trees the 3rd week as the 2nd week?

2. In the addition at the right, the first number is read "19 thousand, 2 hundred, 63." It means 19 thousands, 2 hundreds, 6 tens, and _?_ ones. It is a *5-place* number.

Read the other numbers in the addition. The figures to the left of the comma tell how many thousands. What do the figures to the right of the comma tell?

```
19,263
17,102
27,076
20,807
─────
84,248
```

Read these numbers:

	a	b	c	d	e
3.	46,003	70,506	35,806	45,632	62,275
4.	35,967	8,007	5,072	50,005	40,240
5.	2,304	27,554	54,024	5,235	99,999

6. Write the numbers in Exs. 3–5 as your teacher dictates them. Be sure to write a comma when she says *thousand*. How many figures must there be after the comma?

7. Show that understanding large numbers is important in reading newspapers and books.

Copy, and put commas in the correct places. Then read the numbers.

8.	5768	24375	73046
9.	5006	20079	35208
10.	3064	75300	28060
11.	6450	72006	40079
12.	4803	30505	70220

32

Problem study

If you have trouble with Problem 1 in Column A, do Problem 1 in Column B. Then go back and try Problem 1 in Column A again, and so on.

A

1. Some Scouts can get a used pair of field glasses for $7.00. They have $5.47. How much more do they need?

2. Jimmie earned $4.00. If he buys a wrist watch for $2.98, how much will he have left?

3. Mark wants a flashlight that costs $.98 and two batteries that cost 10¢ each. How much will the flashlight and batteries cost?

4. Dan wants a harmonica. He can get one for $.25, or a better one for $.59. What is the difference between the prices?

5. Joseph wants to get a box of shoe polish for $.15 and a shoe-brush for $.29. How much will both cost?

6. How much change will John get from a 5-dollar bill if he buys a brief case for $2.79?

7. Tom set out 6 rows of apple trees with 10 trees in a row, and 7 extra trees. How many trees did he set out in all?

B

1. Donald wants to buy a ball. The ball costs 30¢. He has only 20¢. How much more does he need?

2. Clayton has a dollar. If he spends 65¢ for a haircut, how much will he have left?

3. Joe bought a kite that cost 25¢ and 2 balls of string that cost 5¢ each. How much did the string cost? the kite and string both?

4. William is 9 years old. His little brother Tim is 5 years old. What is the difference in their ages?

5. Clifford is going to buy a bicycle light for $1 and a bell for $.45. How much will he have to pay for both?

6. How much change will Ellen get from a quarter after she buys something for 18¢?

7. 6 tens equal __?__.
6 tens and 3 more equal __?__.
6 tens and 5 more equal __?__.
6 tens and 7 more equal __?__.

UNIT

6

*Making sure of multiplica-
tion. Review of facts of
2, 3, 5. Multiplying with
and without carrying*

Meaning of multiplication

▶ You can find that three 2's are 6 by *counting* by twos.

Count the kittens' eyes by 2's.

▶ You can find that three 2's are 6 by *adding*.

Do this addition: $2 + 2 + 2$.

▶ When you say "three 2's are 6" or "3 times 2 is 6," you find three 2's by **multiplying**. You multiply 2 by 3.

The example may be written this way: ⟶

$$\begin{array}{r} 2 \\ \times 3 \\ \hline 6 \end{array}$$

You remember the sign **×**. It stands for *times*. It tells you to *multiply*.

$$3 \times 2 = 6$$

The example may also be written this way: ⟶
It is read "3 times 2 is 6" or "3 times 2 equals 6."

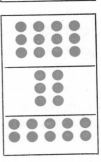

1. Which of the pictures at the right shows that 3 fours are 12 and that 4 threes are 12? Which shows that 3 twos are 6 and that 2 threes are 6? Which shows that $2 \times 5 = 10$ and that $5 \times 2 = 10$?

What multiplication facts do these additions teach?

2. $8 + 8$ $5 + 5 + 5$ $3 + 3 + 3$ $2 + 2 + 2 + 2$

3. $7 + 7$ $8 + 8 + 8$ $2 + 2 + 2$ $5 + 5 + 5 + 5$

4. $4 \times 2 = 8$, so $2 \times 4 = \underline{\ ?\ }$.

5. $3 \times 9 = 27$, so $9 \times 3 = \underline{\ ?\ }$.

6. $5 \times 3 = 15$, so $3 \times 5 = \underline{\ ?\ }$.

7. $5 \times 8 = 40$, so $8 \times 5 = \underline{\ ?\ }$.

8. $3 + 3 + 3 + 3 + 3 + 3 = 18$ shows that:

6 threes are 18, or $6 \times 3 = \underline{\ ?\ }$.

9. 2 fives are 10, so 4 fives are *twice as many*, or $\underline{\ ?\ }$. Why?

10. 3 fives are 15, so 6 fives are *twice as many*, or $\underline{\ ?\ }$. Why?

11. Make up some *twice as many* examples like Exs. 9 and 10.

12. Does $6 + 6 + 6 + 6 = 24$ show that $4 \times 6 = 24$, or $6 \times 4 = 24$?

Multiplication problem helps

▶ If 9 boys are needed for one ball team, how many boys are needed for 2 teams? How does the rule below help answer this problem?

> **When you know how many there are in 1 group, to find how many there are in 2 or more groups of the same size, you multiply.**

▶ How does the rule below help you find the cost of 5 pencils at 2¢ each?

> **When you know the cost of 1 article, to find the cost of 2 or more of those same articles, you multiply.**

Two of these problems are not multiplication problems. Which ones are they? Tell all the answers.

1. If one apple costs 4¢, how much will 5 cost?

2. Airmail stamps cost 6¢ each. How much will 3 cost?

3. Alice wants to wear two barrettes that cost 8¢ apiece. How much will the pair cost?

4. Tom has 5 rabbits in one pen and 4 rabbits in another pen. How many has he in the 2 pens?

5. Find the cost of 6 soap-bubble pipes at 5¢ each.

6. If David needs 4 wheels for each cart he is making, how many wheels will he need for 3 carts?

7. How many feet are there in 2 yards? in 3 yards? in 4?

8. Andrew's grandmother sent him a box of candy. There are 8 rows of candy with 3 pieces in each row. How many pieces of candy are there in all?

9. Paul can get 6 fishhooks on a card. How many fishhooks are there on 3 cards?

10. In a target game Ellen had 3 turns. She made 5 points each turn. What was her score then?

11. At 4¢ apiece, what will 5 oranges cost?

12. If apples cost 3¢ apiece and bananas 4¢ apiece, how much will an apple and a banana cost?

13. Do 5 nickels = a quarter?

Earning honor points

1. Charlie has 17 honor points. How many more points must he earn to win a badge? to win a pennant? to win his club letters?

2. Anne Marie has 22 honor points. How many more points must she earn to win a badge? a pennant? her club letters?

3. Joseph had 33 honor points. He has just earned 3 more points for stopping a fist fight. How many points has he now?

4. Martha had 42 honor points. She has just earned 5 more points for knitting a sweater. How many points has she now?

How many more points must she earn to get a club pennant?

5. John had 63 points. He earned 5 more points by repairing a clubroom lamp, and 10 points by waxing the clubroom floor. How many points has he now?

How many more points must he earn to win his club letters?

6. Ann has won an honor badge. How many more points must she earn to get a club pennant?

7. Theodore has won a club pennant. How many more points must he earn to get club letters?

8. Jerry has 76 points. Arthur has 59 points.

Arthur said, "I'll have to earn _?_ more points to catch up with you, Jerry."

Multiplying mentally

1. $2 \times 30 = 2 \times 3$ tens $= 6$ tens $= \underline{\ ?\ }$
2. $2 \times 50 = 2 \times 5$ tens $= 10$ tens $= \underline{\ ?\ }$
3. $2 \times 70 = 2 \times 7$ tens $= 14$ tens $= \underline{\ ?\ }$ hundred and $\underline{\ ?\ }$ tens $= \underline{\ ?\ }$
4. $3 \times 60 = 3 \times 6$ tens $= 18$ tens $= \underline{\ ?\ }$ hundred and $\underline{\ ?\ }$ tens $= \underline{\ ?\ }$
5. $3 \times 70 = 3 \times 7$ tens $= 21$ tens $= \underline{\ ?\ }$ hundreds and $\underline{\ ?\ }$ ten $= \underline{\ ?\ }$

Tell what you think to do these multiplications:

	a	b	c	d	e	f
6.	2×40	3×20	5×20	6×20	7×20	6×50
7.	2×50	3×40	5×30	6×30	7×30	7×50

8. To find 2×76, Jane thought: $2 \times 70 = 140$; $2 \times 6 = 12$; so
$$2 \times 76 = 140 + 12 = \underline{\ ?\ }.$$

Tell what you think to do these multiplications:

	a	b	c	d	e	f
9.	2×43	3×23	4×22	6×21	5×61	2×95
10.	2×84	3×82	4×52	6×32	3×86	2×79

11. To find 5×130, Jane thought: $5 \times 100 = \underline{\ ?\ }$; $5 \times 30 = \underline{\ ?\ }$; so
$$5 \times 130 = 500 + 150 = \underline{\ ?\ }.$$

Tell what you think to do these multiplications:

	a	b	c	d	e	f
12.	3×150	2×240	5×220	2×310	3×120	4×250

13. Jane says that $0 + 0 + 0 = 0$ shows her that $3 \times 0 = 0$. Write an addition to show that $5 \times 0 = 0$.

Make up a rule for multiplying zero by any number.

14. Marcia estimated that 5×29 is about 5×30, or 150. Explain.
15. Is 2×78 about 140 or 160? Explain.
16. Estimate: 3×29 5×98 3×19 2×67 6×18

Test on multiplication facts

Practice saying the answers to these multiplication facts. Try to write all the answers on folded paper in 4 minutes.

Make Help-Yourself Cards for any facts you do not know. The right answers for your cards are on page 308.

Study the cards. Then take the test again. Practice until you can write every answer correctly in 4 minutes.

1.	2 2	6 5	7 2	5 1	3 6	5 9	8 2	1 8	5 7
2.	5 6	3 7	1 6	6 2	5 5	2 5	3 8	4 2	2 9
3.	1 2	7 3	2 6	9 2	8 1	1 7	2 3	9 5	3 5
4.	4 3	1 9	3 1	6 3	7 5	5 3	4 5	5 4	6 1
5.	5 8	3 9	3 2	2 4	7 1	8 5	4 1	3 3	1 4
6.	8 3	9 3	5 2	9 1	2 7	3 4	1 5	3 8	2 8

Just for fun

- Each person in the class choose a secret number.
- Write down your number.
- Multiply the number by 2.
- Add 10. Divide by 2.
- Subtract the number you wrote down at first.
- If no pupil made a mistake, everybody's answer is the same. What is the answer?

Easy multiplying

1. What is the cost of 3 movie tickets at 32¢ each?

① Find the answer to this problem by adding three 32's:——➤

```
32¢
32¢
32¢
____
```

② Find the answer by using toy coins (dimes and pennies).

③ Now find the answer by multiplying 32¢ by 3:——➤

▶ Think, "3 times 2 cents is 6 cents." Write the 6 in the cents column.

```
 32¢
× 3
____
 96¢
```

▶ Think, "3 times 3 dimes is 9 dimes." Write the 9 in the dimes column.

In 3 different ways you found that 3 tickets at 32¢ each will cost _?_ ¢. Which way is quickest? easiest to write?

Copy and multiply:

2. 23¢   21¢   24¢   14¢
     2   4   2   2
   ____   ____   ____   ____

3. 12¢   32¢   12¢   42¢
     3   2   4   2
   ____   ____   ____   ____

4. How much will 2 comic books cost at 14¢ each?

5. Find the cost of 4 notebooks at 21¢ each.

6. James has an order for 3 dozen roses. How many roses should he pick?

① Find the answer to this problem by adding three 12's:——➤

```
12
12
12
__
```

② Find the answer by multiplying 12 by 3:——➤

▶ Think, "3 times 2 ones is 6 ones." Write the 6 in the ones column.

```
 12
× 3
__
 36
```

▶ Think, "3 times 1 ten is 3 tens." Write the 3 in the tens column.

In 2 different ways you found that 3 dozen roses = _?_ roses. Which way is quicker? easier to write?

7. How many eggs are there in 2 dozen? 4 dozen?

8. There are 12 paper plates in a package. How many plates are there in 2 packages? 3? 4?

9. Jane bought 2 boxes of cookies. There were 24 cookies in each box. She bought _?_ cookies.

10. Tom wants to plant 3 rows of tomatoes. He can put 13 plants in each row. How many plants will he need?

On the radio

Nan, Earl, and Peter are saving milk-bottle tops to get a ring they heard about on the radio.

1. Look at the picture on page 41. Nan has 59 bottle tops. How many more does she need for a ring?

2. Earl has 47 milk-bottle tops. How many more does he need for a ring?

3. Peter has 91 milk-bottle tops. He has __?__ more than he needs for a ring.

4. If Peter gives Earl 8 of his extra milk-bottle tops, and Nan gets the rest, how many will Nan get?

5. Here is part of the dial on Peter's radio:

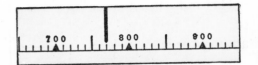

Tell whether the arrow on the dial shows that Peter's radio is set at 770 or at 830.

6. The radio announcer said, "The time is now six fifty-five."

Earl glanced at his watch. This is the way it looked: ⟶

Was it fast or slow? How much?

7. Earl would like to get a ring for himself, and another ring for his best friend. How many bottle tops would he need for the two rings?

8. Peter likes to listen to a Quiz Program on the radio. This is one of the questions he heard asked on the program. Can you give the answer?

• There are 5 blue marbles and 5 red marbles in a bag.

If you reach into the bag in the dark, what is the smallest number of marbles you must take out of the bag before you can be *sure* you have two marbles of the same color?

9. One morning Nan heard over the radio that the temperature would remain in the low twenties all day.

Nan said, "Good! There will be ice on the skating pond."

How did she know that?

10. One radio news reporter said, "About one half the Emerson School children marched in the parade today."

Another reporter said, "About 200 Emerson School children marched in the parade today."

Can you figure out from the news reports about how many children there are in the Emerson School?

SEND 75 PURITY MILK-BOTTLE TOPS FOR A RING THAT SHINES IN THE DARK.

Multiplying without carrying

1. Do these multiplications mentally.

Think, "60¢ = 6 dimes; 3 × 6 dimes = 18 dimes = $1.80."

$.60	$.30	$.50	$.41	$.81	$.92	$.52
× 3	× 4	× 3	× 3	× 3	× 2	× 4

2. Now copy Ex. 1 and write the answers.

▶ Think, "3 × 0 cents = 0 cents." Write the 0 in the cents column.

```
$ .60
 × 3
$1.80
```

▶ Think, "3 × 6 dimes = 18 dimes; 18 dimes = 1 dollar, 8 dimes." Write the 1 in the dollars column and the 8 in the dimes column.

▶ Don't forget to write the dollar sign and cents point.

3. Do these multiplications mentally.

Think, "50 = 5 tens; 3 × 5 tens = 15 tens = 150."

50	60	30	42	41	83	72
× 3	× 2	× 8	× 3	× 5	× 2	× 3

4. Now copy Ex. 3 and write the answers.

▶ Think, "3 × 0 = 0." Write the 0 in the ones column.

```
 50
× 3
150
```

▶ Think, "3 × 5 tens = 15 tens; 15 tens = 1 hundred, 5 tens." Write the 1 in the hundreds column and the 5 in the tens column.

Copy and multiply. Check by multiplying mentally.

	a	b	c	d	e	f
5.	43 × 2	33 × 2	22 × 3	63 × 3	$.21 × 3	$.51 × 5
6.	70 × 5	40 × 4	401 × 2	300 × 3	$2.00 × 4	$3.04 × 2
7.	60 × 5	31 × 2	231 × 2	200 × 4	$4.03 × 2	$.21 × 4
8.	240 × 2	403 × 2	41 × 3	30 × 6	$4.21 × 2	$.30 × 9

Multiplying with carrying

Tom is ordering by mail 4 arrows at $.23 each. How much money should he send?

① Find the answer to this problem by adding:➤

```
$.23
 .23
 .23
 .23
 ───
```

② Use toy money (dimes and cents) to find the answer.

③ Find the answer mentally.

④ Now find the answer by writing down the multiplication:──────────➤

```
$.23
×  4
────
$.92
```

▶ Think, "4 × 3 cents = 12 cents; but 12¢ = 1 dime and 2 cents." Write the 2 in the cents column. *Carry* the 1 dime to the dimes column.

▶ Think, "4 × 2 dimes = 8 dimes and 1 dime to carry = 9 dimes." Write the 9 in the dimes column.

▶ Don't forget to write the dollar sign and cents point.

In 4 different ways you found that 4 arrows at $.23 each will cost __?__.

1. In 4 different ways find the cost of:

4 magnets _____ at $.25 each
3 popguns _____ at $.39 each
5 flags _____ at $.29 each

Do each of these examples in 4 ways: by addition, by using toy coins, mentally, and as written multiplications.

2.
```
$.35        $.48        $.27
× 2         × 2         × 3
```

3.
```
$.48        $.64        $.75
× 3         × 5         × 2
```

Copy and multiply. Check by multiplying mentally.

4.
```
  45          63          37
×  2        ×  3        ×  3
```

5.
```
  35          23          23
×  4        ×  7        ×  9
```

6.
```
  25          35          32
×  8        ×  9        ×  6
```

7.
```
  32          89          67
×  8        ×  3        ×  3
```

8. Find the cost of four 35-cent books.

9. There are 36 inches in a yard. How many inches are there in 2 yards? in 3 yards?

10. Henry has 4 broken links in his bicycle chain. New links cost $.15 each. How much will 4 links cost?

Multiplying with carrying

How much will 2 punching bags cost at $4.62 each?

①Find the answer to this problem by adding:————→

$4.62
4.62
$9.24

②Use toy coins (dollars, dimes, and cents) to find the answer.

③Find the answer mentally.

④Now find the answer by writing the multiplication:–→

$4.62
× 2
$9.24

▶ Think, "2 × 2 cents = 4 cents." Write the 4 in the cents column.

▶ Think, "2 × 6 dimes = 12 dimes; but 12 dimes = 1 dollar and 2 dimes." Write the 2 in the dimes column. *Carry* the 1 dollar to the dollars column.

▶ Think, "2 × 4 dollars = 8 dollars, and 1 dollar to carry is 9 dollars." Write the 9 in the dollars column.

▶ Don't forget to write the dollar sign and cents point.

In 4 different ways you found that 2 punching bags at $4.62 each cost __?__. Most children like the last way best. Do you?

Copy and multiply. Check by estimating to see if each answer is sensible.

	a	b	c	d	e	f
1.	$2.71	$1.83	$4.71	$3.25	$2.81	$3.95
	2	3	2	3	3	2
2.	$2.35	$4.06	$2.08	$6.06	$7.09	$8.86
	2	3	5	2	3	2
3.	389	826	762	307	203	228
	2	2	2	3	2	3
4.	429	176	253	135	105	134
	3	3	7	6	8	5
5.	538	743	297	654	806	352
	2	3	5	3	3	6

Keeping in practice

Copy in columns, add, and check:

1. $7 + 6 + 8 + 5$ **2.** $9 + 6 + 7 + 4$ **3.** $\$7.06 + \$.79 + \$.64$

4. $4 + 3 + 7 + 9$ **5.** $5 + 8 + 9 + 7$ **6.** $\$5 + \$.69 + \$3.48$

Subtract and check:

	a	b	c	d	e	f	g	h
7.	845	743	496	764	934	630	372	700
	532	694	287	364	285	597	134	324
8.	727	736	930	800	700	605	903	845
	79	29	37	54	36	27	46	68

Multiply. Check by going over your work.

	a	b	c	d	e	f	g	h
9.	51	47	76	415	324	603	502	$6.29
	5	3	5	4	5	3	4	2

Read these numbers:

	a	b	c	d	e
10.	6,471	1,409	53,240	62,320	72,403
11.	3,568	6,537	78,704	56,006	45,500
12.	9,072	7,326	55,051	70,032	63,690

Add and check. Use folded paper.

	a	b	c	d	e	f	g
13.	2	27	$.75	243	358	$3.84	$8.00
	4	40	.82	87	796	2.97	3.50
	3	89	.39	532	89	7.63	.74
	6	56	.67	86	653	4.08	9.28
14.	5	38	$.64	356	628	$3.84	$7.01
	6	85	.87	29	532	.79	8.23
	7	50	.39	84	95	.73	9.65
	4	99	.27	703	876	8.65	.49

Multiplication tryout

Copy and multiply. Check by going over your work. If you make more than one mistake in Test I, do Practice Set I on the next page; and so on.

▶ **TEST I**

1. 34	2. 12	3. 41	4. 62	5. 53	6. 92
2	4	5	3	2	3

▶ **TEST II**

1. 25	2. 13	3. 28	4. 39	5. 68	6. 94
3	6	5	3	3	5

▶ **TEST III**

1. $.23	2. $.32	3. $.46	4. $.57	5. $.49	6. $.63
4	3	3	3	2	5

▶ **TEST IV**

1. 122	2. 215	3. 426	4. 335	5. 847	6. 559
4	7	3	4	3	2

▶ **TEST V**

1. 402	2. 503	3. 302	4. 203	5. 804	6. 607
2	3	9	4	3	3

▶ **TEST VI**

1. $2.00	2. $1.15	3. $6.57	4. $4.16	5. $9.85
7	4	3	3	2

▶ **TEST VII**

1. 3×56
2. 5×714
3. 3×48
4. $6 \times \$3.05$
5. 4×205
6. $5 \times \$3.17$

If you need to try again

If you made more than one error on Test I on page 46, do Practice Set I below. Check each answer by going over your work. Then take Test I on page 46 again; and so on.

▶ **PRACTICE SET I**

1. 21	2. 32	3. 42	4. 31	5. 72	6. 93
4	2	3	5	3	3

▶ **PRACTICE SET II**

1. 34	2. 47	3. 69	4. 89	5. 58	6. 74
5	3	3	2	3	3

▶ **PRACTICE SET III**

1. $.42	2. $.31	3. $.74	4. $.86	5. $.69	6. $.38
2	8	5	3	3	2

▶ **PRACTICE SET IV**

1. 231	2. 526	3. 315	4. 647	5. 857	6. 864
9	3	4	5	3	3

▶ **PRACTICE SET V**

1. 604	2. 703	3. 904	4. 706	5. 805	6. 507
2	3	3	5	3	5

▶ **PRACTICE SET VI**

1. $4.00	2. $1.15	3. $7.79	4. $8.17	5. $6.69
5	5	2	3	2

▶ **PRACTICE SET VII**

1. 3×78

2. 5×816

3. 3×59

4. $6 \times \$5.03$

5. 4×305

6. $5 \times \$4.18$

UNIT 7

Using arithmetic. Problem solving and linear measure. Maintenance

Measuring lengths and heights

1. In the craft room at Crestwood School there are several different kinds of measuring sticks. The smallest measuring stick is a ruler a *foot* long.

A ruler is divided into 12 equal parts. Each part is called an *inch*.

Look at a ruler. How many inches are there in 1 foot?

2. How many inches are there in 2 feet? in 3 feet?

Find your answers by adding; by multiplying.

3. The next size measuring stick is a *yard* long. That is divided into 36 inches.

Prove that the yardstick is 3 times as long as the ruler by adding; by multiplying; by using a ruler and a yardstick.

4. There is also a folding measuring stick in the craft room like the one at the right. It is hinged so that it will fold into sections 6 inches long.

Maybe someone in your class can bring a hinged measuring stick like this to school.

When the measuring stick is opened out, it is 72 inches long. In 3 different ways show that 72 inches = 6 feet.

5. Peter is making a bench. It is to be 4 feet long. The folding rule is divided into inches, not into feet. How many inches long should he make the bench?

6. George is making a clothes tree. It is to be 6 feet tall. How many inches tall should he make it?

7. How many inches are there in 5 feet?

8. June said the folding measuring stick is 2 yards long. Prove that she is right by adding; by multiplying.

9. Betty has a tape measure. It is 60 inches long. She needs to measure off 2 yards of ribbon. How can she do it?

10. Would you use inches, feet, or yards to measure the length of your pencil? to measure the material needed for a coat? to measure the height of a room?

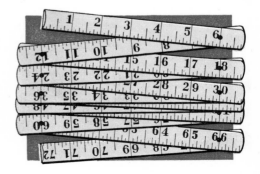

11. Dan knows his father is 6 feet tall. How would that help him estimate the height of a room?

12. Bill said, "I know the rug in our living room is 12 feet long. This room looks about twice as long as our rug. So I estimate the room to be __?__ feet long."

13. *The length of Bill's rug* and *the height of Dan's father* are "helpers" in estimating lengths and heights. Choose some "helpers" so that you can estimate easily.

14. Use your measurement "helpers" to estimate some lengths and heights. How can you check estimates?

15. The doorway in the picture above is $6\frac{1}{2}$ ft. high. Do you think Susan's height is 2 ft., $3\frac{1}{2}$ ft., or $4\frac{1}{2}$ ft.?

16. Dan measured a board. He said it was 15 inches long. Then Burt measured the board and said it was 1 ft. 3 in. long. Show that 1 ft. 3 in. = 15 in.

LEARN THESE FACTS

12 inches (in.) = 1 foot (ft.)
3 feet (ft.) = 1 yard (yd.)
36 inches (in.) = 1 yard (yd.)

How many inches are there in the following?

17. 1 ft. 8 in.   4 ft. 3 in.   1 ft. 9 in.   3 ft. 6 in.

18. 1 yd. 14 in.   1 yd. 27 in.   2 yd. 20 in. $1\frac{1}{2}$ yd.

Put on your thinking cap

▶ Oral review

1. Make a toy clock say: 4:15   5:45   6:30.

2. How long is it from 7:00 A.M. to 7:00 P.M.?

3. 1 min. = _?_ sec.   1 hr. = _?_ min.   1 ft. = _?_ in.

4. 1 day = _?_ hr.   1 yd. = _?_ in.   1 yd. = _?_ ft.

5. Read these numbers: 74,400   65,005   96,060

6. Which is more: 10,010 or 10,001?

7. $7000 + 500 + 40 + 9 = $ _?_.   9. 12 from 60 = _?_.

8. 3×9 is _?_ more than 3×8.   10. $3 \times 70 = $ _?_.

▶ Written review

1. Copy these numbers. Put in the commas.

1301   4076   12057   25255
6340   5505   16700   23006

2. Add $2.75, $3, and $.59.

3. Find the difference between 789 and 832.

4. Do these multiplications:
5×304 $5 \times \$.19$ $6 \times \$.53$

5. Last year Jim planted a young walnut tree. It was 27 in. tall. Now it is 40 in. tall.

Has the tree grown a foot? less than a foot? more than a foot?

Could you say the tree is now 1 yd. 4 in. tall?

6. Dan bought a punching bag for $2.98 and boxing gloves for $2.79. How much did he spend in all?

7. Harry helped his father pack 8 dozen eggs. Was that more or less than 100 eggs?

8. How much change would you get from a 5-dollar bill if you spent $2.47?

9. At 40¢ an hour, how much will Tom earn by working from 9:30 to 11:30?

10. Using the figures 0, 1, 2, and 3, write the largest number you can.

50

Problem study

If you have trouble with Problem 1 in Column A, do Problem 1 in Column B. Then go back and try Problem 1 in Column A again; and so on.

A

1. Sam wants riding breeches that cost $4.98 and boots that cost $5.98. How much will the breeches and the boots cost?

2. Bill is buying a 79-cent pencil sharpener. How much change will he get from a dollar bill?

3. A class wants 6 wigs for a play. How much will it cost to rent them at 25¢ apiece?

4. A camp sent in an order for 6 softballs at $2.05 each. How much will the 6 balls cost?

5. Andrew has saved $4.75. How much more does he need to buy a pair of boots costing $6.98?

6. Camp Carefree would like a new clock. It can get one for $9.00 or a smaller one for $4.75. What is the difference in price?

7. How many paper napkins will Jane get in 3 boxes if there are 80 napkins in each box?

8. If it takes William 18 hours to make 1 model airplane, how long will it take him to make 3 more?

B

1. Molly wants a lunch box that costs 20¢ and a thermos bottle that costs 78¢. How much will both cost?

2. Dan is buying a 40-cent bicycle bell. How much change will he get from a 50-cent piece?

3. A class needs 6 rulers. They cost 10¢ each. How much will the 6 rulers cost?

4. A boys' club is going to buy 3 baseball bats at 75¢ each. How much money does the club need?

5. Ellen wants a victrola record that costs 53¢. She has saved 50¢. How much more does she need?

6. Henry can buy a new book bag for 60¢ or he can buy his brother's old one for 30¢. What is the difference in price?

7. Sue bought 2 bags of popcorn balls. There were 5 balls in each bag. How many balls did she get?

8. If Jean can braid one pigtail in 3 minutes, how long does she need to braid both her pigtails?

Problem Test 1

Reach for a perfect score on this Problem Test.

1. There are 17 boys and 15 girls in a fourth-grade class. How many pupils are there in all?

2. How many days are there in 5 weeks?

3. Sam wants a mouth organ. He can get a red plastic one for 49¢. He has 23¢. How much more does he need to buy the mouth organ?

4. How much will Joseph have left from a dollar if he buys a parachute for 69¢?

5. Sue wants a tiny glass elephant for 19¢, a little rabbit for 23¢, and a dog for 29¢. How much will all three cost?

6. Jean needs 5 balls of yarn for a sweater. At $.59 a ball, what will the yarn cost?

7. Martha needs a suitcase. She can get one for $5.98 or a better one for $7.50. How much more does the one suitcase cost than the other?

8. Jim wants to make a sword. He needs 18 inches of wood for the dagger and 7 inches of wood for the crosspiece. Can he cut both pieces from a strip 2 feet long?

9. Jimmie wants to buy a 25-cent key chain and a 49-cent billfold. How much will both cost?

10. Find the cost of 5 switches for an electric train at $.49 each.

You have just taken Problem Test 1. How many problems did you have right? Give yourself 10 points for each correct answer. What is your mark?

There are 8 Problem Tests in this book. Keep a record of your score on each test.

Now is the time to test yourself

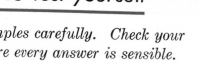

Copy the examples carefully. Check your answers. Be sure every answer is sensible.

1. $43 + 78 + 39$ 2. 3×648 3. From 732 take 274

4. $\$1.34 + \$6 + \$.75$ 5. $\$9 - \$5.63$ 6. Multiply 503 by 4

7. Write the numbers from 8,997 to 9,002.

8. William's uncle gave him a dog for his birthday.

William bought a harness for $.29, a plastic leash for $1, a dog sweater for $1.59, and a wire brush for $.50.

How much did all the things cost?

9. The Boys' Fishing Club gives each new member a club pin. The pins are shaped like fish and cost $.14 each.

How much will the club have to pay for pins for 6 new members?

10. Mary Jane is going to buy a bird cage for $1.29. She wonders how much change she will get from two dollars. Can you tell?

Just for fun

Victor said he knows a quick trick for finding the sum of the numbers from 1 to 19.

As a hint of how to do it, he started to make the drawing shown below.

Victor says the sum of the numbers from 1 to 19 is 9×20 plus 10. Explain his hint.

Can you make up a quick trick for finding the sum of the numbers from 1 to 9? from 1 to 29?

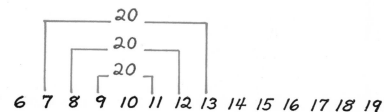

Halves — fourths — thirds

Joe

| $\frac{1}{2}$ | $\frac{1}{2}$ |

Tom

| $\frac{1}{2}$ |
| $\frac{1}{2}$ |

Dick

| $\frac{1}{2}$ / $\frac{1}{2}$ |

Nancy

| $\frac{1}{4}$ | $\frac{1}{4}$ |
| $\frac{1}{4}$ | $\frac{1}{4}$ |

Jane

| $\frac{1}{4}$ | $\frac{1}{4}$ | $\frac{1}{4}$ | $\frac{1}{4}$ |

Sue

| $\frac{1}{4}$ |
| $\frac{1}{4}$ |
| $\frac{1}{4}$ |
| $\frac{1}{4}$ |

May

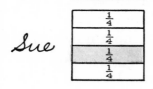

| $\frac{1}{3}$ | $\frac{1}{3}$ | $\frac{1}{3}$ |

Ann

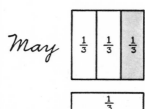

| $\frac{1}{3}$ |
| $\frac{1}{3}$ |
| $\frac{1}{3}$ |

1. Miss Carter gave each child in the class a sheet of paper. Each paper was the same size.

Joe, Tom, and Dick divided their papers into *2 equal parts*. How can Joe prove the 2 parts of his paper are the same size?

Each boy colored one of the 2 equal parts of his paper. He colored *one half* of the paper.

How do you write one half in figures?

2. Joe says $\frac{1}{2}$ of his paper is a *rectangle*. What shape is $\frac{1}{2}$ of Tom's paper? $\frac{1}{2}$ of Dick's?

3. Nancy, Jane, and Sue divided their papers into *4 equal parts*. How can Jane prove the 4 parts of her paper are the same size?

Each girl colored one of the 4 equal parts of her paper. She colored *one fourth* of the paper.

$\frac{1}{4}$ **means one fourth.**

4. Nancy says $\frac{1}{4}$ of her paper is a *square*. What shape is $\frac{1}{4}$ of Jane's paper? $\frac{1}{4}$ of Sue's?

5. May and Ann divided their papers into *3 equal parts*. How can May prove the 3 parts of her paper are the same size?

Each girl colored one of the 3 equal parts of her paper. She colored *one third* of the paper.

$\frac{1}{3}$ **means one third.**

6. What shape is $\frac{1}{3}$ of May's paper? $\frac{1}{3}$ of Ann's?

7. What is the name of each part if something is divided into 2 equal parts? into 3 equal parts? into 4 equal parts?

Peter and Peggy were quarreling over how to share a stick of candy. Just then Willie came along and said, "I'll divide it equally."

- Willie broke the stick into __?__ equal pieces.
- What part of it did Peter get? Peggy? Willie?
- If Peter and Peggy alone had divided the stick equally, what part would each have got?
- Which would you rather have: $\frac{1}{2}$ of a candy stick or $\frac{1}{3}$ of a stick? Which is more: $\frac{1}{2}$ or $\frac{1}{3}$?
- Do you think this set of comics has a good title?

1. In a whole there are __?__ halves; __?__ fourths; __?__ thirds.

2. In $\frac{1}{2}$ the 2 tells into how many equal parts a whole is divided.

When a whole is divided into 2 equal parts, the name of *each part* is a __?__ .

3. In $\frac{1}{3}$ the 3 tells into how many equal parts a whole is __?__ .

When a whole is divided into 3 equal parts, the name of each part is a __?__ .

Is this rectangle divided into thirds?

4. What is the name of each part when a whole is divided into 4 equal parts? 5? 6? 7? 8? 10?

5. In $\frac{1}{4}$ the 4 tells into how many equal parts a whole is divided.

What does the 5 tell in $\frac{1}{5}$? What does the 6 tell in $\frac{1}{6}$?

6. Fold a piece of paper to divide it into halves; fold another to divide it into thirds; fold another to divide it into fourths.

Write in figures on the correct parts: one half; one third; one fourth.

Using fractions

1. Tom had a small cake. He cut it into 2 equal pieces in order to share it with John. Each piece was what part of the cake?

2. Before Tom and John had picked up the pieces of cake, along came Dick and Carl. Then there were __?__ boys. If you had been Tom, how would you have cut the cake then?

3. Tom cut it this way:——→ Then he had __?__ equal pieces.

He said, "I cut each half cake in half. One half of one half is one fourth." How many fourths are there in half the cake? in the whole cake?

4. Tom took 1 fourth of the cake. John took 1 fourth of the cake. Together they took __?__ fourths of the cake.

Show on the picture in Ex. 3 how much they took.

2 fourths may be written this way: $\frac{2}{4}$.

5. Use the picture in Ex. 3 to show that $\frac{2}{4}$ is as much as $\frac{1}{2}$.

6. Three of the boys together ate 3 fourths of the cake. Show on the picture how much they ate.

3 fourths may be written this way: $\frac{3}{4}$.

7. Use the picture to show that $\frac{3}{4}$ is as much as $\frac{1}{2}$ and $\frac{1}{4}$ together.

8. The 4 boys together ate 4 fourths of the cake. 4 fourths may be written this way: $\frac{4}{4}$.

If they ate $\frac{4}{4}$ of the cake, did they eat the whole cake?

Numbers like $\frac{1}{2}$, $\frac{1}{4}$, $\frac{2}{4}$, $\frac{3}{4}$, and $\frac{4}{4}$ are called *fractions*.

9. Draw a circle. Divide it into 4 equal parts.

Color $\frac{1}{4}$ of the circle red. Color $\frac{1}{2}$ of the circle green.

What part of the circle have you colored all together?

Your coloring shows that $\frac{1}{4}$ and $\frac{1}{2}$ together make __?__ fourths.

Write the fraction that tells what part of your circle you have not colored.

56

More about fractions

1. Into how many equal parts is this bar divided? What is the name of each part?

2. How many fourths of the bar are colored? In the fraction $\frac{3}{4}$, the 4 tells the number of equal parts into which the bar is divided. The name of each part is a __?__. The 3 tells how many parts are colored.

3. What part of the bar in Ex. 1 is not colored?

4. In $\frac{1}{4}$, what does the 4 tell? What does the 1 tell?

5. Fold a piece of paper into 4 equal parts. Show $\frac{1}{4}$; $\frac{2}{4}$; $\frac{3}{4}$; $\frac{4}{4}$.

6. Use your ruler to draw a line 1 in. long; $\frac{1}{2}$ in. long; $\frac{1}{4}$ in.; $\frac{3}{4}$ in.

7. Does $\frac{2}{4}$ in. = $\frac{1}{2}$ in.?

8. Does $\frac{2}{2}$ in. = $\frac{4}{4}$ in.?

9. Jane divided this stick of chalk into 3 equal parts to share with Joy and Molly. Each piece is what part of the stick?

10. Jane kept $\frac{1}{3}$ of the chalk (Ex. 9). What part did she give to Joy? to Molly?

What part of the chalk did she give away all together?

11. What part of this chocolate bar will be gone when Albert eats 1 piece? 2 pieces? 3 pieces? 4 pieces? 5 pieces?

12. After Albert has eaten 2 pieces, what part of the bar will be left?

13. In $\frac{3}{5}$, what does the 5 tell? the 3?

14. Copy these fractions. Then write them as your teacher dictates them.

$$\frac{1}{4} \qquad \frac{1}{2} \qquad \frac{3}{4} \qquad \frac{2}{5} \qquad \frac{2}{3} \qquad \frac{4}{5} \qquad \frac{1}{5}$$

15. Draw a picture to show what each fraction in Ex. 14 means.

16. Ann cut a pie into 4 equal pieces. She served Jane and Bob each a piece.

How many different fractions can you write to show what part of the pie she gave them in all?

Making discoveries with fractions

1. One day when Joan was cutting grapefruit for breakfast, she made these discoveries about halves:

2 half grapefruit = 1 whole grapefruit $\frac{2}{2} = 1$
4 half grapefruit = 2 whole grapefruit $\frac{4}{2} = 2$
6 half grapefruit = __?__ whole grapefruit $\frac{6}{2} =$ __?__
8 half grapefruit = __?__ whole grapefruit $\frac{8}{2} =$ __?__

2. Joan also found that:

3 half grapefruit = one and one-half grapefruit $\frac{3}{2} = 1\frac{1}{2}$
5 half grapefruit = two and one-half grapefruit $\frac{5}{2} =$ __?__
7 half grapefruit = three and one-half grapefruit $\frac{7}{2} =$ __?__

3. Point to the grapefruit and count them by halves:

$\frac{1}{2}$ 1 $1\frac{1}{2}$ __?__ $2\frac{1}{2}$ __?__   __?__   4

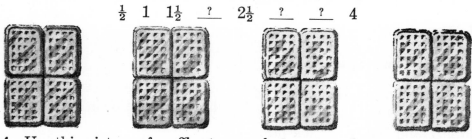

4. Use this picture of waffles to see what you can learn about fourths.

$\frac{2}{4} = \frac{?}{2}$ $\frac{2}{2} = \frac{?}{4}$ $\frac{7}{4} =$ __?__ $\frac{9}{4} =$ __?__ $3 = \frac{?}{4}$ $3\frac{1}{2} = \frac{?}{4}$

$2 = \frac{?}{4}$ $\frac{6}{4} =$ __?__ $2\frac{1}{2} = \frac{?}{4}$ $\frac{10}{4} =$ __?__ $\frac{5}{4} =$ __?__ $\frac{13}{4} =$ __?__

5. Point to the waffles and count them by fourths:

$\frac{1}{4}$ $\frac{1}{2}$ $\frac{3}{4}$ __?__ $1\frac{1}{4}$ $1\frac{1}{2}$ __?__   2 $2\frac{1}{4}$ __?__ $2\frac{3}{4}$ __?__ $3\frac{1}{4}$ $3\frac{1}{2}$ $3\frac{3}{4}$ __?__

58

Using division

The Outdoor Club is having a picnic. Ann, Molly, and June are to make the sandwiches.

The girls know they need 2 slices of bread for each sandwich. They know there are 18 slices of bread in a loaf.

They wonder how many sandwiches they can make from a loaf of bread. Do you know? Try to find out without help.

① Ann is drawing the picture at the left to help her find how many sandwiches they can make from a loaf of bread. First she drew the 18 slices. Count them by twos. Now she is drawing a line around each group of 2 slices. How many groups of 2 will she find there are in 18? How many sandwiches can they make from 18 slices of bread?

② Molly started with 18 slices of bread, and kept subtracting 2 slices until she had no slices left. Look at her work in this box:——————➝ How many times did she take 2 slices away? Her subtraction shows there are __?__ twos in 18. She said, "We can make __?__ sandwiches."

③ June said, "I find the answer by *dividing*. To find how many groups of 2 slices there are in 18 slices, I *divide* 18 by 2. 18 *divided by* 2 is 9. We can make 9 sandwiches out of 18 slices of bread."

18 divided by 2 may be written in these two ways: $18 \div 2$, or $2\overline{)18}$. The sign $\div$ is read "divided by." It is the *division sign*.

$$
\begin{array}{r}
18 \\
-\ 2 \quad\surd \\
\hline
16 \\
-\ 2 \quad\surd \\
\hline
14 \\
-\ 2 \quad\surd \\
\hline
12 \\
-\ 2 \quad\surd \\
\hline
10 \\
-\ 2 \quad\surd \\
\hline
8 \\
-\ 2 \quad\surd \\
\hline
6 \\
-\ 2 \quad\surd \\
\hline
4 \\
-\ 2 \quad\surd \\
\hline
2 \\
-\ 2 \quad\surd \\
\hline
0
\end{array}
$$

1. How do you read these divisions?

$16 \div 2 = 8$ $10 \div 2 = 5$ $12 \div 2 = 6$ $14 \div 2 = 7$

2. "$18 \div 2 = $ __?__ " asks the question, "How many 2's are there in 18?" What questions do these divisions ask?

$14 \div 2 = $ __?__ $8 \div 2 = $ __?__ $2\overline{)6}$ $2\overline{)12}$ $2\overline{)10}$

59

Using division

1. Use Ann's drawing on page 59 to find how many sandwiches you can make from 4 slices of bread; 6 slices; 8; 10; 12; 14; 16.

2. Use Molly's subtractions to find how many sandwiches you can make from 4 slices; 6; 8; 10; 12; 14; 16.

3. Divide to find how many sandwiches you can make from 4 slices; 6; 8; 10; 12; 14; 16.

Think, "If one sandwich takes 2 slices, from 4 slices I can make as many sandwiches as there are 2's in 4."

To find how many 2's there are in 4, divide 4 by 2. $4 \div 2 = 2$. You can make 2 sandwiches out of 4 slices of bread.

4. How many 2-cent stamps can you buy for 8¢? 10¢? 18¢? 14¢? Prove your answers with toy coins.

5. At 2 for 1¢, how much will 6 paper clips cost? 8? 10?

6. If 16 children line up two-by-two, how many pairs of children will there be?

7. How many clothespins will Ann need to hang up 14 socks if she hangs 2 socks with each pin?

8. How many sheets of paper would you need to make an 18-page notebook? Use sheets of paper to prove your answer.

Show that each sheet makes 2 pages. The front of the first sheet is page 1; the back of it is page 2.

9. Tom can trade 10 one-cent stamps for __?__ two-cent stamps.

10. For a hoop dance each pair of children needs a hoop. How many hoops do 8 children need? 12? 16? 20?

Using division

1. One peanut bar costs 5¢. How many can you get for 20¢? Can you find out without help?

Think, "If 1 bar costs 5¢, for 20¢ I can buy as many bars as there are 5's in 20."

● Show how many 5's there are in 20 by a drawing; then show it by starting with 20 and subtracting 5 over and over.

● To find how many 5's there are in 20, you *divide 20 by 5*.

$20 \div 5 = 4$. You can get __?__ bars for 20¢.

2. Tell what you think to find how many 5-cent balloons you can buy for 15¢; 20¢; 25¢; 35¢; 40¢; 45¢; 30¢; 10¢.

3. Tell what you think to find how many 3-cent stamps you can buy for 6¢; 9¢; 12¢; 15¢; 18¢; 21¢; 24¢; 27¢.

4. Which picture below shows:

● that there are 3 fours in 12, and 4 threes in 12?

● that $8 \div 2 = 4$, and $8 \div 4 = 2$?

● that there are 2 threes in 6, and 3 twos in 6?

```
▲ ▲ ▲ ▲  │ ▲ ▲ │ ▲ ▲ ▲ ▲
▲ ▲ ▲ ▲  │ ▲ ▲ │ ▲ ▲ ▲ ▲
▲ ▲ ▲ ▲  │ ▲ ▲ │
```

5. $27 \div 3 = 9$, so $27 \div 9 = $ __?__

6. $18 \div 6 = 3$, so $18 \div 3 = $ __?__

7. $45 \div 9 = 5$, so $45 \div 5 = $ __?__

8. $35 \div 5 = 7$, so $35 \div 7 = $ __?__

9. These 4 facts belong to a Number Family. Why?

$$4 \times 5 = 20 \qquad 20 \div 5 = 4$$
$$5 \times 4 = 20 \qquad 20 \div 4 = 5$$

10. Name 3 other facts in the family of each of these:

$$7 \times 2 = 14 \qquad 21 \div 7 = 3$$
$$7 \times 5 = 35 \qquad 18 \div 3 = 6$$
$$8 \times 3 = 24 \qquad 16 \div 2 = 8$$
$$9 \times 5 = 45 \qquad 27 \div 3 = 9$$

11. $5 \times 8 = 40$, so $40 \div 8 = $ __?__

12. $7 \times 3 = 21$, so $21 \div 3 = $ __?__

13. $2 \times 9 = 18$, so $18 \div 9 = $ __?__

14. How does $9 + 9 + 9 = 27$ show that $27 \div 9 = 3$?

15. How does $8 + 8 = 16$ show that $16 \div 8 = 2$?

16. Use a ruler to show how many 3-inch lengths there are in 12 inches.

17. Write the division that Ex. 16 teaches.

Finding $\frac{1}{2}$ of a number

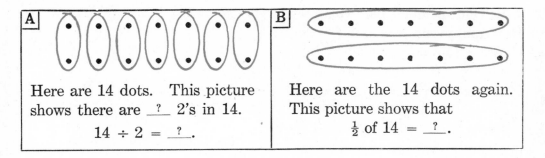

A Here are 14 dots. This picture shows there are __?__ 2's in 14.

$$14 \div 2 = \underline{\ ?\ }.$$

B Here are the 14 dots again. This picture shows that

$$\frac{1}{2} \text{ of } 14 = \underline{\ ?\ }.$$

1. Picture A above shows that $14 \div 2 = 7$. Picture B shows that $\frac{1}{2}$ of 14 *also* equals 7. Do you agree?

2. Peter said, "Any number divided by 2 is as many as $\frac{1}{2}$ of the number. I can prove it by the pictures below."

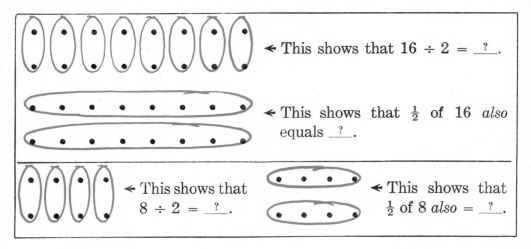

← This shows that $16 \div 2 = \underline{\ ?\ }$.

← This shows that $\frac{1}{2}$ of 16 *also* equals __?__.

← This shows that $8 \div 2 = \underline{\ ?\ }$.

← This shows that $\frac{1}{2}$ of 8 *also* $= \underline{\ ?\ }$.

3. Doris and Ethel want to share 18 gumdrops equally. How many should each girl take?

Think, "To divide 18 gumdrops equally between 2 girls, give each $\frac{1}{2}$ of 18 gumdrops.

"To find $\frac{1}{2}$ of 18, divide 18 by 2. $18 \div 2 = 9$." Use counters to prove your answer.

4. Tell what you think when you find how many gumdrops each girl gets if 2 girls share 10 gumdrops; 8 gumdrops; 16; 20; 14; 6. Use counters to prove your answers.

| To find $\frac{1}{2}$ of a number, divide the number by 2.

62

$\frac{1}{3}$ of a number — $\frac{1}{5}$ of a number

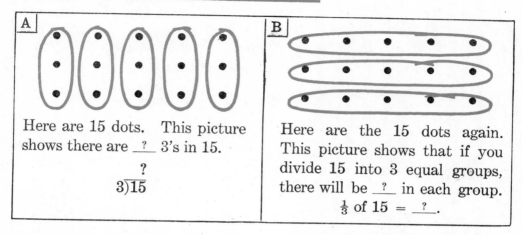

A Here are 15 dots. This picture shows there are __?__ 3's in 15.

$$3\overline{)15}^{?}$$

B Here are the 15 dots again. This picture shows that if you divide 15 into 3 equal groups, there will be __?__ in each group. $\frac{1}{3}$ of 15 = __?__.

1. Picture A above shows you that $15 \div 3 =$ __?__.

Picture B shows that $\frac{1}{3}$ of 15 *also* equals __?__.

To find $\frac{1}{3}$ of 15, divide 15 by __?__. To find $\frac{1}{3}$ of any number, divide the number by __?__.

2. How many pennies can you put in each of 3 equal piles if you have 6 pennies? 9 pennies? 12? 15? 18? 21? 24? 27?

3. Use toy coins to prove your answers in Ex. 2.

4. Three boys caught 24 fish. They want to share the fish equally. How many fish should each boy take?

Think, "To divide 24 fish equally among 3 boys, give each boy $\frac{1}{3}$ of the fish. To find $\frac{1}{3}$ of 24, divide 24 by 3. $24 \div 3 = 8$. Each boy should take __?__ fish."

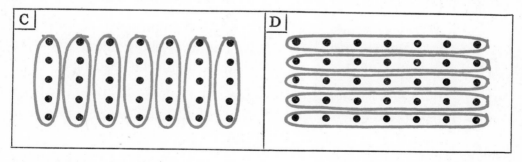

5. Picture C shows you that $35 \div 5 =$ __?__. Picture D shows that $\frac{1}{5}$ of 35 = __?__.

6. To find $\frac{1}{5}$ of 35, divide 35 by __?__. To find $\frac{1}{5}$ of any number, divide the number by __?__.

33 Broad Street
Windsor, Ohio
October 10, 195–

Good's Sport Shop
Bangor, Ohio

Dear Mr. Good:

Will you please send me two 15-cent arrow tips? I am enclosing 30¢ in stamps.

Yours truly,
William Rogers

Ordering by mail

1. Read William's letter. To pay for the arrow tips, he has:

    10 one-cent stamps
    12 two-cent stamps
    8 three-cent stamps
    1 five-cent stamp

2. Does he have enough 3-cent stamps to pay for the arrow tips?

3. If William sends the 10 one-cent stamps, can he send the rest of the 30¢ in three-cent stamps? Why not?

4. If William sends the 12 two-cent stamps, how many one-cent stamps should he send?

5. If William sends the 8 three-cent stamps, how many two-cent stamps should he send?

6. If William sends the 10 one-cent stamps, how many two-cent stamps should he send?

7. If William sends 6 two-cent stamps, how many three-cent stamps should he send?

8. If William sends 10 one-cent stamps and 1 five-cent stamp, can he send the rest of the 30¢ in two-cent stamps? in three-cent stamps?

9. William found 10 different ways to pay for the arrow tips by using the stamps he had. See if your class can find more than 10 ways.

10. When William mails his letter, what kind of stamp or stamps will be put on the envelope?

11. If William had sent coins to pay for the arrow tips, he would have needed a coin holder. Why?

12. What is the smallest number of coins William could have sent to pay for the arrow tips? What coins are they?

13. Would you like to make a coin holder like the one shown at the bottom of the page? Use heavy paper. Measure carefully.

14. Nancy is ordering by mail 4 twelve-cent calendars. How much should she send to pay for them?

15. What is the smallest number of coins Nancy can send to make 48¢? What coins are they?

16. If Nancy sends 10 one-cent stamps and 10 two-cent stamps, how many three-cent stamps will she also have to send to pay for the calendars?

17. What is the smallest number of coins Jack could send to make 68¢? 72¢? 77¢? 84¢? What coins are they in each case?

Second—fold here

Third—fold here

First—fold here

PLACE COINS HERE

COIN HOLDER

Use for sending coins through the mails

Test on division facts

Practice saying the answers to these divisions. Try to write all the answers on folded paper in 5 minutes.

Make and study Help-Yourself Cards for any facts you do not know. See page 309. Practice taking the test until you can write every answer correctly in 5 minutes.

	a	b	c	d	e	f	g	h
1.	4)8	2)6	3)9	1)5	1)7	2)4	5)10	4)12
2.	3)12	5)20	1)4	9)27	3)15	8)24	2)8	1)3
3.	5)5	5)45	3)3	2)2	2)18	5)15	3)6	5)40
4.	6)30	3)18	2)16	5)35	3)21	6)18	6)12	4)20
5.	1)8	8)16	3)24	1)9	5)30	2)10	5)25	3)27
6.	9)45	2)12	7)35	8)40	7)21	1)2	2)14	9)18

Watch the signs

	a	b	c	d	e
1.	$8 + 7$	$13 - 5$	3×8	$9 + 4$	$27 \div 3$
2.	2×9	$8 + 9$	$14 - 8$	$8 \div 4$	$8 + 8$
3.	$20 \div 4$	3×9	$9 + 7$	$12 - 8$	5×9
4.	$14 - 7$	$24 \div 3$	4×3	$6 + 9$	$11 - 3$
5.	$9 + 5$	$10 - 8$	$12 \div 4$	$18 \div 3$	$17 - 9$

6. $\underline{?} \times 2 = 0$ $\underline{?} \times 3 = 0$ $\underline{?} \times 4 = 0$
$\underline{?} \div 2 = 0$ $\underline{?} \div 3 = 0$ $\underline{?} \div 4 = 0$

Be your own teacher

You have never been taught how to do the problems on this page. But in arithmetic you can be your own teacher.

See how many different ways the pupils in your class can find to solve these problems.

1. Herbert received 40 cents an hour for mowing lawns. One Saturday he worked from 9:30 A.M. till noon. How much did he earn?

2. Joe knew that numbers like 2, 4, 6, 8, and so on, are *even numbers;* and that numbers like 1, 3, 5, 7, 9, and so on, are *odd numbers.* He decided that:
- the sum of two even numbers is an _?_ number.
- the sum of two odd numbers is an _?_ number.
- the sum of an even number and an odd number is an _?_ number.

3. Tom needs 60 inches of rope to tie his dog at night. The rope he wants is sold by the foot. How many feet should he ask for?

4. Each of the 24 pupils in a fourth-grade class earned a quarter for the Junior Red Cross. How much did they earn all together?

5. Joan practices her music lesson a half hour every day. How many hours does she practice in a week?

6. Billy can get 3 peanut bars for a dime. How much will he have to pay for a dozen of the peanut bars? Draw a picture of the problem.

7. Mary is making corn-meal mush. The recipe says, "Use 3 cups of boiling water to 1 cup of corn meal."

Mary wants to make half the recipe. How much corn meal should she use? How much water should she use?

8. Jim has saved **32 quarters.** He wants them **changed into dollar** bills.

How many dollar bills can he get for the 32 quarters? Will a picture help you?

9. Betty bought 20¢ worth of apples. Apples were selling at 3 for 5 cents. How many apples did she buy? Draw a picture of the problem.

10. Alice bought $2\frac{1}{2}$ pounds of bird food at 10¢ a pound. How much did she spend?

To the Teacher: See Note 1 on page 310.

SEASIDE SNACK STAND

$\frac{1}{2}$ of 6 dimes = 3 dimes

$\frac{1}{2}$ of 60¢ = 30¢

Using dimes in division

1. Bob and Sue have 60¢. If they share the money equally, how much can each spend at the Snack Stand?

Bob figured out the answer to this problem in the sand. Explain his work. Is it correct?

Study the pictures of dimes. Then tell the missing numbers.

2.

$\frac{1}{2}$ of 4 dimes = __?__ dimes
$\frac{1}{2}$ of 40¢ = __?__ ¢

3.

$\frac{1}{2}$ of 8 dimes = __?__ dimes
$\frac{1}{2}$ of 80¢ = __?__ ¢

4.

$\frac{1}{2}$ of 6 dimes = __?__ dimes
$\frac{1}{2}$ of 60¢ = __?__ ¢

5.

$\frac{1}{2}$ of 10 dimes = __?__ dimes
$\frac{1}{2}$ of 100¢ = __?__ ¢

6.

$\frac{1}{2}$ of 12 dimes = __?__ dimes
$\frac{1}{2}$ of 120¢ = __?__ ¢

Uneven division facts

1. Sam has saved 17 pennies in his penny-saving bank. He wants to have the pennies changed into nickels. How many nickels can he get for 15 pennies? for 17 pennies? Use coins to prove your answer.

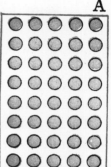
A

2. Sam said that 17 pennies = 3 nickels and 2 pennies. $17 \div 5 = 3$ and 2 left over. The 2 that is left over is called the *remainder*.

3. In Picture A, how many circles are there in each row?

4. Picture A shows that in 6 there is 1 five and 1 left over; in 8 there is 1 five and 3 over; in 11 there are 2 fives and ___?___ over.

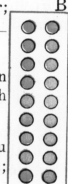
B

5. Use Picture A to help you tell how many 5's there are in each number from 12 to 45. Also tell the remainder in each division.

6. Use Picture A to help you tell how many nickels you can get for 14¢; for 18¢; for 22¢; for 28¢; for 31¢; for 37¢; for 44¢; for 48¢.

7. Use Picture B to help you tell how many 2's there are in each number from 2 to 18. Tell the remainder in each division.

C

8. Use Picture B to help you tell how many 2-cent balloons you can buy for 3¢; for 9¢; for 5¢; 7¢; 13¢; 19¢; 11¢; 15¢.

9. Use Picture C to help you tell how many 3's there are in each number from 3 to 27. Tell the remainder in each division.

10. Use Picture C to help you tell how many 3-cent stamps you can buy for 4¢; 7¢; 11¢; 13¢; 17¢; 19¢; 23¢; 25¢; 29¢.

Helping Numbers

1. Count from 5 to 50 by 5's. Do any of these numbers have a remainder when divided by 5?

2. Count from 2 to 20 by 2's. These are all *even numbers*.

Do any of these numbers have a remainder when divided by 2?

3. Count from 1 to 19 by 2's. These are all *odd numbers*.

Do any of these numbers have a remainder when divided by 2?

4. Count from 3 to 30 by 3's. Do any of these numbers have a remainder when divided by 3?

5. Sam said, "When I divide by 5, these are my Dividing-by-Five Helping Numbers: 5, 10, 15, 20, 25, 30, 35, 40, 45, 50"

Tell why Sam calls them Helping Numbers.

6. When Sam finds how many 5's there are in 23, he must *first* think, "20 is my Helping Number. How many 5's are there in 20?"

Next Sam thinks, "There are *four* 5's in 20."

How does he then find the remainder?

7. Why did Sam choose 20 for his Helping Number in Ex. 6?

8. What Helping Number would you use in finding how many 5's there are in each of these numbers?

29	41	26	38	32	36
18	13	9	28	27	39
42	19	43	12	31	48

9. Can you make a rule to explain how to choose the correct Helping Numbers in Ex. 8?

10. In dividing each number in Ex. 8 by 5, what subtraction must you do to find the remainder?

11. Divide each of the numbers in Ex. 8 by 5.

Say, "In 29 there are five 5's, and 4 left over"; and so on.

12. Joy has 23¢. How many 5-cent bags of popcorn can she buy?

How many cents will she have left over? Use toy money to prove your answers.

13. Draw a picture to show the meaning of: In 17 there are three 5's and 2 left over.

14. $5 + 5 + 5 + 4 = 19$ proves that in 19 there are 3 fives and 4 left over. Explain.

Uneven division facts

1. What Helping Number do you use in finding how many 3's there are in each of the following numbers?

7	16	22	10	13
8	25	29	19	11
28	17	20	23	14

2. Can you make a rule to explain how to choose the correct Helping Numbers in Ex. 1?

3. In dividing each number in Ex. 1, what subtraction must you do to find the remainder?

4. Divide each number in Ex. 1 by 3. In the first number say, "In 7 there are 2 threes, and 1 left over"; and so on.

5. When you find **how many** 5's there are in 17, you may write the example this way: ⟶

$$5 \overline{)17} \quad 3\ r2$$

r2 means a remainder of 2. It tells that there are _?_ left over.

Notice where the 3 is written.

6. Explain each of these divisions. Use counters.

$$3\overline{)20}\ 6\ r2 \qquad 3\overline{)25}\ 8\ r1 \qquad 4\overline{)22}\ 5\ r2 \qquad 3\overline{)29}\ 9\ r2$$

$$3\overline{)26}\ 8\ r2 \qquad 4\overline{)19}\ 4\ r3 \qquad 5\overline{)49}\ 9\ r4 \qquad 4\overline{)23}\ 5\ r3$$

7. Copy the examples in Ex. 6 without the answers. Work each one. Then look to see if your answers are right and written in the correct place.

Do these divisions orally. Then copy and divide. Be sure to write each answer in the correct place.

	a	b	c	d	e	f	g
8.	5)9	3)25	5)19	3)8	5)21	3)12	5)32
9.	3)11	3)9	5)46	2)13	3)28	2)15	5)34
10.	5)42	3)18	5)14	3)24	3)23	2)19	2)19
11.	2)17	5)38	3)21	3)15	5)28	3)27	5)18
12.	3)19	2)11	3)29	3)14	3)10	5)12	2)9
13.	2)7	3)13	5)24	3)20	3)3	3)22	5)27

UNIT
10

Two-place quotients with-
out carrying. Three-place
quotients without carrying

Oral practice in dividing

1. Don and Bill want to share 40 rubber bands equally.

Don said, "40 = 4 tens; $\frac{1}{2}$ of 4 tens = 2 tens = 20. We should each take __?__ rubber bands."

2. How many rubber bands should each of 2 boys take if they share equally 20 bands? 60? 80? 100? 120? 140? 180? 200?

$\frac{1}{2}$ of 6 = __?__ $\frac{1}{2}$ of 60 = __?__

3. $\frac{1}{2}$ of 60 = $\frac{1}{2}$ of 6 tens = 3 tens = __?__.   60 ÷ 2 = __?__

4. $\frac{1}{2}$ of 80 = $\frac{1}{2}$ of 8 tens = 4 tens = __?__.   80 ÷ 2 = __?__

5. $\frac{1}{2}$ of 100 = $\frac{1}{2}$ of 10 tens = 5 tens = __?__.   100 ÷ 2 = __?__

6. $\frac{1}{2}$ of 120 = $\frac{1}{2}$ of 12 tens = 6 tens = __?__.   120 ÷ 2 = __?__

7. $\frac{1}{2}$ of 200 = $\frac{1}{2}$ of 2 hundreds = 1 hundred.   200 ÷ 2 = __?__

8. $\frac{1}{2}$ of 400 = $\frac{1}{2}$ of 4 hundreds = 2 hundred.   400 ÷ 2 = __?__

9. $\frac{1}{3}$ of 60 = $\frac{1}{3}$ of 6 tens = __?__ tens = __?__.   60 ÷ 3 = __?__

10. $\frac{1}{3}$ of 90 = $\frac{1}{3}$ of 9 tens = __?__ tens = __?__.   90 ÷ 3 = __?__

11. $\frac{1}{3}$ of 120 = $\frac{1}{3}$ of 12 tens = __?__ tens = __?__.   120 ÷ 3 = __?__

12. $\frac{1}{3}$ of 180 = $\frac{1}{3}$ of 18 tens = __?__ tens = __?__.   180 ÷ 3 = __?__

13. $\frac{1}{5}$ of 100 = $\frac{1}{5}$ of 10 tens = __?__ tens = __?__.   100 ÷ 5 = __?__

14. $\frac{1}{5}$ of 150 = $\frac{1}{5}$ of 15 tens = __?__ tens = __?__.   150 ÷ 5 = __?__

15. $\frac{1}{5}$ of 200 = $\frac{1}{5}$ of 20 tens = __?__ tens = __?__.   200 ÷ 5 = __?__

16. Five boys want to share 150 paper clips. How many clips should each boy take?

17. Three girls are buying a victrola record. It costs 60¢. If they share the cost equally, how much should each girl pay?

18. Miss Jones asked Bill and Don to carry 80 books from the book closet. If they share the work equally, how many books should each boy carry?

19. If 3 boys share equally 120 stamps, each will get __?__ stamps.

Jack's test paper

This is Jack White. He just got back his arithmetic test paper. Did the teacher mark his examples correctly?

Tell how you would correct Jack's mistakes.

Jack White   November 4

1. $ 3.19
    .75
    .86
   2.04
   ‾‾‾‾‾
   $6.84 ✓

2.   28
    506
     34
    827
   ‾‾‾‾
   1385 ✗

3.   7 r 2
     5) 37   ✓

4. 26 ÷ 3 = 7 r 5
              ✗

5. $9.82
  −4.79
  ‾‾‾‾‾
  $5.03 ✓

6. $4.85
    × 3
   ‾‾‾‾
   $14.55 ✓

7. 302
    × 9
   ‾‾‾‾
   2718 ✓

8. 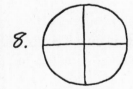 This circle shows that $\frac{2}{4} = \frac{1}{2}$ ✓

9.   948 + 56 − 56 = 948 ✓

10. You could trade 160 pennies
     for 1 dollar and 6 dimes. ✓

Oral practice in dividing

1. Betsy and Sue want to share 46 pine cones equally. How many should each girl take?

46 = 4 tens and 6 ones

$\frac{1}{2}$ of 4 tens = 20

$\frac{1}{2}$ of 6 ones = 3

So $\frac{1}{2}$ of 46 = 20 + 3 = __?__

2. How many cones should each girl take if they share equally 48 cones? 64 cones? 86 cones? 108? 126?

3. How many shells should each of 2 boys take if they share equally 68 shells? 146 shells?

4. $\frac{1}{2}$ of 64 ➤ $\frac{1}{2}$ of 60 plus $\frac{1}{2}$ of 4 = 30 + 2, or __?__.   64 ÷ 2 = __?__

5. $\frac{1}{2}$ of 86 ➤ $\frac{1}{2}$ of 80 plus $\frac{1}{2}$ of 6 = 40 + 3, or __?__.   86 ÷ 2 = __?__

6. $\frac{1}{2}$ of 106 ➤ $\frac{1}{2}$ of 100 plus $\frac{1}{2}$ of 6 = 50 + 3, or __?__.   106 ÷ 2 = __?__

7. $\frac{1}{2}$ of 124 ➤ $\frac{1}{2}$ of 120 plus $\frac{1}{2}$ of 4 = 60 + 2, or __?__.   124 ÷ 2 = __?__

8. $\frac{1}{3}$ of 36 ➤ $\frac{1}{3}$ of 30 plus $\frac{1}{3}$ of 6 = 10 + 2, or __?__.   36 ÷ 3 = __?__

9. $\frac{1}{3}$ of 99 ➤ $\frac{1}{3}$ of 90 plus $\frac{1}{3}$ of 9 = 30 + 3, or __?__.   99 ÷ 3 = __?__

10. $\frac{1}{3}$ of 126 ➤ $\frac{1}{3}$ of 120 plus $\frac{1}{3}$ of 6 = 40 + 2, or __?__.   126 ÷ 3 = __?__

11. $\frac{1}{3}$ of 159 ➤ $\frac{1}{3}$ of 150 plus $\frac{1}{3}$ of 9 = 50 + 3, or __?__.   159 ÷ 3 = __?__

12. $\frac{1}{5}$ of 155 ➤ $\frac{1}{5}$ of 150 plus $\frac{1}{5}$ of 5 = 30 + 1, or __?__.   155 ÷ 5 = __?__

13. If 3 boys share 69 walnuts equally, how many will each get?

14. Two girls are buying a game. It costs 48¢. If they share the cost equally, how much should each girl pay?

15. If 5 boys share 205 seeds equally, how many will each get?
Prove your answer by doing an addition.

16. Mike had a rope 108 inches long. He cut it into 2 equal pieces. Each piece was __?__ inches long.

17. Esther baked 96 cookies. She wants to divide them equally among her mother, her aunt, and her best friend. How many should she give to each?

18. 43 + 43 + 43 = 129 shows that $\frac{1}{3}$ of 129 = __?__.

74

Writing divisions

1. Jane and Sue are making puppets. Jane has made 26 wooden hands. That is enough hands for how many puppets?

Each puppet needs 2 hands; so 26 hands will make as many puppets as there are 2's in 26. $26 \div 2 =$ ___?___.

$$\begin{array}{r} 13 \\ 2\overline{)26} \end{array}$$

▶ Think, "How many 2's in 2? One." Write 1 above the 2.

▶ Think, "How many 2's in 6? Three." Write 3 above the 6.

▶ There are ___?___ twos in 26.

▶ Check the division this way: $20 \div 2 = 10$; $6 \div 2 = 3$. So $26 \div 2 = 10 + 3$, or 13.

2. Check each division in this example by thinking this way:

$$40 \div 2 = 20; \quad 8 \div 2 = 4; \text{ so}$$
$$48 \div 2 = 20 + 4, \text{ or } \underline{}.$$

$$\begin{array}{r} 24 \\ 2\overline{)48} \end{array} \qquad \begin{array}{r} 32 \\ 3\overline{)96} \end{array} \qquad \begin{array}{r} 51 \\ 5\overline{)255} \end{array} \qquad \begin{array}{r} 42 \\ 3\overline{)126} \end{array}$$

3. Copy the examples in Ex. 2 without the answers. Work them, then look to see if your answers are right. Be sure to write each figure in exactly the right place.

4. Which division in Ex. 2 shows that 126 pennies will make 42 piles with 3 pennies in each pile?

Do these divisions orally. Then copy and divide.

	a	b	c	d	e	f
5.	$3\overline{)156}$	$4\overline{)168}$	$5\overline{)55}$	$2\overline{)86}$	$3\overline{)189}$	$4\overline{)208}$
6.	$3\overline{)210}$	$5\overline{)455}$	$4\overline{)80}$	$2\overline{)184}$	$5\overline{)400}$	$3\overline{)273}$
7.	$5\overline{)200}$	$4\overline{)88}$	$3\overline{)123}$	$5\overline{)300}$	$4\overline{)204}$	$3\overline{)150}$
8.	$5\overline{)355}$	$6\overline{)186}$	$4\overline{)124}$	$5\overline{)450}$	$3\overline{)270}$	$4\overline{)128}$

To the Teacher: See note 2 on page 310.

Harder divisions

Sue has made 29 wooden feet for puppets. She did this division and said, "29 feet are enough feet for 14 puppets and there will be 1 *puppet* left over."

$$\begin{array}{r} 14\text{ r}1 \\ 2\overline{)29} \end{array}$$

Andrew said, "Oh, no! There will be 1 *foot* left over."

What do *you* think the division shows?

1. Check the divisions below this way:

$$\begin{aligned} 40 \div 2 &= 20 \\ 7 \div 2 &= \underline{\ 3\text{ r}1} \\ \text{So } 47 \div 2 &= 23\text{ r}1 \end{aligned}$$

$$\begin{array}{ccc} 23\text{ r}1 & 41\text{ r}2 & 31\text{ r}3 \\ 2\overline{)47} & 5\overline{)207} & 4\overline{)127} \end{array}$$

2. Copy the divisions above without answers. Work them. Then see if your answers are right.

Divide orally. Then copy and divide.

3. $3\overline{)155}$ $\quad$ $4\overline{)209}$ $\quad$ $5\overline{)358}$

4. $4\overline{)127}$ $\quad$ $3\overline{)217}$ $\quad$ $2\overline{)189}$

5. $4\overline{)205}$ $\quad$ $5\overline{)409}$ $\quad$ $3\overline{)129}$

6. $3\overline{)244}$ $\quad$ $4\overline{)86}$ $\quad$ $5\overline{)456}$

7. $5\overline{)307}$ $\quad$ $3\overline{)187}$ $\quad$ $4\overline{)205}$

8. Check the divisions below this way:

$$\begin{aligned} 300 \div 3 &= 100 \\ 90 \div 3 &= 30 \\ 9 \div 3 &= \underline{\ \ 3} \\ \text{So } 399 \div 3 &= 133 \end{aligned}$$

$$\begin{array}{ccc} 133 & 432\text{ r}1 & 402 \\ 3\overline{)399} & 2\overline{)865} & 2\overline{)804} \end{array}$$

$$\begin{array}{ccc} 302 & 501 & 900 \\ 4\overline{)1208} & 5\overline{)2505} & 3\overline{)2700} \end{array}$$

9. Copy the divisions above without the answers. Work them. Then see if your answers are right.

10. $2\overline{)684}$ $\quad$ $5\overline{)1505}$ $\quad$ $5\overline{)1500}$

11. $2\overline{)847}$ $\quad$ $3\overline{)1806}$ $\quad$ $2\overline{)1805}$

12. $5\overline{)4500}$ $\quad$ $3\overline{)2409}$ $\quad$ $2\overline{)1648}$

13. $4\overline{)2008}$ $\quad$ $2\overline{)1247}$ $\quad$ $3\overline{)2168}$

14. One half of the 486 children in the Rosemont School are boys. How many boys are there in the school? How many girls?

15. Bill is driving 426 miles with his father. His father says when they have gone half the distance they will eat their lunch.

How far will they drive before lunch? after lunch?

Do each division in Exs. 16–21 in these two ways:

Oral Way

648 = 600 + 40 + 8

$$600 \div 2 = 300$$
$$40 \div 2 = 20$$
$$8 \div 2 = 4$$

So 648 ÷ 2 = 324

Written Way

Write the division this way: $2\overline{)648}$ with 324

Think, "6 ÷ 2 = 3." Write the 3.
Think, "4 ÷ 2 = 2." Write the 2.
Think, "8 ÷ 2 = 4." Write the 4.
The division shows that 648 ÷ 2 = 324.

	a	b	c	d	e	f
16.	$2\overline{)648}$	$3\overline{)937}$	$4\overline{)808}$	$5\overline{)3505}$	$3\overline{)1809}$	$4\overline{)1209}$
17.	$2\overline{)684}$	$4\overline{)448}$	$3\overline{)603}$	$2\overline{)1800}$	$4\overline{)2008}$	$5\overline{)4500}$
18.	$5\overline{)555}$	$2\overline{)806}$	$2\overline{)408}$	$3\overline{)1507}$	$2\overline{)1604}$	$4\overline{)2004}$
19.	$3\overline{)696}$	$4\overline{)846}$	$3\overline{)903}$	$4\overline{)1208}$	$5\overline{)4005}$	$3\overline{)2100}$
20.	$4\overline{)884}$	$3\overline{)965}$	$2\overline{)808}$	$5\overline{)3007}$	$3\overline{)1209}$	$5\overline{)1000}$
21.	$5\overline{)539}$	$2\overline{)487}$	$4\overline{)815}$	$4\overline{)1220}$	$3\overline{)690}$	$4\overline{)1280}$

Whose answer to each of these divisions is sensible? Tell why.

		JANE'S ANSWER	BILL'S ANSWER	TOM'S ANSWER
22.	2109 ÷ 3	73	703	730
23.	1680 ÷ 2	804	84	840
24.	1260 ÷ 3	42	402	420
25.	455 ÷ 5	901	910	91
26.	4505 ÷ 5	91	901	910
27.	2760 ÷ 3	902	920	92
28.	3500 ÷ 5	50	900	700
29.	1809 ÷ 3	630	63	603
30.	1664 ÷ 2	832	82	83

Checking division

Pat is making a treasure chest. He bought a box of 48 brass-headed tacks. He wants to use half the tacks to decorate each end of the chest. He wonders how many tacks he can use for each end.

He found $\frac{1}{2}$ of 48 as shown here: ⟶

Pat said, "$\frac{1}{2}$ of 48 is 24. I can prove it.

"Two groups of 24 make 48 all together.

"$2 \times 24 = 48$. So I can use 24 tacks for each end."

$$\begin{array}{r} 24 \\ 2\overline{)48} \end{array}$$

Check
$$\begin{array}{r} 24 \\ \times\ 2 \\ \hline 48 \end{array}$$

1. $\frac{1}{2}$ of 80 = 40. Can you prove it? $(2 \times 40 = \underline{\ ?\ })$

2. $\frac{1}{4}$ of 48 = 12. Can you prove it? $(4 \times 12 = \underline{\ ?\ })$

3. $\frac{1}{3}$ of 36 = 12. Can you prove it? $(3 \times 12 = \underline{\ ?\ })$

4. $\frac{1}{5}$ of 105 = 21. Can you prove it? $(5 \times 21 = \underline{\ ?\ })$

> To check a division example, multiply the answer by the number you divided by. This should give you the number you divided.

Divide. Check your answers.

	a	*b*	*c*	*d*	*e*
5.	$\frac{1}{4}$ of 128	$\frac{1}{5}$ of 355	$2\overline{)188}$	$5\overline{)255}$	$3\overline{)93}$
6.	$\frac{1}{2}$ of 64	$\frac{1}{3}$ of 249	$2\overline{)86}$	$3\overline{)270}$	$3\overline{)210}$
7.	$\frac{1}{4}$ of 208	$\frac{1}{3}$ of 129	$3\overline{)276}$	$3\overline{)240}$	$2\overline{)186}$
8.	$\frac{1}{3}$ of 186	$\frac{1}{5}$ of 270	$2\overline{)184}$	$5\overline{)300}$	$3\overline{)189}$

Dick grew a pumpkin. He made a jack o'lantern out of it for Halloween and saved the seeds to sell. He has 407 seeds and wants to put them in envelopes, with 5 seeds in each envelope.

To find how many envelopes he needs, Dick did this division. He found there are 81 fives in 407 and 2 left over.

This is the way to check his work: Multiply 81 by 5. Add the remainder of 2. The answer should equal the number divided. Does it?

$$
\begin{array}{r}
81 \text{ r}2 \\
5\overline{)407} \\
\text{Check} \\
81 \\
\times\ 5 \\
\hline
405 \\
+\ 2 \\
\hline
407
\end{array}
$$

> To check a division example with a remainder, first multiply the answer by the number you divided by. Then add the remainder. This should give you the number you divided.

1. Divide each of these numbers by 3. Check.

246   128   275   184   155   247   215   279

2. Find $\frac{1}{2}$ of each of these numbers. Check.

164   486   408   187   149   68   123   243

3. Find $\frac{1}{5}$ of each of these numbers. Check.

157   250   408   200   300   459   357   456

Tell the missing numbers:

4. $25 + \underline{\ ?\ } = 29$

5. $32 + \underline{\ ?\ } = 37$

6. $42 + \underline{\ ?\ } = 46$

7. $26 + \underline{\ ?\ } = 29$

8. $24 + \underline{\ ?\ } = 31$

9. $13 + \underline{\ ?\ } = 17$

10. $37 - 35 = \underline{\ ?\ }$

11. $42 - 40 = \underline{\ ?\ }$

12. $18 - 16 = \underline{\ ?\ }$

Practice makes perfect

Multiply. Check by seeing if the answer is sensible.

	a	b	c	d	e	f
1.	42 3	51 4	30 6	54 2	23 3	71 5
2.	32 6	32 7	53 8	53 9	35 6	67 3
3.	513 3	322 4	934 2	513 6	728 5	353 4
4.	305 4	607 5	503 9	203 8	306 5	502 7

Divide and check:

	a	b	c	d	e
5.	3)187	4)126	5)359	2)167	3)248
6.	3)2406	3)2709	2)1004	3)1806	3)960
7.	5)3500	2)1406	4)2008	3)1509	4)2000

Add and check:

8.	97 36 48 70	236 847 490 654	607 86 594 735	$3.00 .79 2.25 8.68	$9.75 1.34 .49 .67

Subtract and check:

9.	867 523	742 429	834 628	$7.20 6.98	$9.00 3.64
10.	907 459	650 594	763 709	$8.75 4.68	$8.00 7.77

Problem study

If you have trouble with Problem 1 in Column A, do Problem 1 in Column B. Then try Problem 1 in Column A again.

A

1. Henry wants a football that costs $3.29. He has only $.75. How much more does he need?

2. Blanche has 65¢. How many 2-cent stamps can she buy? Will she have any money left over?

3. Three boys found $39. They cannot find the owner. If they share the money equally, how much will each boy get?

4. There are 50 rubber bands in a package. How many rubber bands will Tom get in 3 packages?

5. Oliver bought a knife for $2.98, a chain for $.79, and a whistle for $.88. How much did he pay in all?

6. If Oliver (Ex. 5) paid with a 5-dollar bill, how much change should he have received?

7. Joseph has 43 Indian-head pennies. Paul has 27. How many more has Joseph than Paul?

8. At the movies there are 25 seats in each row. How many children will fill 8 rows of seats?

B

1. Eve lost her skate key. A new one costs 5¢. She has 3¢. How much more does she need?

2. How many 3-cent apples can you get for 25¢? Will you have any money left over?

3. Two boys have found 16¢. They want to share the 16¢ equally. How many cents should each boy take?

4. If you can carve 3 rabbits from 1 cake of soap, how many can you carve from 2 cakes? from 3?

5. Sam broke a pane of window glass. He spent 10¢ for a new pane and a nickel for putty. How much did the glass and putty cost?

6. How much change will Fay get from a dime if she spends 4¢? 5¢? 6¢? 7¢? 9¢?

7. Jenny made 11 puppets. Barbara made 8. How many more did Jenny make than Barbara?

8. If there are 10 stamps in one row, how many are there in 2 rows? in 3 rows? in 4? 5? 6? 7? 8?

Going to the movies

1. This is the movie house to which Barbara sometimes goes. What movie will be showing on November second? Look at your calendar and see what day of the week that is.

2. Barbara is 10 years old. If she goes to the movies with her 15-year-old sister, how much will they both have to pay?

3. Barbara's sister has one dollar. How much change will she get when she buys their tickets?

4. How much will Barbara's sister (Ex. 3) have left after she buys two 10-cent bags of popcorn?

5. It takes Barbara 20 minutes to walk from home to the movies. She likes to get there ten minutes before the show starts.

At what time does she leave home for the first show?

6. Will Barbara need to keep her coat on in the movies? How do you know?

7. Do you ever go to a Saturday-afternoon movie? How much do you have to pay?

8. How much would it cost you to see a Saturday-afternoon movie, buy a bag of popcorn, and after the movie to have a soda?

Addition and subtraction review

Add and check. Use folded paper.

	a	b	c	d	e	f
1.	654	123	498	748	750	970
	837	45	371	193	312	186
	292	678	625	325	946	52
	134	90	576	162	898	434
2.	235	819	254	234	309	596
	764	970	163	15	418	87
	710	586	379	379	527	712
	689	457	488	858	735	94
3.	$8.12	$3.51	$9.51	$3.65	$8.76	$9.84
	3.67	.26	.27	7.14	4.59	1.37
	8.45	.74	3.86	7.92	.23	8.62
	9.54	8.98	9.45	8.98	9.78	7.59

Subtract and check. Use folded paper.

	a	b	c	d	e	f
4.	206	874	463	564	605	549
	147	568	278	557	574	248
5.	648	537	567	476	543	786
	399	295	498	394	398	697
6.	870	506	581	609	483	517
	299	297	478	399	290	309
7.	905	550	670	800	800	605
	850	430	208	709	270	430
8.	$5.63	$6.72	$4.98	$5.83	$8.75	$7.89
	1.72	4.75	3.85	3.24	6.37	5.64

Facts of fours

At the State Fair the boys in Miss Green's class will do a dance called The Last Round-Up. The boys are to dress in cowboy suits and dance in groups.

There will be 4 boys in each group. How many boys will be needed for 6 groups?

▶ Tom did this addition to find six 4's: ──────▶ How many boys did he find are needed?

$$
\begin{array}{r}
4 \\
4 \\
4 \\
4 \\
4 \\
4 \\
\hline
24
\end{array}
$$

▶ Don multiplied to find six 4's. Is his answer the same as Tom's?

$$
\begin{array}{r}
4 \\
\times\ 6 \\
\hline
24
\end{array}
$$

1. Count by 4's from 4 to 40.

2. In the picture below, how many boys are there in 1 group? 2 groups? 3? 4? 5? 6? 7? 8? 9?

Use the picture below to find these missing numbers:

3. 2 fours = _?_   4 fours = _?_

4. 3 fours = _?_   6 fours = _?_

5. 8 fours = _?_   9 fours = _?_

6. Look at the picture below. How many groups of 4 boys can be made from 8 boys? 12 boys? 16? 24? 32? 20? 28? 36?

7. In 16 there are _?_ fours.

8. In 24 there are _?_ fours.

1. Shirley made this table to help her learn facts of fours.

She drew __?__ circles in each row across. She drew __?__ rows of circles. Then she numbered the circles from 1 to 40.

2. You can see without counting that 2 fours are __?__; that 3 fours are __?__.

3. How many are 4 fours?

4. In 6 rows of 4 each, there are __?__; in 7 rows there are __?__.

5. The table shows that 10 fours are __?__; 9 fours are __?__; 8 fours are __?__; and 7 fours are __?__.

Table of Fours

1	2	3	4
5	6	7	8
9	10	11	12
13	14	15	16
17	18	19	20
21	22	23	24
25	26	27	28
29	30	31	32
33	34	35	36
37	38	39	40

Look at Shirley's table to help you complete the following:

6. It takes __?__ fours to make 24.   __?__ × 4 = 24   24 ÷ 4 = __?__

7. It takes __?__ fours to make 32.   __?__ × 4 = 32   32 ÷ 4 = __?__

8. It takes __?__ fours to make 16.   __?__ × 4 = 16   16 ÷ 4 = __?__

9. It takes __?__ fours to make 28.   __?__ × 4 = 28   28 ÷ 4 = __?__

10. It takes __?__ fours to make 36.   __?__ × 4 = 36   36 ÷ 4 = __?__

Use Shirley's table to help you do these problems:

11. How much will 8 candy canes cost at 4¢ each?

12. How many 4-cent balls can you get for 24¢?

13. Bill has 7 boxes of cookies. There are 4 cookies in each box. In all, he has __?__ cookies.

14. Doris has 6 gallons of sirup to pour into quart jars. How many jars will she need? (4 qt. = 1 gal.)

15. Shirley says her table (Ex. 1) teaches her both the multiplication and the division facts of fours. Explain what she means.

Multiplication facts of fours

1. Count the trees by 4's. Now count them by 6's. How many trees are there?

2. The trees show that:

6 fours = _?_. In 24 there are _?_ fours.
4 sixes = _?_. In 24 there are _?_ sixes.

3. Count the balls by 4's; by 7's. How many balls are there?

4. The balls show that:

7 fours = _?_. In 28 there are _?_ fours.
4 sevens = _?_. In 28 there are _?_ sevens.

5. Count the hearts by 4's; by 8's. How many hearts are there?

6. The hearts show that:

8 fours = _?_. In 32 there are _?_ fours.
4 eights = _?_. In 32 there are _?_ eights.

7. Count the blocks by 4's; by 9's. How many blocks are there?

8. The blocks show that:

9 fours are _?_. In 36 there are _?_ fours.
4 nines are _?_. In 36 there are _?_ nines.

9. Read the multiplication facts below.

Multiplication Facts of Fours

$$\frac{\begin{array}{r}4\\1\end{array}}{4} \quad \frac{\begin{array}{r}4\\2\end{array}}{8} \quad \frac{\begin{array}{r}4\\3\end{array}}{12} \quad \frac{\begin{array}{r}4\\4\end{array}}{16} \quad \frac{\begin{array}{r}4\\5\end{array}}{20} \quad \frac{\begin{array}{r}4\\6\end{array}}{24} \quad \frac{\begin{array}{r}4\\7\end{array}}{28} \quad \frac{\begin{array}{r}4\\8\end{array}}{32} \quad \frac{\begin{array}{r}4\\9\end{array}}{36}$$

$$\frac{\begin{array}{r}1\\4\end{array}}{4} \quad \frac{\begin{array}{r}2\\4\end{array}}{8} \quad \frac{\begin{array}{r}3\\4\end{array}}{12} \quad \frac{\begin{array}{r}4\\4\end{array}}{16} \quad \frac{\begin{array}{r}5\\4\end{array}}{20} \quad \frac{\begin{array}{r}6\\4\end{array}}{24} \quad \frac{\begin{array}{r}7\\4\end{array}}{28} \quad \frac{\begin{array}{r}8\\4\end{array}}{32} \quad \frac{\begin{array}{r}9\\4\end{array}}{36}$$

Using fours in multiplying

Multiply. Practice until you can say every answer.

1.
4	7	4	1	4	4	4	3	4
1	4	9	4	5	2	4	4	8

2.
5	4	2	6	4	9	4	8	4
4	3	4	4	7	4	6	4	4

3. Make and study Help-Yourself Cards for the multiplication facts of fours on page 86.

4. Add 1 to each answer in Ex. 1; add 2; add 3.

5. Copy Exs. 1–2 and write the answers.

a	b	c	d	e	f	g
6. 143	435	425	534	254	134	345
× 7	× 6	× 5	× 8	× 9	× 6	× 9

7. $4.04	$5.04	$2.40	$4.02	$4.25	$3.04	$4.67
× 9	× 8	× 6	× 7	× 6	× 8	× 4

8. If gumdrops are 4 for a cent, how many gumdrops can you get for 6¢? (Draw a picture if you need to.)

9. How much will 8 balloons cost at 4¢ each?

10. Dick has 3 gallons of honey. He wants to put it in quart jars. How many quart jars will he need? (1 gal. = 4 qts.)

11. Ada, Kay, Lee, and Rose each want to make a doll's bed like this. They will each use 4 clothespins. How many clothespins will they need for the 4 beds?

Division facts of fours

1. Susan is making bookmarks. How many pieces 4 inches long can she cut from a yard of ribbon?

▶ On a blackboard draw a line a yard long. Find how many 4-inch lengths there are in 36 inches.

▶ Now find how many 4's there are in 36 by subtracting. Start with 36. Subtract 4 over and over, as many times as you can. Your subtractions show that 36 is made up of __?__ 4's.

When you find how many 4's there are in 36, you divide 36 by 4. 36 divided by 4 equals 9.

2. How many 4-cent pencils can you buy for 32¢? for 36¢? 24¢? 28¢? 20¢? 12¢? 8¢? 16¢? 4¢?

3. Nancy can get 4 gumdrops for a cent. How many cents' worth of gumdrops will she need to buy if she wants 8 gumdrops? 16? 12? 28? 20? 32? 24? 36?

4. How many groups of 4 marbles each can be made with 16 marbles? 20 marbles? 8 marbles? 12 marbles? 4? 24? 32? 36? 28?

5. Make and study Help-Yourself Cards for these facts of fours:

				Division Facts of Fours				
1	2	3	4	5	6	7	8	9
4)4	4)8	4)12	4)16	4)20	4)24	4)28	4)32	4)36
4	4	4	4	4	4	4	4	4
1)4	2)8	3)12	4)16	5)20	6)24	7)28	8)32	9)36

Say the answers to these examples. Then copy the examples and write the answers.

	a	b	c	d	e	f	g	h	i
6.	4)4	4)24	4)28	1)4	4)32	4)16	6)24	4)20	8)32
7.	3)12	7)28	5)20	4)12	9)36	2)8	4)36	4)8	4)16

8. If you know that $36 \div 4 = 9$, then you know that $36 \div 9 = $ __?__.

9. If you know that $7 \times 4 = 28$, then you know that $28 \div 4 = $ __?__.

Finding $\frac{1}{4}$ of a number

1. Deal out 24 cards into 4 equal piles. How many cards are there in each pile? Each pile contains one __?__ of the cards.

2. How many cards will there be in each pile if you deal out 32 cards into 4 equal piles? 28 cards? 36 cards?

> To find $\frac{1}{4}$ of a number, divide the number by 4.

3. Exs. 1 and 2 show that:

$\frac{1}{4}$ of 24 = __?__ $\frac{1}{4}$ of 32 = __?__

$\frac{1}{4}$ of 28 = __?__ $\frac{1}{4}$ of 36 = __?__

4. Find $\frac{1}{4}$ of 16; 12; 20; 32; 36; 28; 24.

5. If you divide an apple into 4 equal parts, each part is called one __?__ of the apple. Each part could be called **one quarter** instead of one fourth.

One quarter and *one fourth* mean the same thing.

6. One fourth of 8 is __?__. One quarter of 8 is __?__.

7. One quarter of 16 equals __?__. What is one quarter of 32? of 24? of 36? 8? 12? 20? 28? 40?

8. How many inches are there in a yard?

9. How many inches are there in a quarter of a yard?

10. How many *ounces* are there in a pound? in a quarter of a pound?

11. How many 25-cent pieces are there in a dollar?

12. Why do we call a 25-cent piece a quarter?

13. If you divide an hour into 4 equal parts, what do you call each part?

14. How does this addition prove there are 15 minutes in a quarter of an hour?

15
15
15
15
60

15. What do you mean when you say that the time is "quarter after 9"? "quarter of 12"?

16. Find the cost of a quarter of a pound of potato chips at 80¢ a pound.

17. Find the cost of a quarter of a yard of ribbon that sells for 28¢ a yard.

18. Find the cost of a quarter of a pound of salted peanuts at 84¢ a pound.

Leftovers

1. At 4¢ each, how many pears can you get for:

8¢? 9¢? 10¢? 11¢? 12¢? 13¢? 14¢? 15¢? 16¢?

2. Look at the picture above. Study it and say:

"In 5 there is 1 four and 1 left over; in 6 there is 1 four and 2 left over"; and so on for each of the numbers in the circles.

3. What are the Dividing-by-Four Helping Numbers?

4. What Dividing-by-Four Helping Number would you use in finding how many 4's there are in each of these numbers?

17	27	6	33	14	39
35	9	18	15	25	37
31	23	38	7	30	11
21	5	19	10	22	29

5. If you are dividing the numbers in Ex. 4 by 4, what subtractions must you do to find the remainders?

6. Divide each of the numbers in Ex. 4 by 4.

Bob writes his divisions this way: ⟶

$$\begin{array}{r} 4\text{ r}1 \\ 4\overline{)17} \end{array}$$

Jane writes her divisions this way: ⟶

She writes down her Helping Number, and shows the subtraction she does to find the remainder.

$$\begin{array}{r} 4\text{ r}1 \\ 4\overline{)17} \\ \underline{16} \\ 1 \end{array}$$

7. Divide the numbers in Ex. 4 by 4. Write the divisions. Use Jane's way.

8. 1 gal. = 4 qt. How many gallons are there in each of these numbers of quarts:

8 qt.? 9 qt.? 13 qt.? 15 qt.? 17 qt.? 18 qt.?

9. If you divide 38 pennies into piles of 4 pennies, how many piles will you have?

10. How many quarters are there in one dollar?

11. How many dollars can you get for each of these?

12 quarters	23 quarters
13 quarters	32 quarters

90

Using fours in division

1. Four girls want to share equally 248 sea shells. Can you tell without help how many each should take?

Each girl should get $\frac{1}{4}$ of 248 shells. Here are two ways to find $\frac{1}{4}$ of 248. Explain each way.

Oral Way:

$248 = 240 + 8 = 24$ tens $+ 8$

$\frac{1}{4}$ of $240 = \frac{1}{4}$ of 24 tens $= 6$ tens $= 60$

$\frac{1}{4}$ of $8 = 2$

$\frac{1}{4}$ of $248 = 60 + 2 = $ _?_

Each girl should take _?_ shells.

Written Way:

$\frac{1}{4}$ of $248 = 248 \div 4$

Write the division as shown: $\longrightarrow$

Think, "$24 \div 4 = 6$." Write the 6.

Think, "$8 \div 4 = 2$." Write the 2.

Each girl should take _?_ shells.

$4\overline{)248}$

$\overset{62}{4\overline{)248}}$

Do these divisions orally. Use the oral way shown above.

	a	b	c	d	e	f
2.	$4\overline{)124}$	$4\overline{)328}$	$3\overline{)275}$	$4\overline{)280}$	$5\overline{)250}$	$4\overline{)368}$
3.	$4\overline{)240}$	$3\overline{)243}$	$4\overline{)84}$	$3\overline{)217}$	$4\overline{)88}$	$4\overline{)320}$
4.	$4\overline{)324}$	$3\overline{)187}$	$4\overline{)204}$	$4\overline{)128}$	$5\overline{)200}$	$4\overline{)164}$
5.	$3\overline{)155}$	$2\overline{)165}$	$4\overline{)288}$	$5\overline{)100}$	$4\overline{)364}$	$5\overline{)307}$
6.	$4\overline{)360}$	$3\overline{)126}$	$2\overline{)187}$	$3\overline{)97}$	$3\overline{)68}$	$6\overline{)248}$
7.	$4\overline{)165}$	$4\overline{)209}$	$4\overline{)366}$	$4\overline{)249}$	$3\overline{)278}$	$7\overline{)287}$
8.	$9\overline{)369}$	$4\overline{)89}$	$4\overline{)326}$	$4\overline{)120}$	$8\overline{)320}$	$5\overline{)356}$

9. Now copy Exs. 2–8 and divide. Use the written way shown above. Check each answer by multiplying.

Multiplication and division facts of sixes

The members of the West Side Boys' Club are going to sell candy bars on Saturday to earn money to buy a football. They will sell the candy bars for 6¢ each.

They use this table of sixes to tell how much to charge for any number of bars at 6¢ each.

A Helping Chart for Sixes

1	2	3	4	5	6
7	8	9	10	11	12
13	14	15	16	17	18
19	20	21	22	23	24
25	26	27	28	29	30
31	32	33	34	35	36
37	38	39	40	41	42
43	44	45	46	47	48
49	50	51	52	53	54
55	56	57	58	59	60

---

1. Count the numbers in the chart by 6's.

Use the chart to help you do Exs. 2–15.

2. How much should the boys charge for 2 six-cent bars? 4? 6? 3? 5? 8? 7? 9?

3.
$2 \times 6 = \underline{\ ?\ }$ $5 \times 6 = \underline{\ ?\ }$
$3 \times 6 = \underline{\ ?\ }$ $6 \times 6 = \underline{\ ?\ }$
$4 \times 6 = \underline{\ ?\ }$ $7 \times 6 = \underline{\ ?\ }$

4.
$8 \times 6 = \underline{\ ?\ }$ $3 \text{ sixes} + 2 = \underline{\ ?\ }$
$9 \times 6 = \underline{\ ?\ }$ $4 \text{ sixes} + 3 = \underline{\ ?\ }$
$10 \times 6 = \underline{\ ?\ }$ $5 \text{ sixes} + 4 = \underline{\ ?\ }$

5. $2 \times 6 = 12$, so $4 \times 6 = \underline{\ ?\ }$.

6. $2 \times 6 = 12$, so $6 \times 6 = \underline{\ ?\ }$.

7. $2 \times 6 = 12$, so $8 \times 6 = \underline{\ ?\ }$.

8. $3 \times 6 = 18$, so $6 \times 6 = \underline{\ ?\ }$.

9. $3 \times 6 = 18$, so $9 \times 6 = \underline{\ ?\ }$.

10. $4 \times 6 = 24$, so $8 \times 6 = \underline{\ ?\ }$.

11. Make a multiplication table of 6's. The table is started for you. Go up as far as $10 \times 6 = 60.$ ⟶

$1 \times 6 = 6$
$2 \times 6 = 12$

12. Bill helped his father plant little pine trees. They planted 6 trees in each row. How many trees did they plant in 3 rows? in 5? 7? 8? 9?

13. How many 6-cent candy bars should the boys give for 12¢? 18¢? 30¢? 24¢? 36¢? 42¢? 54¢?

14. In 18 there are $\underline{\ ?\ }$ 6's
In 24 there are $\underline{\ ?\ }$ 6's
In 36 there are $\underline{\ ?\ }$ 6's

15. In 48 there are $\underline{\ ?\ }$ 6's
In 54 there are $\underline{\ ?\ }$ 6's
In 42 there are $\underline{\ ?\ }$ 6's

Use the chart on page 92 to help you do Exs. 1–6 on this page.

1. In 13 there are __?__ 6's, and __1__ left over. $13 \div 6 = 2\,r1$

2. In 14 there are __?__ 6's, and __2__ left over. $14 \div 6 =$ __?__

3. In 19 there are __?__ 6's, and __?__ left over. $19 \div 6 =$ __?__

4. In 23 there are __?__ 6's, and __?__ left over. $23 \div 6 =$ __?__

5. In 40 there are __?__ 6's, and __?__ left over. $40 \div 6 =$ __?__

6. In 49 there are __?__ 6's, and __?__ left over. $49 \div 6 =$ __?__

7. Tom said that he could go from a multiplication table of 6's to a division table of 6's. "Anybody who knows that $5 \times 6 = 30$ also knows that $30 \div 6 =$ __?__."

8. Make a division table of 6's. The table is started for you. Go up as far as $60 \div 6 = 10.$ →

$$6 \div 6 = 1$$
$$12 \div 6 = 2$$
$$18 \div 6 = 3$$

9. When Jane couldn't remember how many 7 sixes are, she thought, "5 sixes are 30, and 2 sixes are 12. So 7 sixes are __?__."

10. When Jane forgot how many 9 sixes are, she thought, "10 sixes are 60. So 9 sixes are $60 - 6$, or __?__." Explain.

11. Make a drawing of dots to show that 4 sixes are as many as 6 fours.

Your drawing shows there are __?__ 6's in 24 and __?__ 4's in 24.

12. If you couldn't remember how many 8 sixes are, which of these ways of helping yourself would you use?

- Ask the teacher.
- Look it up in a book.
- Write down 8 sixes, and add.
- Make 8 rows of pennies, with 6 pennies in a row, and then count the pennies.
- Think of some number of sixes that you do know. You might think, "5 sixes are 30, and 3 sixes are 18. So 8 sixes are 48."
- Think, "2 sixes are 12, so 8 sixes are 4×12, or 48."

13. Alice calls these four facts a Number Family:

$$4 \times 6 = 24 \qquad 24 \div 6 = 4$$
$$6 \times 4 = 24 \qquad 24 \div 4 = 6$$

Tell the other three facts in the Number Family of each of these:

$$7 \times 6 = 42 \qquad 54 \div 6 = 9$$
$$48 \div 6 = 8 \qquad 30 \div 6 = 5$$

Multiplication facts of sixes

1. At 6¢ each, find the cost of 4 ice-cream cones; of 5 ice-cream cones; 7; 6; 9; 8.

Multiply.   Practice until you can say every answer.

2. 6	6	6	6	6	6
1	4	7	2	5	8

3. 6	6	6	5	8	2
3	6	9	6	6	6

4. 3	6	7	9	4	1
6	6	6	6	6	6

5. Copy the examples in Exs. 2–4 and write the answers.

6. Make Help-Yourself Cards for facts you did not know in Ex. 5.   Then do Ex. 5 again.

7. Find the cost of 6 pencils at 5¢ each; at 6¢ each; 9¢; 8¢; 7¢; 4¢; 3¢.

8. Which would cost more: nine 5-cent balls, or eight 6-cent balls?

9. If 3 sevens are 21, then 6 sevens are 42.   Why?

10. If 3 eights are 24, then 6 eights are _?_.   Why?

11. 6 weeks = _?_ days.

12. A quart of ice cream serves 8 persons.   How many persons will 6 quarts of ice cream serve?

13. An airmail stamp costs 6¢. Find the cost of 9 airmail stamps; 7 airmail stamps.

14. Six nickels = _?_ cents.

15. Carl did 8 rows of examples with 6 examples in each row.   In all, he did _?_ examples.

16. Tom's chickens laid 6 eggs a day for a week.   During the week they laid _?_ eggs.

Multiplication Facts of Sixes

6	6	6	6	6	6	6	6	6
1	2	3	4	5	6	7	8	9
6	12	18	24	30	36	42	48	54

1	2	3	4	5	6	7	8	9
6	6	6	6	6	6	6	6	6
6	12	18	24	30	36	42	48	54

Thinking about zeros

Good thinkers can figure out the answers to the last example in each of these exercises. Can you?

1. $4 \times 3 = 12$
   $4 \times 2 = 8$
   $4 \times 1 = 4$
   $4 \times 0 = \underline{}$

2. $5 \times 3 = 15$
   $5 \times 2 = 10$
   $5 \times 1 = 5$
   $5 \times 0 = \underline{}$

3. $6 \times 3 = 18$
   $6 \times 2 = 12$
   $6 \times 1 = 6$
   $6 \times 0 = \underline{}$

4. $7 \times 3 = 21$
   $7 \times 2 = 14$
   $7 \times 1 = 7$
   $7 \times 0 = \underline{}$

5. Any number times zero is $\underline{}$.

6. $3 \times 8 = 24$
   $2 \times 8 = 16$
   $1 \times 8 = 8$
   $0 \times 8 = \underline{}$

7. $3 \times 4 = 12$
   $2 \times 4 = 8$
   $1 \times 4 = 4$
   $0 \times 4 = \underline{}$

8. $3 \times 9 = 27$
   $2 \times 9 = 18$
   $1 \times 9 = 9$
   $0 \times 9 = \underline{}$

9. $3 \times 6 = 18$
   $2 \times 6 = 12$
   $1 \times 6 = 6$
   $0 \times 6 = \underline{}$

10. Zero times any number is $\underline{}$.

11. $12 \div 4 = 3$
    $8 \div 4 = 2$
    $4 \div 4 = 1$
    $0 \div 4 = \underline{}$

12. $9 \div 3 = 3$
    $6 \div 3 = 2$
    $3 \div 3 = 1$
    $0 \div 3 = \underline{}$

13. $6 \div 2 = 3$
    $4 \div 2 = 2$
    $2 \div 2 = 1$
    $0 \div 2 = \underline{}$

14. $18 \div 6 = 3$
    $12 \div 6 = 2$
    $6 \div 6 = 1$
    $0 \div 6 = \underline{}$

15. Zero divided by any number is $\underline{}$.

16. $9 + 2 = 11$
    $9 + 1 = 10$
    $9 + 0 = \underline{}$

17. $17 + 2 = 19$
    $17 + 1 = 18$
    $17 + 0 = \underline{}$

18. $2 + 7 = 9$
    $1 + 7 = 8$
    $0 + 7 = \underline{}$

19. $2 + 16 = 18$
    $1 + 16 = 17$
    $0 + 16 = \underline{}$

20. Any number plus zero is the $\underline{}$; zero plus any number is the $\underline{}$.

21. $9 - 2 = 7$
    $9 - 1 = 8$
    $9 - 0 = \underline{}$

22. $37 - 2 = 35$
    $37 - 1 = 36$
    $37 - 0 = \underline{}$

23. $9 - 7 = 2$
    $9 - 8 = 1$
    $9 - 9 = \underline{}$

24. $100 - 98 = 2$
    $100 - 99 = 1$
    $100 - 100 = \underline{}$

25. How much is left when you take zero from a number? Why?

26. How much is left when you take a number from itself? Why?

27. Can you tell the answers to these examples in just a second?

$9 \times 8 \times 7 \times 4 \times 6 \times 0 = \underline{}$

$6 \times 5 \times 7 \times 0 \div 2 = \underline{}$

A page of practice

Multiply.   Check by seeing if your answers are sensible.

	a	b	c	d	e	f
1.	323 2	412 4	523 3	804 6	731 3	702 2
2.	$8.59 2	$7.16 4	$9.06 5	$8.65 3	$4.06 9	$7.69 6
3.	$8.10 6	$6.09 4	$5.06 6	$6.12 8	$6.03 9	$6.26 8

4. Find the cost of 4 tennis rackets at $4.69 each.

5. Ann bought 3 papers of pins. There are 160 pins in each paper. How many pins did she buy in all?

6. Find the sum of:

52   306   257   79   632

7. Find the difference between 386 and 603.

8. 700 is __?__ more than 427.

9. Multiply 406 by 7.

10. Multiply 624 by 6.

11. Is 6 × 198 closer to 600 or to 1200?   Why?

12. Is 7 × 59 closer to 350 or to 420?   Why?

13. Does   1500 − 699   equal about 800 or 900?

14. How many sheets of paper are there in 6 packages if there are 450 sheets in each package?

15. How much will 9 baseball suits cost at $6.65 each?

16. 4 × 25 is 100, so 12 × 25 = __?__ ; 16 × 25 = __?__ .

17. Is the sum of 295 + 301 + 409 about 900 or 1000?

18. Divide 1208 by 4.

19. Does $\frac{1}{3}$ of 309 equal $\frac{1}{3}$ of 300 plus $\frac{1}{3}$ of 9?

20. Does $\frac{1}{2}$ of 168 equal $\frac{1}{2}$ of 160 plus $\frac{1}{2}$ of 8?

21. Take the addition test on page 11.

22. Take the subtraction test on page 21.

96

Division facts of sixes

1. Find how many 6-inch badges you can cut from a yard of ribbon.

When you find how many 6-inch lengths there are in 36 inches, you are dividing 36 by __?__ .

2. Draw a dot picture to show that $12 \div 6 = 2$ and $12 \div 2 = 6$.

3. $54 \div 6 = 9$, so $54 \div 9 = $ __?__ .

4. $48 \div 6 = 8$, so $48 \div 8 = $ __?__ .

5. For 42¢ you can get __?__ 6-cent candy bars, or __?__ 7-cent bars.

6. Read the division facts of sixes at the bottom of the page.

Practice until you can say the answers to all these examples:

a	b	c	d	e
7. 6)24	7)42	6)18	8)48	6)36
8. 3)18	6)12	4)24	6)54	6)30
9. 9)54	6)48	6)6	6)42	2)12
10. 6)48	6)36	5)30	6)54	1)6

11. Copy Exs. 7–10 and write the answers.

12. Make Help-Yourself Cards for any facts you did not know in Ex. 11. Study the cards. Then do Ex. 11 again.

13. Tell all the numbers from 6 to 60 which can be divided by 6 without a remainder. Write them. These are your Dividing-by-Six Helping Numbers.

14. Which of the following numbers can be divided by 6 without a remainder?

16   26   24   44   54   18   21   48

15. How many 6-inch tags can be cut from a strip of wood 54 inches long? 42 inches long? 36? 48? 30? 24? 60? 12? 18?

16. How many 8-cent bus tickets can you buy for 48¢? How much money will you have left over?

Division Facts of Sixes

1	2	3	4	5	6	7	8	9
6)6	6)12	6)18	6)24	6)30	6)36	6)42	6)48	6)54

6	6	6	6	6	6	6	6	6
1)6	2)12	3)18	4)24	5)30	6)36	7)42	8)48	9)54

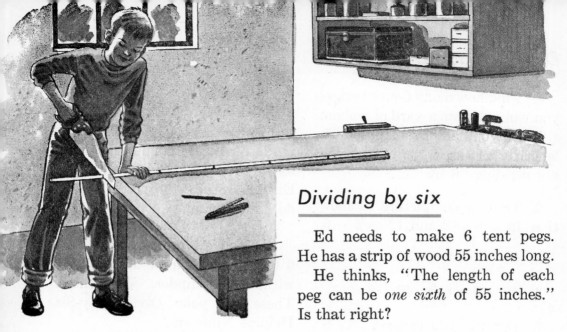

Dividing by six

Ed needs to make 6 tent pegs. He has a strip of wood 55 inches long.

He thinks, "The length of each peg can be *one sixth* of 55 inches." Is that right?

❚ **To find $\frac{1}{6}$ of a number, divide the number by 6.**

You know how to divide 55 by 6 this *short way:* ──────→
The short way is easy when you divide by small numbers.

Below is a *long way* to use when you divide by larger numbers like 6. Study it. It is like the short way except that you write more of the work to keep from making mistakes.

To divide 55 by 6, write the example this way: ──────→

▶ Divide. First think, "My Helping Number is 54. $54 \div 6 = 9$." Write the 9 as shown in this box: ──────→

▶ Multiply. 9 times 6 is 54. Write 54 under the 55. ──→

▶ Subtract 54 from 55. Write 1. The work shows that in 55 there are nine 6's, and 1 over. Write r1 in the answer.

▶ Check. $6 \times 9 = 54.$ $54 + 1 = 55.$

If Ed makes 6 pegs from a 55-inch strip, how long can each peg be? How many inches of wood will be left?

$$\begin{array}{r} 9\text{ r}1 \\ 6\overline{)55} \end{array}$$

$$6\overline{)55}$$

$$\begin{array}{r} 9 \\ 6\overline{)55} \\ 54 \\ \hline \end{array}$$

$$\begin{array}{r} 9\text{ r}1 \\ 6\overline{)55} \\ 54 \\ \hline 1 \end{array}$$

1. If 6 boys share 45¢, each boy will get __?__ ¢ and there will be __?__ ¢ left over.

2. Does $19 \div 6 = 2$ r7 or 3 r1?

3. If you deal out 50 cards to 6 children, each child will get __?__ cards and you will have __?__ extra cards to put in the center of the table.

Dividing-by-six Helping Numbers

Tell how these divisions are done. Then copy them without the answers and work them.

1.

7 r4	4 r1	8 r2	6 r4	7 r3	5 r5
6)46	6)25	6)50	6)40	6)45	6)35
42	24	48	36	42	30
4	1	2	4	3	5

2. Peter needed to divide 43 by 6. He found 43 on this chart and thought, "I must first find my Helping Number. It is 42. $42 \div 6 = \underline{\ ?\ }$. $43 \div 6 = \underline{\ ?\ }$."

3. Tell how the chart can help you when you are dividing 20 by 6; when you are dividing 37 by 6; 50 by 6; 46 by 6; 57 by 6.

4. The first 54 numbers on this chart are written in __?__ rows with 6 numbers in a row.

A Helping Chart for Sixes

1	2	3	4	5	6
7	8	9	10	11	12
13	14	15	16	17	18
19	20	21	22	23	24
25	26	27	28	29	30
31	32	33	34	35	36
37	38	39	40	41	42
43	44	45	46	47	48
49	50	51	52	53	54
55	56	57	58	59	60

Copy and divide by 6. First tell each Helping Number.

	a	b	c	d	e	f	g	h	i
5.	34	47	48	35	10	40	52	20	49
6.	36	58	9	56	19	38	21	11	33
7.	8	51	44	37	39	18	32	12	22
8.	57	23	17	41	29	54	13	31	7
9.	24	15	55	26	30	28	50	6	14

10. What is the largest remainder you can have when you are dividing by 6? Can you give an illustration?

Watching remainders

To find out how many 6-cent bulbs he should give Jenny for 50 cents, Joseph divided like this:————————————➤

He said, "For 50¢ I should give seven 6-cent bulbs, and 8¢ change." Was that right?

Jenny said, "You can give 8 bulbs. That 8¢ change will buy another bulb."

Joseph forgot to *compare*. He should have looked at the remainder, 8, to see if it was more than 6. It was; so he should have known there was one more 6 in the 50.

For 50¢ he can give eight 6-cent bulbs and 2¢ change:——➤

Wrong
7
6)50
42
8

Right
8
6)50
48
2

In a division example always compare, to be sure that the remainder is smaller than the number you divide by.

What mistakes can you find in these divisions?

	6 r4		9 r6		3 r5		8 r4		7 r7
1.	6)40	**2.**	6)60	**3.**	6)23	**4.**	6)52	**5.**	6)49
	36		54		18		48		42
	4		6		5		4		7

Selling seeds

Tom borrowed $5.00 from his father to pay for a case of vegetable seeds. It contained:

>   40 ten-cent packages
>   40 five-cent packages

How much will Tom take in if he sells:

1. 10 ten-cent packages?

2. 40 ten-cent packages?

3. 20 five-cent packages?

4. 40 five-cent packages?

5. If Tom sells all the seeds in the case, how much will he earn?

6. If you know how much you pay for something and how much you sell it for, how can you find how much you earn? Illustrate.

7. Tom has sold all his seeds except:

>   10 ten-cent packages
>   5 five-cent packages

He has taken in $4.75. How can Tom tell whether $4.75 is the amount of money he should have?

8. How many more packages of seeds must Tom sell before he can pay back the $5.00 he borrowed from his father?

Oral practice in dividing by six

1. Carl discovered this way of finding how many 6's there are in 180. Explain his work. Do you know a better way?

60	$60 \div 6 = 10$
60	$60 \div 6 = 10$
60	$60 \div 6 = 10$
$\overline{180}$	$\overline{180 \div 6 = 30}$

2. This is the way Mary discovered how many 6's there are in 180. Explain her work.

$18 \div 6 = 3$
$18 \text{ tens} \div 6 = 3 \text{ tens}$
$180 \div 6 = 30$

3. $12 \div 6 = \underline{\ ?\ }$
$12 \text{ tens} \div 6 = \underline{\ ?\ } \text{ tens}$
$120 \div 6 = \underline{\ ?\ }$

4. $24 \div 6 = \underline{\ ?\ }$
$24 \text{ tens} \div 6 = \underline{\ ?\ } \text{ tens}$
$240 \div 6 = \underline{\ ?\ }$

5. $\frac{1}{6}$ of $36 = \underline{\ ?\ }$
$\frac{1}{6}$ of $36 \text{ tens} = \underline{\ ?\ } \text{ tens}$
$\frac{1}{6}$ of $360 = \underline{\ ?\ }$

6. $\frac{1}{6}$ of $42 = \underline{\ ?\ }$
$\frac{1}{6}$ of $42 \text{ tens} = \underline{\ ?\ }$
$\frac{1}{6}$ of $420 = \underline{\ ?\ }$

7. $\frac{1}{6}$ of $48 = \underline{\ ?\ }$
$\frac{1}{6}$ of $48 \text{ tens} = \underline{\ ?\ }$
$\frac{1}{6}$ of $480 = \underline{\ ?\ }$

8. $\frac{1}{6}$ of $54 = \underline{\ ?\ }$
$\frac{1}{6}$ of $54 \text{ tens} = \underline{\ ?\ }$
$\frac{1}{6}$ of $540 = \underline{\ ?\ }$

9. If you know that $18 \div 6 = 3$, then you know that $180 \div 6 = \underline{\ ?\ }$.

10. If you know that $24 \div 6 = 4$, then you know that $240 \div 6 = \underline{\ ?\ }$.

11. If you know that $30 \div 6 = 5$, then you know that $300 \div 6 = \underline{\ ?\ }$.

12. Tell the missing numbers:

$48 \div 6 = \underline{\ ?\ }$ $54 \div 6 = \underline{\ ?\ }$
$480 \div 6 = \underline{\ ?\ }$ $540 \div 6 = \underline{\ ?\ }$

13. If $30 \times 6 = 180$, does $180 \div 6 = 30$?

14. Does $300 \div 6 = \underline{\ ?\ }$ ask the question, "How many 6's are there in 300?"

15. $540 \div 6 = \underline{\ ?\ }$ asks the question, "How many $\underline{\ ?\ }$ are there in $\underline{\ ?\ }$?"

16. $40 \times 6 = 240$, so you know that there are $\underline{\ ?\ }$ 6's in 240.

17. $50 \times 6 = 300$, so you know that there are $\underline{\ ?\ }$ 6's in 300.

18. $70 \times 6 = 420$, so you know that there are $\underline{\ ?\ }$ 6's in 420.

19. $90 \times 6 = 540$, so you know that there are $\underline{\ ?\ }$ 6's in 540.

To the Teacher: See Note 3 on page 310.

Multiplying and dividing

1. $2 \times 6 = 12$, so $20 \times 6 = 120$ $20 \times 6 = 120$, so $120 \div 6 = \underline{\ ?\ }$

2. $3 \times 6 = 18$, so $30 \times 6 = 180$ $30 \times 6 = 180$, so $180 \div 6 = \underline{\ ?\ }$

3. $4 \times 6 = 24$, so $40 \times 6 = 240$ $40 \times 6 = \underline{\ ?\ }$, so $240 \div 6 = \underline{\ ?\ }$

4. Make a rule for finding 10×6; 20×6; 30×6; 40×6; 50×6.

Use the table to help you answer Exs. 5 to 8.

5. How many 6's does it take to make 480? 360? 240? 180? 540? 600? 120?

6. If it takes 20 sixes to make 120, then the answer to $120 \div 6$ is $\underline{\ ?\ }$.

7. If it takes 30 sixes to make 180, then the answer to $180 \div 6$ is $\underline{\ ?\ }$.

8. If $50 \times 6 = 300$, then the answer to the division $6\overline{)300}$ is $\underline{\ ?\ }$.

$$
\begin{array}{rcl}
10 \times 6 & = & 60 \\
20 \times 6 & = & 120 \\
30 \times 6 & = & 180 \\
40 \times 6 & = & 240 \\
50 \times 6 & = & 300 \\
60 \times 6 & = & 360 \\
70 \times 6 & = & 420 \\
80 \times 6 & = & 480 \\
90 \times 6 & = & 540 \\
100 \times 6 & = & 600 \\
\end{array}
$$

9. Don said, "I don't need a table of sixes to divide 240 by 6. I just cover the 0 of the 240 with my finger. I divide the 24 by 6. $24 \div 6 = 4$ gives me the hint that $240 \div 6 = 40$."

To find $420 \div 6$, Don thinks, "$42 \div 6 = 7$ gives me the hint that $420 \div 6 = \underline{\ ?\ }$."

Use Don's Hint System to do these:

10. $6\overline{)360}$ $6\overline{)180}$ $6\overline{)540}$

11. $6\overline{)480}$ $6\overline{)120}$ $6\overline{)300}$

12. Explain these divisions:

$$
\begin{array}{r}
90\ r2 \\
6\overline{)542} \\
540 \\
\hline
2
\end{array}
\qquad
\begin{array}{r}
50\ r4 \\
6\overline{)304} \\
300 \\
\hline
4
\end{array}
\qquad
\begin{array}{r}
40\ r5 \\
6\overline{)245} \\
240 \\
\hline
5
\end{array}
$$

Copy, divide, and check. Use Don's Hint System.

13. $6\overline{)301}$ $6\overline{)425}$ $6\overline{)243}$

14. $6\overline{)543}$ $6\overline{)63}$ $6\overline{)481}$

15. $6\overline{)185}$ $6\overline{)364}$ $6\overline{)182}$

16. $6\overline{)484}$ $6\overline{)423}$ $6\overline{)124}$

$$10 \times 6 = 60$$
$$20 \times 6 = 120$$
$$30 \times 6 = 180$$
$$40 \times 6 = 240$$
$$50 \times 6 = 300$$
$$60 \times 6 = 360$$
$$70 \times 6 = 420$$
$$80 \times 6 = 480$$
$$90 \times 6 = 540$$

TODAY'S PLANS

Starting our Science Notebooks

Learning to divide large numbers

Allowing 6 sheets of paper to a notebook, how many notebooks can be made from 150 sheets?

Miss Allison said, "We should divide 150 by 6. We'll use the Helping Facts table on the board."

1. Can you use the table to find how many 6's there are in 150?

2. Joe said, "150 sheets are more than 120 sheets, so we can make more than 20 notebooks." Explain.

3. Don said, "150 sheets are not as many as 180 sheets, so we can't make 30 notebooks." Explain.

Paul said, "I see. We can make *20 some* notebooks. But I still don't know just how many."

4. Bill suggested, "Let's start by making up 20 notebooks."

That used up 20×6 sheets, or _?_ sheets. Miss Allison had left $150 - 120$, or _?_ sheets.

5. Next the class made notebooks from the 30 sheets. How many notebooks could they make from 30 sheets? $30 \div 6 = $ _?_.

6. Then they had $20 + 5$, or _?_ notebooks.

104

7. Next Miss Allison showed the class how to divide 150 by 6 this way:

The 2 in tens place shows the 20 notebooks they made at first.

What does the 120 show? the 30? the 5?

```
    25
6)150
   120
    30
    30
```

8. Don says he uses a Hint System to find how many 6's there are in a large number.

In the division at the right he covers the 2 with his finger. Then, looking at the 13, he thinks, "13 ÷ 6 is a little more than 2, so 132 ÷ 6 is *20 some.*" Explain his thinking.

```
6)132
```

Tell *about how many 6's* there are in each of the numbers in Ex. 9–13.

Answer this way: "In dividing 198 by 6, I find 19 ÷ 6 is a little more than 3, so 198 ÷ 6 is *30 some.*"

9.	198	253	490	300
10.	78	450	200	164
11.	382	274	312	500
12.	560	83	493	264
13.	145	442	206	318

14. If 6 boys share 162 sheets of notebook paper equally, will each boy get *20 some* or *30 some* sheets?

Dividing large numbers by six

Six girls want to share 192 jelly beans equally. How many should each girl take?

First they wrote: 6)192

Joy said, "To find how many 6's there are in 192, I use the Hint System.

"I cover the 2 in the 192. Then I think: 19 ÷ 6 is a little more than 3, so 192 ÷ 6 is *30 some.*"

1. If each of the 6 girls takes 30 beans, how many is that in all?

2. Then how many beans will be left?

3. If the 6 girls share the 12 beans that are left, how many more beans will each get?

4. How many beans does each girl get in all?

5. Look at the division in the picture below. The 3 in tens place shows the 30 beans each took out at first. What does the 180 show? the 12? the 2? the 32?

6. Explain the division in this box. →

What does the 4 in tens place show? the 240? the 20? the 3? the 18? the 2? the 43?

```
      43 r2
6)260
    240
    ----
     20
     18
     --
      2
```

7. Six boys bought a pack of 250 elastic bands. How many bands should each boy take?

Dan gathered 192 eggs. He wants to pack them in boxes, 6 eggs to the box. To find how many boxes he needs, he should divide 192 by __?__. Here are the steps he should take:

▶ Write 6)192. Then use the Hint System. 19 ÷ 6 is a little more than 3, so 192 ÷ 6 = "30 some." *Write 3 in the tens place* in the answer. Does 3 in tens place mean 30?

▶ Multiply: 30 × 6 = 180. Write the 180.

▶ Subtract 180 from 192. Write the 12.

▶ Divide: 12 ÷ 6 = 2. Write the 2 in the ones place.

▶ Finish and check the division. Dan needs __?__ boxes.

```
      32
  6)192
    180
     12
     12
     ——

  Check
     32
    × 6
    ———
    192
```

Explain how these divisions are done. Next copy them without the work. Divide. Then look to see if your work is right.

```
        15 r1   CHECK              84 r3   CHECK            24    CHECK
1.  5)76         15      2.  6)507          84      3.  6)148      24
      50        × 5           480          × 6          120      × 6
      ——        ———          ———          ———          ———      ———
      26         75            27          504           28      144
      25        + 1            24          + 3           24      + 4
      ——        ———           ——          ———           ——      ———
       1         76             3          507            4      148
```

107

Dividing large numbers

Divide and check:

	a	b	c	d	e	f	g
1.	4)56	6)90	4)74	5)88	6)160	6)443	6)497
2.	6)96	6)92	6)72	6)84	6)207	6)520	6)412
3.	5)69	2)99	6)82	6)80	4)293	3)256	6)315
4.	6)74	6)98	6)83	6)81	5)79	4)375	3)198
5.	6)88	6)75	5)75	6)77	2)111	5)464	4)340
6.	3)76	3)48	4)96	6)94	5)128	6)539	6)354
7.	6)67	5)65	6)78	6)69	6)203	2)138	6)504
8.	5)78	6)70	6)85	6)99	2)178	3)225	4)347
9.	6)79	6)89	6)71	6)73	6)258	6)498	5)375

10. If 6 pupils can ride in a car, how many cars will be needed to take 84 pupils to the zoo?

11. Molly bought a package of drawing paper. There were 72 sheets of paper in the package.

If 6 girls share the package equally, how many sheets of paper will each girl get?

12. Molly bought a set of 6 paintbrushes for 96¢. Judy wants to buy one from Molly. How much should Molly charge for one brush?

13. If 144 cedar trees are set out in rows of 6 trees, how many rows will there be?

14. If 324 Scouts march 6 abreast, how many rows of Scouts will there be in the parade?

15. Tom wants to pack 144 eggs in boxes, 6 eggs to a box. How many boxes does he need?

16. Mrs. Allen bought a box of 100 drinking straws. If the Allen children use 6 straws a day, how many days will the straws last?

A shorter way of writing divisions

1. Explain John's way of finding $84 \div 6$. ───→

2. Now look at Peter's way of dividing 84 by 6. ──────→

How does Peter's way differ from John's way?

Did Peter write the 6 in tens place under the 8, instead of writing the whole 60?

Peter

$$\begin{array}{r} 1\ 4 \\ 6\overline{\smash{)}84} \\ 6 \\ \hline 24 \\ 24 \\ \hline \end{array}$$

John

$$\begin{array}{r} 1\ 4 \\ 6\overline{\smash{)}84} \\ 60 \\ \hline 24 \\ 24 \\ \hline \end{array}$$

These are the steps in Peter's division:

▶ Write $6\overline{)84}$. Then use the Hint System. $8 \div 6$ is a little more than 1, so $84 \div 6$ is a little more than 10. Write 1 in tens place, over the 8. Does 1 in tens place mean 10?

▶ Multiply: $10 \times 6 = 60$. Write 6 in tens place, under the 8. Does 6 in tens place mean 60?

▶ Subtract 6 from 8. Write the 2.

▶ Bring down the 4 and write it in ones place beside the 2.

▶ Divide: $24 \div 6 = 4$. Write 4 in ones place in the answer.

▶ The division shows that $84 \div 6 = \underline{\ ?\ }$. Prove it.

3. Do each of these divisions, first by using John's way, then by using Peter's way:

$$90 \div 6 \qquad 72 \div 6 \qquad 78 \div 6 \qquad 96 \div 6 \qquad 84 \div 6 \qquad 66 \div 6$$

Explain how these divisions are done. Next copy them without the work. Divide. Then see if your work is right.

4.
$$\begin{array}{r} 58 \\ 6\overline{\smash{)}348} \\ 30 \\ \hline 48 \\ 48 \\ \hline \end{array}$$

CHECK
$$\begin{array}{r} 58 \\ \times\ 6 \\ \hline 348 \end{array}$$

5.
$$\begin{array}{r} 64\ \text{r}2 \\ 6\overline{\smash{)}386} \\ 36 \\ \hline 26 \\ 24 \\ \hline 2 \end{array}$$

CHECK
$$\begin{array}{r} 64 \\ \times\ 6 \\ \hline 384 \\ +\ 2 \\ \hline 386 \end{array}$$

6.
$$\begin{array}{r} 88\ \text{r}4 \\ 6\overline{\smash{)}532} \\ 48 \\ \hline 52 \\ 48 \\ \hline 4 \end{array}$$

CHECK
$$\begin{array}{r} 88 \\ \times\ 6 \\ \hline 528 \\ +\ 4 \\ \hline 532 \end{array}$$

7. Now do the divisions on page 108, using Peter's short way.

Making change at the carnival

The Rosedale School is giving a carnival. When Sue bought a 10-cent carnival ticket from Andrew, she gave Andrew a quarter.

Andrew said, "10¢ for the ticket." Then, dropping a nickel into Sue's hand, he said, "15." Dropping a dime into her hand, he said, "25. Thank you."

Ann gave Dick a nickel for a ticket to see the snake charmer. The ticket cost 1¢. Dick said, "1." Then, dropping 4 cents into Ann's hand, he said, "5."

1. Tell what Dick would say and what coins he would give in change from a nickel when selling 2 one-cent tickets; 3 tickets; 4.

2. Tell what Dick would say and what coins he would give in change from a dime when selling 6 one-cent tickets; 7 tickets; 8; 9; 5; 4; 3; 2; 1.

3. What would Fred say and what coins would he give in change from a quarter after these sales?

20¢	17¢	13¢	8¢	3¢
22¢	16¢	12¢	6¢	1¢
24¢	18¢	15¢	9¢	4¢

4. What would Marie say and what coins would she give in change from a half dollar after these sales?

46¢	37¢	28¢	21¢	14¢
43¢	33¢	26¢	17¢	9¢
40¢	30¢	25¢	15¢	3¢

SCHOOL CARNIVAL
ADMISSION 10¢

Problem Test 2

Reach for a perfect score on this Problem Test.

1. Ralph is buying a fountain pen for $1.69. If he gives the clerk two dollars, how much change will he receive?

2. If Andrew buys a notebook for $.42, a book for $1.19, a ruler for $.10, and pencil leads for $.05, how much will his bill be?

3. The carpenter's tool set Alfred wants costs $19.75. He has $9.87. How much more does he need?

4. Alice would like 6 nature books. At $1.79 each, how much will 6 books cost?

5. One rainy day 4 boys were playing at Paul's house. Paul's older brother gave them a box with 132 stamps in it and said, "Here, divide these among you."
How many stamps should each boy have taken?

6. How many 6-inch badges can Jean make from a piece of ribbon a yard long?

7. What will Esther have to pay for 6 victrola records at $.53 each?

8. May's dog is 1 ft. 9 in. tall. Ed's dog is 21 in. tall. Whose dog is taller?

9. Benny plans to buy a hammer for 19¢, a saw for 79¢, a file for 30¢, a screw driver for 35¢, and nails for 25¢. How much money does he need?

10. Alice has baked 192 cookies for a school food sale. She will pack them in cellophane bags, with 6 cookies in a bag. How many bags will she need?

Be sure to write your score on your Problem Test Record.

A page of practice

Add and check. Use folded paper.

	a	b	c	d	e	f
1.	6 5 9 8	8 7 4 7	8 6 5 7	9 6 7 5	8 9 3 7	6 8 4 8
2.	$.76 .48 .05 .32	$3.89 9.10 4.35 7.63	$7.00 7.49 5.75 3.75	$ .39 4.50 8.89 7.35	$ .79 .50 9.49 6.25	$7.46 .29 .04 8.00

Subtract and check. Use folded paper.

	a	b	c	d	e	f
3.	726 349	986 389	843 367	657 98	7930 5297	8762 3847
4.	$7.42 2.99	$6.39 2.89	$8.46 .37	$7.10 3.83	$26.96 13.70	$16.00 4.07
5.	$7.63 3.95	$8.74 3.47	$9.86 8.94	$9.61 3.75	$34.82 29.17	$25.00 19.55

Multiply. Check by seeing if the answer is sensible. Use folded paper.

	a	b	c	d	e	f
6.	314 7	419 6	837 2	928 3	925 4	825 3
7.	$.35 4	$.55 9	$.24 6	$.80 4	$.25 3	$.30 6
8.	$4.13 5	$2.16 6	$8.25 3	$3.18 4	$9.15 5	$4.10 5

112

Put on your thinking cap

▶ Oral review

1. Tell what you would say and what coins you would give in change from a half dollar if you were a clerk and a shopper bought something costing 14¢.

2. Count by 6's from 6 to 60.

3. Find these answers without using a pencil:

$$2\overline{)486} \qquad 4\overline{)804} \qquad 5\overline{)150} \qquad 4\overline{)1204}$$

4. Copy these numbers on the board and put the commas where they belong. Then read the numbers.

27500   60307   28007   71633

5. Find $\frac{1}{4}$ of: 28; 36; 24; 32.

6. Count by halves from $\frac{1}{2}$ to 5.

7. What does 7:30 A.M. mean?

▶ Written review

1. Ellen rides to school on the bus and walks home. She goes to school 5 days a week and the bus fare is 6¢. How much does she pay for bus fares for one week?

2. A magic show will be given at 2:30 P.M. Saturday. It takes Donald 10 minutes to walk to the theater. At what time should he leave home?

3. Martha can get three pieces of chalk for a cent. How many pieces can she get for a nickel?

4. Henry has 384 stamps in his stamp book. Janet has 403 stamps. Who has more? How many more?

5. If 80 paper napkins are in a package, how many napkins are there in 4 packages?

6. Some Cub Scouts are going on a hike. They plan to cook their lunch over a campfire. They are taking three dozen eggs. How many eggs is that?

7. Four girls bought a box of paper handkerchiefs. There were 100 handkerchiefs in the box. If the girls share them equally, how many should each girl take?

8. If you had 78 pennies, how many piles of 5 pennies could you make? How many pennies would be left over?

Addition practice

Add and check.   Use folded paper.

1. 1 9	**2.** 5 3	**3.** 7 6	**4.** 9 6	**5.** 2 8
3 2	7 6	6 5	8 5 9	4 0 0
8 9	7 0	7	6 2	4 3
8 2	3 6	8 7	9 8	6 3 7
5 6	4 4	4 9	4 6 2	4 5
2 6	3 5	6	9 0	8 7

Copy, add, and check:

6. 28 + 430 + 50 + 7

7. 220 + 500 + 63 + 75

8. 696 + 10 + 5 + 839

9. 750 + 92 + 8 + 65

10. 47 + 477 + 6 + 35

11. 280 + 48 + 50 + 304

12. \$69.50 + \$25.05 + \$7.39

13. \$19.85 + \$.75 + \$15

14. \$17.39 + \$14.48 + \$8.97

15. \$52.65 + \$29.33 + \$9.75

16. \$17.83 + \$4.69 + \$14.98

17. \$87.07 + \$6.46 + \$40

Subtraction practice

Subtract and check.   Use folded paper.

1. 9 5 4	**2.** 5 0 0	**3.** 2 7 4	**4.** 9 6 8
2 8 6	2 8 7	1 8 2	8 5 6

5. \$1 9.6 2	**6.** \$1 7.9 5	**7.** \$7 4.7 8	**8.** \$9 2.0 0
9.6 3	8.7 6	1 6.3 5	8 3.6 9

Find the differences between these numbers and check:

9. 5095 and 5389

10. 900 and 327

11. \$75.40 and \$84.32

12. 2380 and 628

13. 6397 and 3700

14. \$47.85 and \$27.96

15. 1965 and 684

16. 5000 and 287

17. \$10.00 and \$7.85

18. 904 and 1086

19. 900 and 1346

20. \$25.02 and \$35.50

Golden Fruit Punch

I pt. sugar syrup
I cup lemon juice
I cup orange juice
I pt. pineapple juice
I qt. ginger ale
I qt. cracked ice
I dozen cherries

Liquid measure

1. Miss Miller's class is having a Mothers' Visiting Day. The children want to make and serve punch.

How many glasses of punch will they need in order to serve one glass to each of the 24 children, 16 mothers, and Miss Miller?

2. In the picture above you can see their punch recipe. How many glasses of punch will the recipe make?

You may use the table at the bottom of the page if you need help.

3. Joan says that if they double the recipe they will have 2 × 14 glasses, or _?_ glasses. Will that be enough?

4. Molly says if they make 3 times the recipe they will have 3 × 14 glasses, or _?_ glasses. Will that be enough? more than enough?

5. Miss Miller has a bowl that holds 3 gallons. The children wonder if that will be large enough to hold the 42 glasses of punch.

Do you think it will? These exercises will help you decide.

1 pt. = _?_ glasses
1 qt. = _?_ glasses
1 gal. = _?_ glasses
3 gal. = _?_ glasses

6. If there are 42 glasses of punch, and 41 persons, how many persons can have 2 glasses of punch?

LEARN THIS

2 glasses = 1 pint (pt.)
2 pints = 1 quart (qt.)
4 quarts = 1 gallon (gal.)

Self-Help Test 1

If you make any mistakes in a Self-Help Test, the number at the right of an example tells you on what page you can find help. Where can you find help for Ex. 1?

1.
```
   936
   548
   705
 + 367  (83)
```

2.
```
  $7.67
    .89
   8.25
 + 5.00  (83)
```

3.
```
   7673
 − 3098  (112)
```

4. $66.00 − $34.26 (112)

5.
```
  804
 × 6  (44)
```

6.
```
  756
 × 6  (44)
```

7.
```
  $4.78
  × 4  (44)
```

8. 6)57 (98–99)

9. 6)92 (107–109)

10. 6)449 (107–109)

Self-Help Test 2

1. What part of this circle is white? In your answer what does the 4 tell? the 3? (56–57)

2. Joe's dog Toby has fleas. Joe wants to get rid of the fleas.

He bought some flea soap for 25¢, a comb for 29¢, a brush for 50¢, and a can of meat as a reward for Toby for 10¢.

How much did Joe spend? (13–15)

3. Find the cost of 3 dresses at $3.79 each. (44)

4. Sally collects match folders. A week ago she had 39. Now she has 56. How many did she get this week? (24–25)

5. If 6 children share 144 paper clips equally, how many paper clips will each child get? (107–109)

6. Penny has 39¢. How many 6-cent apples can she buy? How many cents will she have left? (98)

7. If you were selling hot dogs at a school field meet, what coins would you give in change from a dollar after a 32-cent sale? (110)

8. What is wrong with this division? Copy it and work it correctly. (100)

Now is the time to test yourself

Copy the examples correctly. Work carefully. Check your work. Be sure your answers are sensible.

1. Divide 504 by 6.

2. Find $\frac{1}{6}$ of 86.

3. Multiply $2.58 by 6.

4. Add: $78 + 400 + 76 + 248$

5. If you buy a 38-cent puzzle and hand the clerk a half dollar, what coins might you get in change?

6. Betsy has a quart bottle of grape juice. If she adds a quart of water to the quart of grape juice, how many glasses of the drink will she have to serve to her friends?

7. Four boys helped Mr. Adams pick apples. When they finished, he gave them a basket of apples to divide equally.

There were 112 apples in the basket. How many apples should each boy get?

8. If one ball point pen costs $1.69, how much will two pens cost?

9. How many 6-inch book marks can Sally make from a strip of leather 45 inches long?

10. If a pound of food for your dog costs 30¢, how much will a half pound cost?

Just for fun

Copy each example. Then figure out what signs are missing between the numbers. The first example is done for you.

1. $6 + 7 - 4 \times 3 = 27$

2. $9 \ ? \ 6 \ ? \ 8 \ ? \ 4 = 6$

3. $28 \ ? \ 4 \ ? \ 2 \ ? \ 4 = 10$

4. $8 \ ? \ 4 \ ? \ 9 \ ? \ 3 = 6$

5. $7 \ ? \ 5 \ ? \ 1 \ ? \ 6 = 6$

6. $21 \ ? \ 7 \ ? \ 6 \ ? \ 9 = 0$

7. $9 \ ? \ 5 \ ? \ 6 \ ? \ 8 = 3$

8. $5 \ ? \ 6 \ ? \ 2 \ ? \ 8 = 4$

9. $54 \ ? \ 6 \ ? \ 9 \ ? \ 3 = 6$

10. $8 \ ? \ 6 \ ? \ 6 \ ? \ 6 = 9$

11. $7 \ ? \ 7 \ ? \ 7 \ ? \ 7 = 6$

12. $8 \ ? \ 8 \ ? \ 8 \ ? \ 8 = 9$

13. $5 \ ? \ 5 \ ? \ 5 \ ? \ 5 = 3$

14. $6 \ ? \ 9 \ ? \ 2 \ ? \ 8 = 7$

To the Teacher: See Note 4 on page 310.

A pet show

Miss Andrews' class is having a pet show.   These are the pets in the show:

1 goat	1 monkey
5 rabbits	1 sheep
6 dogs	2 roosters
4 cats	3 turtles
1 pony	1 guinea pig
2 canaries	2 mice
6 goldfish	2 ducks

1. How many pets are in the show?

2. Which of the following ways of finding the number of pets in the show do you like best?

• Harry wrote the numbers of all the pets in a column and added.

• Doris added mentally without copying the numbers.

• Jane found the sum of the number of pets in the first column. She found the sum in the second column.   Then she added the 2 sums.

• Below is the way Jim found how many pets there were.

Can you figure out how he did it?   Is his answer correct?

$$5 \times 1 \text{ pet } = 5 \text{ pets}$$
$$4 \times 2 \text{ pets} = 8 \text{ pets}$$
$$1 \times 3 \text{ pets} = 3 \text{ pets}$$
$$1 \times 4 \text{ pets} = 4 \text{ pets}$$
$$1 \times 5 \text{ pets} = 5 \text{ pets}$$
$$2 \times 6 \text{ pets} = \underline{12} \text{ pets}$$
$$37 \text{ pets}$$

3. The class decided to give a blue-ribbon prize to:

The friendliest pet
The funniest pet
The most unusual pet
The best-cared-for pet
The biggest pet
The smallest pet
The prettiest pet

How many prizes were needed?

4. They bought a yard of blue ribbon. How would you divide a yard of ribbon into 7 prizes?

5. Which of the following suggestions for dividing the ribbon do you like best?

● Molly said, "$36 \div 7 = 5$ r1. Let's make each prize 5 in. long and throw 1 in. of ribbon away."

● Jim said, "Let's make each prize a little bit more than 5 inches long and not throw any ribbon away."

● Bill said, "Let's make six 5-inch prizes and one 6-inch prize."

6. Allowing 12 ft. of rope for each animal, how many feet of rope were needed to tie 8 animals to stakes? Were two 50-ft. rolls of rope enough?

7. At $2.39 a roll, how much did 2 rolls of rope cost?

8. The class sold 55 ten-cent tickets to the show. How much did they take in?

Did they take in enough to pay for the ribbon prizes ($.39) and the rope ($4.78)?

Thinking about sevens

Roy has a game called "Lucky Seven." When he gets a ball into the "Lucky Cup," he gets 7 points. On the lid of the box is this help for scoring.

Lucky Seven Scoring Chart						
1	2	3	4	5	6	7
8	9	10	11	12	13	14
15	16	17	18	19	20	21
22	23	24	25	26	27	28
29	30	31	32	33	34	35
36	37	38	39	40	41	42
43	44	45	46	47	48	49
50	51	52	53	54	55	56
57	58	59	60	61	62	63
64	65	66	67	68	69	70

1. Count the numbers on the chart by 7's.

2. Look at the chart. How many points does Roy win when he gets 2 balls in the Lucky Cup? 3? 5? 4? 6? 9? 8? 7?

Look at the chart to find:

3.

2×7	5×7	8×7
3×7	6×7	9×7
4×7	7×7	10×7

4.

4 sevens + 3	3 sevens + 1
5 sevens + 4	6 sevens + 3
9 sevens + 6	8 sevens + 2

5. How many balls does Roy have in the Lucky Cup when he wins 7 points? 14? 21? 35? 49? 28? 42? 63? 56?

6.

14 = _?_ 7's	56 = _?_ 7's
21 = _?_ 7's	28 = _?_ 7's

7.

49 = _?_ 7's	35 = _?_ 7's
63 = _?_ 7's	42 = _?_ 7's

8. $4 \times 7 = 28$, so you know that $28 \div 7 = \underline{?}$.

9. $9 \times 7 = 63$, so you know that $63 \div 7 = \underline{?}$.

10. Make up a multiplication table of sevens. Use the Lucky Seven Scoring Chart to help you. The table is started. ⟶
Go to $10 \times 7 = 70$.

$1 \times 7 = 7$
$2 \times 7 = 14$

11. Use your table to find the cost of 3 soap-bubble pipes at 7¢ each; of 4 pipes; 6; 7; 9; 8.

12. Jo said, "If you can make a multiplication table of sevens, you can make a division table of sevens. $3 \times 7 = 21$, so $21 \div 7 = \underline{?}$.

13. Make a division table of sevens. The table is started. ⟶
Go to $70 \div 7 = 10$.

$7 \div 7 = 1$
$14 \div 7 = 2$

In Exs. 1–6, explain how you get each answer.

1. $5 \times 7 = 35$, so $10 \times 7 = \underline{\ ?\ }$.

2. $2 \times 7 = 14$, so $4 \times 7 = \underline{\ ?\ }$.

3. $3 \times 7 = 21$, so $6 \times 7 = \underline{\ ?\ }$.

4. $4 \times 7 = 28$, so $8 \times 7 = \underline{\ ?\ }$.

5. $6 \times 7 = 42$, so $7 \times 6 = \underline{\ ?\ }$.

6. $10 \times 7 = 70$, so $9 \times 7 = \underline{\ ?\ }$.

7. $4 \times 7 = 28$; $3 \times 7 = 21$; so $7 \times 7 = 49$. Why?

8. $3 \times 7 = 21$; $2 \times 7 = 14$; so $5 \times 7 = \underline{\ ?\ }$. Why?

9. Peter calls these four facts a Number Family:

$6 \times 7 = 42$ $42 \div 7 = 6$
$7 \times 6 = 42$ $42 \div 6 = 7$

Tell the other three members in the Number Family of each of these facts:

$8 \times 7 = 56$ $63 \div 7 = 9$
$4 \times 7 = 28$ $35 \div 7 = 5$

10. One day Jerry said, "Five weeks from today is Christmas Day." Do you know how many days there are in 5 weeks?

11. Tell how many days there are in 1 week; in 2 weeks; in 3; 4; 5; 6; 7; 8; 9; 10.

Multiply. Practice until you can say every answer.

| 12. | 2 | 7 | 5 | 8 | 9 |
| | 7 | 4 | 7 | 7 | 7 |

| 13. | 3 | 7 | 6 | 7 | 7 |
| | 7 | 9 | 7 | 3 | 7 |

| 14. | 7 | 7 | 7 | 4 | 7 |
| | 1 | 8 | 5 | 7 | 6 |

15. Copy Exs. 12–14 and write the answers.

16. Make and study Help-Yourself Cards for any facts you did not know in Ex. 15. Then do Ex. 15 again.

Multiplication Facts of Sevens

7	7	7	7	7	7	7	7	7
1	2	3	4	5	6	7	8	9
7	14	21	28	35	42	49	56	63

1	2	3	4	5	6	7	8	9
7	7	7	7	7	7	7	7	7
7	14	21	28	35	42	49	56	63

Practice in multiplying and dividing

Multiply each of these numbers by 7; by 6:

	a	*b*	*c*	*d*	*e*	*f*
1.	21	37	45	73	83	60
2.	$.67	$.78	$.94	$.49	$.77	$.50
3.	709	369	548	807	657	360
4.	$3.50	$6.46	$4.89	$5.27	$4.86	$9.75

5. How much will 7 movie tickets cost at $.65 each?

6. Find the cost of 3 Halloween costumes at $2.79 each.

7. From Jerry's home to his uncle's farm is 36 miles. To the farm and back again is __?__ miles.

8. If 9 boys buy caps for $.75 each, how much will they spend?

Tell the missing numbers. Use counters to prove you are right.

9. $14 \div 2 = 7$, so $14 \div 7 = $ __?__.
$21 \div 3 = 7$, so $21 \div 7 = $ __?__.

10. $28 \div 4 = 7$, so $28 \div 7 = $ __?__.
$35 \div 5 = 7$, so $35 \div 7 = $ __?__.

11. $7 \times 6 = 42$, so $42 \div 6 = $ __?__.
$6 \times 7 = 42$, so $42 \div 7 = $ __?__.

12. $5 \times 7 = $ __?__. $3 \times 7 = $ __?__.
So $8 \times 7 = 35 + 21 = $ __?__.

13. $5 \times 7 = $ __?__. $4 \times 7 = $ __?__.
So $9 \times 7 = 35 + 28 = $ __?__.

14. If you have 35¢, how many 5-cent toys can you buy? how many 7-cent toys?

15. For 42¢ how many 6-cent tickets can you buy? how many 7-cent tickets?

16. What will be the date 3 weeks from November 2?

17. On Christmas Day, Ted said, "Two weeks ago today was my birthday." Ted's birthday was Dec. __?__.

18. Write 9 sevens in a column and add. The sum is __?__.

19. Start with 49. Subtract 7 over and over. How many subtractions can you do?
Your subtractions show there are __?__ 7's in 49.

20. In how many different ways can you discover how many 7's there are in 63?

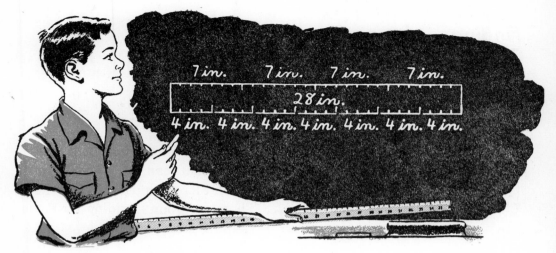

7 in. 7 in. 7 in. 7 in.
28 in.
4 in. 4 in. 4 in. 4 in. 4 in. 4 in. 4 in.

Division facts of sevens

1. Charlie's drawing shows that from a strip of wood 28 inches long he can make __?__ boats 7 inches long, or __?__ boats 4 inches long.

2. In 28 there are __?__ 7's.
$28 \div 7 =$ __?__

3. In 28 there are __?__ 4's.
$28 \div 4 =$ __?__

4. Count by 7's from 7 to 70.

5. Tell the other facts in the Number Family of each of these:

$8 \times 7 = 56$ $5 \times 7 = 35$
$6 \times 7 = 42$ $9 \times 7 = 63$

Say the answers. Then copy the examples and write the answers.

6. $7\overline{)42}$ $3\overline{)21}$ $4\overline{)28}$ $7\overline{)35}$

7. $8\overline{)56}$ $7\overline{)49}$ $2\overline{)14}$ $7\overline{)56}$

8. $7\overline{)28}$ $5\overline{)35}$ $7\overline{)63}$ $7\overline{)7}$

9. $9\overline{)63}$ $7\overline{)21}$ $6\overline{)42}$ $7\overline{)14}$

10. Make and study Help-Yourself Cards for any facts you missed in Exs. 6–9.

11. How many 7-cent balls can you buy for 35¢? 21¢? 42¢?

Division Facts of Sevens

1	2	3	4	5	6	7	8	9
$7\overline{)7}$	$7\overline{)14}$	$7\overline{)21}$	$7\overline{)28}$	$7\overline{)35}$	$7\overline{)42}$	$7\overline{)49}$	$7\overline{)56}$	$7\overline{)63}$

7	7	7	7	7	7	7	7	7
$1\overline{)7}$	$2\overline{)14}$	$3\overline{)21}$	$4\overline{)28}$	$5\overline{)35}$	$6\overline{)42}$	$7\overline{)49}$	$8\overline{)56}$	$9\overline{)63}$

Finding $\frac{1}{7}$ of a number

1. How many counters do you have in each pile if you deal out:
- 14 counters into 7 equal piles?
- 21 counters into 7 equal piles?
- 28 counters into 7 equal piles?

2. Ex. 1 shows: $\frac{1}{7}$ of 14 = _?_ ; $\frac{1}{7}$ of 21 = _?_ ; $\frac{1}{7}$ of 28 = _?_ .

3. $\frac{1}{7}$ of 14 = 14 ÷ _?_ .

$\frac{1}{7}$ of 21 = 21 ÷ _?_ .

$\frac{1}{7}$ of 28 = 28 ÷ _?_ .

> To find $\frac{1}{7}$ of a number, divide the number by 7.

4. If 7 girls share equally the work of writing 21 invitations, how many should each girl write?

If 3 girls share the work, how many should each write?

5. If 7 boys share equally 35 pennies, how many should each boy take?

If 5 boys share the pennies, how many should each take?

6. If 7 boys share equally 56 shells, how many should each boy take?

If 8 boys share the shells, how many should each get?

7. What number facts did you use in Ex. 4? Ex. 5? Ex. 6?

8. Find $\frac{1}{7}$ of these numbers:

28	14	42	0	35
7	63	21	56	49

9. Tell all the numbers from 7 to 70 that can be divided by 7 without a remainder. Write them. These are your Dividing-by-Seven Helping Numbers.

10. Tell all the numbers from 70 to 7 that can be divided by 7 without a remainder. Write them.

11. Which of these numbers can be divided by 7 without a remainder?

36	45	42	54	48
32	24	28	63	56

12. $\frac{1}{7}$ of 42 = 6; $\frac{1}{6}$ of 42 = _?_

$\frac{1}{7}$ of 56 = 8; $\frac{1}{8}$ of 56 = _?_

$\frac{1}{7}$ of 63 = 9; $\frac{1}{9}$ of 63 = _?_

13. If you arrange 56 coins in 7 equal piles, how many coins will you have in each pile?

14. Seven girls bought a record for 63¢. If they share the cost equally, each should pay _?_ ¢.

15. Bill paid 21¢ for a pound of plums. There were 7 plums in the pound. He paid _?_ ¢ apiece for them.

Uneven division facts of sevens

Penny has 51 gumdrops. She wants to divide them equally among 7 baskets. How many should she put in each basket?

If Penny divides 51 gumdrops into 7 equal parts, she puts $\frac{1}{7}$ of the gumdrops in each part.

$$\begin{array}{r} 7\ r2 \\ 7\overline{)51} \\ 49 \\ \hline 2 \end{array}$$

Penny did the division at the left and said, "I can put 7 gumdrops in each basket. I'll eat the 2 that are left."

Prove that Penny's work is right.

Dividing-by-Seven Helping-Number Chart						
1	2	3	4	5	6	7
8	9	10	11	12	13	14
15	16	17	18	19	20	21
22	23	24	25	26	27	28
29	30	31	32	33	34	35
36	37	38	39	40	41	42
43	44	45	46	47	48	49
50	51	52	53	54	55	56
57	58	59	60	61	62	63
64	65	66	67	68	69	70

1. Louise needed to divide 37 by 7. She found 37 on the chart above and thought, "I must first find my Helping Number. It is 35. $35 \div 7 = \underline{\ ?\ }$. $37 \div 7 = \underline{\ ?\ }$."

Divide each of the following numbers by 7. First find each Helping Number. You may use the chart.

2. 31   62   40   27   18   54   48   51   53   61

3. 34   39   43   30   15   20   35   52   60   55

Uneven division facts of sevens

1. How many numbers between 7 and 70 can you name that can be divided by 7 without a remainder?

2. Starting with 70, subtract 7 over and over until you have nothing left. Your subtractions show there are __?__ 7's in 70.

3. Which of these numbers can be divided by 7 without a remainder?

49   54   37   56   63

4. What is the largest remainder you can have when you are dividing by 7?

Tell what your Helping Number is in dividing each of the numbers below by 7. Then divide each number by 7. How many of the divisions can you do without a pencil?

	a	b	c	d	e	f	g	h	i	j
5.	40	8	33	47	13	39	55	56	54	65
6.	27	22	9	34	48	15	20	66	42	35
7.	46	31	23	10	36	50	16	41	58	68
8.	59	64	29	24	11	37	53	17	43	57
9.	51	60	14	30	25	12	38	21	18	44
10.	61	52	62	69	32	26	45	67	28	19

Find $\frac{1}{7}$ of each of the following numbers:

11.	23	65	37	16	44	26	50	33	57	47
12.	64	24	66	38	19	45	29	50	33	58

13. It takes 52 cards to play "Sky Pilot." If 7 girls play, each girl will get __?__ cards and there will be __?__ cards left over.

14. In Ed's spelling notebook he writes 7 words on a page. To write 65 words he needs __?__ pages.

15. If a quart of ice cream serves 7 persons, how many quarts will be needed to serve 34 persons?

16. How many 7-inch stakes can George cut from a pole 60 inches long? Will he have a piece of pole left over?

Dividing large numbers by seven

On July 10 Bill counted on the calendar to see how many days it was until Christmas. He said, "It's a long time, 168 days. I wonder how many weeks it is."

Bill thought, "1 week = 7 days; 10 weeks = 70 days; 20 weeks = 140 days; 30 weeks = 210 days."

1. Then Bill knew that in 168 days there were more than 20 weeks, but not as many as 30 weeks. He decided that $168 \div 7 =$ "20 some." Explain. Can you check his estimate on the calendar?

2. To divide 168 by 7, Bill thought, "16 ÷ 7 is a little more than 2; so 168 ÷ 7 is a little more than 20." Then he wrote the 2 in tens place, as shown in the division at the right. How did he get the 14? Explain his division.

$$
\begin{array}{r}
24 \\
7)\overline{168} \\
14 \\
\hline
28 \\
28 \\
\hline
\end{array}
$$

*Use the Hint System to help you find **about how many 7's** there are in each number in Ex. 3–6. Say, "In 225 there are '30-some' 7's; in 182 there are '20-some' 7's"; and so on.*

	a	b	c	d	e	f	g
3.	225	182	232	298	100	197	258
4.	185	247	315	600	120	340	624
5.	132	75	620	325	370	462	98
6.	204	235	262	300	400	500	600

7. Divide each number in Exs. 3–6 by 7. Check each division.

8. How many weeks are there in 98 days? in 119 days? in 252 days?

9. Find $\frac{1}{7}$ of 364; of 448; of 665; of 558; of 595.

127

A page of practice

Copy, divide, and check:

	a	b	c	d	e	f
1.	7)84	7)91	7)343	7)329	7)364	7)476
2.	7)94	7)86	6)106	7)540	7)659	7)597
3.	7)98	7)89	7)462	7)373	7)510	7)252
4.	4)64	6)96	5)295	2)196	3)228	7)623
5.	3)75	2)98	4)378	6)379	7)675	4)176
6.	7)96	5)87	3)263	5)428	6)490	7)547

Copy, add, and check:

7.	34	72	109	728	600	804
	98	9	324	63	729	36
	26	38	873	401	45	275
	73	65	246	642	302	43
	45	24	512	374	461	500

Copy and multiply. Check by going over your work.

8.	643	789	737	674	752	670
	7	5	3	8	7	8

Copy, subtract, and check:

9.	72	84	923	725	604	800
	48	69	387	78	38	362
10.	84	63	846	546	705	700
	37	29	638	83	96	684

128

Multiplying by 10, 20, 30, 40

1. George was trying to discover how to multiply any number by 10. He experimented with the numbers shown in the yellow box. Tell the missing numbers.

$$10 \times 3 = 30$$
$$10 \times 8 = \underline{\ ?\ }$$
$$10 \times 9 = \underline{\ ?\ }$$
$$10 \times 12 = 120$$
$$10 \times 15 = \underline{\ ?\ }$$

2. George made this rule for multiplying by 10:

❙ To multiply a number by 10, put a zero after the number.

Look at the yellow box. Did George make a good rule? Tell how you know. Use the rule to multiply each of these numbers by 10:

14   20   99   100   101   1000

$$20 \times 3 = 60$$
$$20 \times 12 = 240$$
$$20 \times 15 = 300$$
$$20 \times 36 = 720$$
$$20 \times 44 = 880$$

3. Study the multiplications in the blue box. Then tell a good way to multiply a number by 20.

4. Jane made this rule for multiplying by 20:

❙ To multiply a number by 20, you first multiply the number by 10, and then by 2.

Does Jane's rule work for the numbers in the blue box?

5. Tom made this rule for multiplying by 20:

❙ To multiply a number by 20, first multiply the number by 2, and then by 10.

Does Tom's rule work for the numbers in the blue box?

6. Multiply each of these numbers by 20:   16   25   75   100

7. Make a rule for multiplying by 30; by 40.

8. Multiply each of these numbers by 10; by 20; by 30; by 40.

6   7   20   65   47   10   82   21   31

9. $10 \times 21\cancel{c} = \underline{\ ?\ }\cancel{c} = \$2.10$; $10 \times \$.21 = \underline{\ ?\ }$; $20 \times \$.21 = \underline{\ ?\ }$

10. $30 \times 25\cancel{c} = \underline{\ ?\ }\cancel{c} = \$7.50$; $30 \times \$.25 = \underline{\ ?\ }$; $20 \times \$.25 = \underline{\ ?\ }$

129

Multiplying by a two-place number

Miss Holt's 36 pupils earned $.25 apiece for the Red Cross. In all, they earned 36 × $.25.

Here is the way 3 pupils found 36 × $.25:

```
                  Tom
        6 × $.25 = $1.5 0
       30 × $.25 =   7.5 0
   So  36 × $.25 = $9.0 0
```

```
     Jane              Mary
   $  .2 5           $  .2 5
       3 6               3 6
   ───────           ───────
     1 5 0             1 5 0
     7 5 0               7 5
   ───────           ───────
   $ 9.0 0           $ 9.0 0
```

1. Explain Tom's multiplication.

2. Explain Jane's multiplication. How did she get the 150? the 750? the $9.00?

3. How are Tom's and Jane's multiplications alike? different?

4. Now look at the way Mary multiplied. How did she get the 150?

5. Next Mary found 30 × $.25. Why?

6. To find 30 × 25, she thought, "3 × 25 = 75; 10 × 75 = _?_."

7. Do you see that Mary didn't write all of the 750 in her multiplication?

She wrote 7 in hundreds place, 5 in tens place, and then instead of writing 0 in ones place, she just left a blank space.

8. How did Mary finish her multiplication?

9. How is Mary's work like Jane's? How is it different?

10. Tom, Jane, and Mary all found that 36 × $.25 = _?_.

11. Most fourth-grade pupils use Mary's way to multiply. Exs. 12–13 are done by Mary's way. Explain them.

Copy Exs. 12–13 without the work. Multiply. Then look to see if your work is correct.

	a	b	c
12.	2 5	1 2	4 3
	1 8	2 6	1 7
	2 0 0	7 2	3 0 1
	2 5	2 4	4 3
	4 5 0	3 1 2	7 3 1
13.	$ .3 5	$ .6 7	$ .6 3
	2 6	3 4	4 7
	2 1 0	2 6 8	4 4 1
	7 0	2 0 1	2 5 2
	$9.1 0	$2 2.7 8	$2 9.6 1

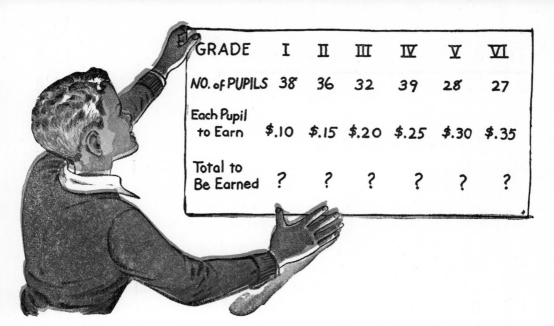

GRADE	I	II	III	IV	V	VI
NO. of PUPILS	38	36	32	39	28	27
Each Pupil to Earn	$.10	$.15	$.20	$.25	$.30	$.35
Total to Be Earned	?	?	?	?	?	?

The Hamilton School is raising money for the Junior Red Cross.

1. Look at John's table. How many pupils are there in each grade?

2. How much money is each first-grade pupil to earn? each second-grade pupil? each pupil in the other grades?

How much money is each grade to earn? the entire school?

Multiply. Check by going over your work.

	a	*b*	*c*	*d*	*e*	*f*	*g*
3.	28 14	69 37	74 49	35 62	84 57	40 36	37 75
4.	35 52	90 76	48 63	29 47	75 35	37 48	82 74
5.	65 47	72 65	80 43	66 32	49 76	84 15	57 29

Remember to put the dollar sign and the cents point in your answer to each of these multiplication examples:

6.	$.54 18	$.49 23	$.63 37	$.15 64	$.20 79	$.72 35	$.38 27

There are many ways to multiply

1. To find 4×15, Jane thinks:
   "4×10 is 40; 4×5 is 20; so 4×15 is $40 + 20$, or _?_."

   Use Jane's method to find:

2. 5×13 6×13 9×12 6×25 7×43

3. 4×16 7×15 9×21 8×35 8×34

4. 3×18 8×21 7×31 9×25 9×17

5. Miss Allison's pupils had a contest to see how many different ways they could find 12×25.

Here are some of the ways they used.   Explain each way. Whose way is quickest?   Whose way is easiest to write?

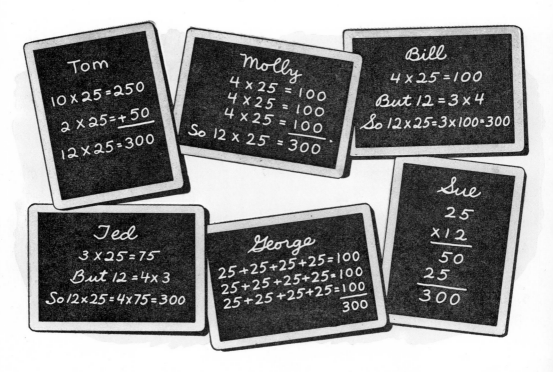

Tom
$10 \times 25 = 250$
$2 \times 25 = +50$
$12 \times 25 = 300$

Molly
$4 \times 25 = 100$
$4 \times 25 = 100$
$4 \times 25 = 100$
So $12 \times 25 = 300$

Bill
$4 \times 25 = 100$
But $12 = 3 \times 4$
So $12 \times 25 = 3 \times 100 = 300$

Ted
$3 \times 25 = 75$
But $12 = 4 \times 3$
So $12 \times 25 = 4 \times 75 = 300$

George
$25 + 25 + 25 + 25 = 100$
$25 + 25 + 25 + 25 = 100$
$25 + 25 + 25 + 25 = 100$
300

Sue
25
$\times 12$
50
25
300

6. See how many different ways your class can find to do these multiplications:

a) 24×25 *b)* 16×32 *c)* 15×36 *d)* 18×27 *e)* 14×22

132

Dividing dollars and cents

Bob made 6 puppets. The materials cost $1.62. To find how much each puppet cost, he needed to divide $1.62 by 6.

▶ Explain his division. Notice that the answer is written with a dollar sign and cents point. Why?

▶ The division shows that the cost of one puppet is __?__ .

1. If Bob had been able to make only 3 puppets from $1.62 worth of material, what would each puppet have cost?

```
       $ .2 7
   6)$1.6 2
       1 2
       4 2
       4 2
```

Check:
6 × $.27 = $1.62

Divide and check:

	a	*b*	*c*	*d*	*e*
2.	3)$2.49	4)$2.72	5)$2.95	7)$5.81	7)$6.09
3.	5)$4.80	6)$4.56	6)$5.76	7)$3.99	5)$4.95
4.	6)$5.58	7)$6.65	6)$1.32	4)$3.04	7)$3.57
5.	4)$3.36	7)$6.72	5)$3.75	7)$4.97	6)$5.04

A page of problems

1. The boys in the West Side Club are giving a show. They have sold 49 tickets, so they will need 49 chairs for the people to sit on.

They now have 34 chairs. How many chairs must they borrow?

2. There is room to put 7 chairs in a row. How many rows of 7 chairs will 49 chairs make?

3. For a fourth-grade party, Ann can get a package of 50 paper napkins for 10¢.

Will 2 packages be enough for the 95 persons invited to the party? How much will 2 packages cost?

4. Ann can get a package of 25 drinking straws for 19¢. Will 2 packages be enough for 95 persons? 3 packages? 4 packages? How much will 4 packages cost?

5. Ann can get 12 paper cups in a package for 10¢. Will 6 packages be enough for 95 persons? 7 packages? 8 packages? How much will 8 packages cost?

6. If Ann spends $.20 for napkins, $.76 for straws, and $.80 for cups, how much will she spend in all?

7. Ann has $3.00 to spend for the party. If she spends $1.76, how much money will she have left?

8. For her party Sue wants to cut a cake into 8 equal parts. Can you show her the easiest way to do it? Draw a picture. Use your picture to show that:

$\frac{1}{2}$ of $\frac{1}{2} = \frac{1}{4}$ $\qquad$ $\frac{2}{2} = \frac{4}{4}$ $\qquad$ $\frac{1}{2} = \frac{4}{8}$

$\frac{1}{2}$ of $\frac{1}{4} = \frac{1}{8}$ $\qquad$ $\frac{4}{4} = \frac{8}{8}$ $\qquad$ $\frac{1}{4} = \frac{2}{8}$

$\frac{1}{4}$ of $\frac{1}{2} = \frac{1}{8}$ $\qquad$ $\frac{2}{2} = \frac{8}{8}$ $\qquad$ $\frac{3}{4} = \frac{6}{8}$

9. Bill has a half dollar to spend for colored pencils. How many pencils can he get if he buys:

5-cent pencils $\qquad$ 8-cent pencils

6-cent pencils $\qquad$ 9-cent pencils

7-cent pencils $\qquad$ 10-cent pencils

10. Bill (Ex. 9) said, "The less I pay for each pencil, the more pencils I can get for 50¢." Do you agree?

11. If you know that you can get 3 roller-coaster tickets for a quarter, can you think of an easy way to find the cost of 6 tickets?

12. If you know that 10 oranges cost 62¢, can you think of an easy way to find the cost of 5 oranges?

Using your head

Two of these divisions are **incorrect**. Find the **mistakes**. Then do the divisions correctly and check.

	20 r4	CHECK		21 r2	CHECK		70 r8	CHECK
1.	6)124	20	**2.**	7)149	21	**3.**	7)498	70
	12	× 6		14	× 7		49	× 7
	4	120		9	147		8	490
		+ 4		7	+ 2			+ 8
		124		2	149			498

	41 r1	CHECK		80 r3	CHECK		91 r2	CHECK
4.	6)247	41	**5.**	7)563	80	**6.**	6)549	91
	24	× 6		56	× 7		54	× 6
	7	246		3	560		9	546
	6	+ 1			+ 3		6	+ 2
	1	247			563		2	549

Many fourth-grade children can do these divisions without using a pencil. If you try hard, you can, too. The Hint System will help you.

	a	b	c	d	e	f
7.	6)305	6)240	7)630	5)453	4)320	6)363
8.	7)497	7)560	7)496	5)400	4)282	3)240
9.	6)481	6)540	7)425	3)272	5)352	4)361
10.	6)422	4)324	6)426	3)273	5)255	4)284
11.	6)368	7)568	4)366	7)148	3)184	7)359
12.	7)429	6)548	7)638	4)286	6)367	6)486
13.	6)547	7)639	6)488	6)427	7)499	6)306
14.	4)248	6)540	7)568	6)429	7)637	5)300

Oral practice

1. Jimmie is making 12 airplanes. He has finished 7. How many more must he make?

2. Jean is making and filling 21 red Christmas stockings. She has finished $\frac{1}{3}$ of the stockings. How many has she finished?

3. Jean can cut 7 stockings from a yard of red material. For 21 stockings she will need __?__ yd.

4. Nine girls want red hair bows. For each bow 10 inches of ribbon are needed. How many inches are needed for 9 bows?

Divide. Do not use a pencil.

5. $2\overline{)84}$ $3\overline{)96}$ $4\overline{)128}$ $2\overline{)188}$ $3\overline{)396}$ $4\overline{)1208}$

6. $2\overline{)160}$ $3\overline{)273}$ $4\overline{)1604}$ $3\overline{)2400}$ $2\overline{)1208}$ $3\overline{)219}$

7. Add 6 to each of these numbers: 49 37 28 93 56

8. Add 7 to each of these numbers: 67 59 84 38 35

9. Add 8 to each of these numbers: 34 67 56 45 78

10. Add 9 to each of these numbers: 32 54 21 43 65

11. From 55 subtract: 25 48 20 49 54 26 37

12. From 67 subtract: 40 37 64 60 63 48 51

136

Subtraction review

1. Take the subtraction test on page 21.

   Subtract and check:

	a	b	c	d	e	f	g
2.	693	825	743	800	904	732	842
	479	683	278	36	459	39	79

	a	b	c	d	e	f	g
3.	$9.23	$9.00	$8.63	$6.13	$5.05	$8.00	$7.65
	8.10	4.26	3.49	4.68	1.89	2.27	4.50

4. From $10 subtract $3.63.

5. Subtract $2.75 from $5.

6. 742 is __?__ more than 469.

7. 237 is __?__ less than 400.

8. $9 − $3.87 = __?__ .

9. 286 − __?__ = 197.

10. __?__ − 246 = 385.

11. 635 is __?__ larger than 276.

12. 349 and __?__ = 743.

13. __?__ and 260 = 890.

14. 247 is __?__ smaller than 500.

15. Take $6.94 from $7.

Addition review

1. Take the addition test on page 11.

2. Add $2.48, $5.07, $3.54, and $7.23.

3. Add $5, $3.50, $4.27, and $.60.

4. Find the sum of $4.67 + $2.98 + $5 + $.75.

5. Find the sum of $8.32 + $10 + $2.46 + $.09.

6. Add and check:

a	b	c	d	e	f	g	h
7	8	48	79	27	6	70	83
9	4	62	30	8	40	9	29
3	6	37	67	52	62	57	17
5	8	83	54	43	38	7	6

Choosing the easier way to multiply

Janet is going to send 29 Christmas cards. She needs 29 three-cent stamps.

To find how much the stamps will cost, Janet thought, "If 1 stamp costs 3¢, 29 stamps will cost 29 × 3¢."

● Look at the multiplications below. Explain how Janet and Roy each found the cost of 29 three-cent stamps. Whose way do you like better?

● Janet looked at Roy's multiplication. She said, "That's funny. We wanted to find 29 times 3¢. You found 3 times 29¢. But you got the right answer anyway."

● Roy answered, "Yes, the answer to 3 × 29¢ is the same as the answer to 29 × 3¢. I chose the easier way to multiply."

● Explain what Roy meant when he said, "I chose the easier way to multiply."

Janet found
$29 × 3$ →
$$\begin{array}{r} 3 \\ 29 \\ \hline 27 \\ 6 \\ \hline 87\,(\text{¢}) \end{array}$$

Roy found
$3 × 29$ →
$$\begin{array}{r} 29 \\ 3 \\ \hline 87\,(\text{¢}) \end{array}$$

1. Would it be easier to find $\begin{array}{r} 5 \\ \times\,27 \end{array}$ or $\begin{array}{r} 27 \\ \times\,5 \end{array}$? Would the answers be the same?

2. Does $20 × 5\text{¢} = 5 × 20\text{¢}$?
$5 × 20\text{¢} = \underline{\ ?\ }\text{¢} = \$1.00$

3. Does $30 × 4\text{¢} = 4 × 30\text{¢}$?
$4 × 30\text{¢} = \underline{\ ?\ }\text{¢} = \$1.20$

4. Does $40 × 3\text{¢} = 3 × 40\text{¢}$?
$3 × 40\text{¢} = \underline{\ ?\ }\text{¢} = \$1.20$

5. Does $50 × 5\text{¢} = 5 × 50\text{¢}$?
$5 × 50\text{¢} = \underline{\ ?\ }\text{¢} = \underline{\ ?\ }$

6. Does $60 × 4\text{¢} = 4 × 60\text{¢}$?
$4 × 60\text{¢} = \underline{\ ?\ }\text{¢} = \underline{\ ?\ }$

7. Does $80 × 5\text{¢} = 5 × 80\text{¢}$?
$5 × 80\text{¢} = \underline{\ ?\ }\text{¢} = \underline{\ ?\ }$

8. Does $70 × 3\text{¢} = 3 × 70\text{¢}$?
$3 × 70\text{¢} = \underline{\ ?\ }\text{¢} = \underline{\ ?\ }$

9. How much is $60 × 5\text{¢}$?

In the illustration: **SALE!**

GIANT PENCILS	4¢
CRAYONS	7¢
RULERS	8¢
ERASERS	3¢
NOTEBOOKS	9¢
PADS	5¢
PENCIL SHARPENERS	6¢
RED PENCILS	2¢

PENCIL SHARPENERS 6¢

Buying school supplies

Use the easier way to multiply. Show whether your answer is cents, dollars, or dollars and cents. At the sale find the cost of:

1. 16 giant pencils

2. 50 erasers

3. 12 pencil sharpeners

4. 24 boxes of crayons

5. 25 notebooks

6. 3 dozen red pencils

7. 36 rulers

8. 48 pads

9. 100 red pencils

Without doing any multiplications, tell which would cost more:

10. 25 five-cent pencils, or four 25-cent pens?

11. 36 eight-cent tops, or nine 36-cent kites?

12. 45 seven-cent balls, or seven 44-cent bats?

13. Make up some problems about buying supplies for your class at the sale.

14. Find the cost of 2 dozen apples at 4¢ each.

15. How much will 25 five-cent Christmas cards cost?

16. How much will a sheet of 50 three-cent stamps cost?

17. Find the cost of 75 two-cent stamps.

18. Can you buy 25 four-cent cards for a dollar?

Estimating answers

1. Would you *estimate* the cost of 3 dolls at $1.98 each to be *about* $3, $6, or $9?

To make the estimate, think, "$1.98 is almost $2. Three dolls at $2 each would cost _?_ dollars."

2. Would you estimate the change from a 10-dollar bill after spending $4.97 to be about $6, $4, or $5?

3. Bill wanted to buy a dozen tickets that cost 24¢ each.

He thought, "24¢ is almost 25¢. Four tickets will cost almost $1.00, so 12 tickets will cost 3 × $1.00, or _?_."

4. Paul has $4. If he spends $1.98 for a stamp book, will he have about $3 or $2 left?

5. Peter bought 5 pounds of grapes at 21¢ a pound. Estimate the charge for the grapes.

6. About how much should you pay for two dozen lemons at 39¢ a dozen?

7. Sue needs 30 in. of ribbon. She said, "I'll buy a half yard of ribbon."

Would you estimate that a half yard would be enough?

8. In order to serve each of 7 children a glass of milk, would you need about 1 quart of milk? 2 qt.? 3 qt.?

9. If the Recreation Center uses 6 tons of coal at $9.95 a ton to heat the Center, will it pay about $50, $60, or $70 for the coal?

10. If you buy a coat for $7.98 and a hat for $2.98, will they both cost about $9, $10, or $11?

11. If you get 5 victrola records in a set for $3.98, would you estimate the cost of each to be about 70¢, 80¢, or 60¢?

12. Estimate the cost of 16 tickets at 24¢ each.

13. Estimate the cost of a dozen pictures at 49¢ each.

14. Estimate the cost of 2 dozen young chicks at 26¢ each.

15. Estimate the cost of 18 gifts at 98¢ each.

16. Estimate the cost of 10 books if a set of 5 costs $8.98.

17. Estimate the cost of one plate if a set of 6 costs $5.98.

18. Estimate the cost of 9 cantaloupes which sell at 3 for 29¢.

140

Telling the missing word

Complete each of the following sentences by one of these words: add, subtract, multiply, divide.

1. To find the total cost of five Christmas gifts at different prices, you should __?__.

2. If you know the cost of six candy canes, to find the cost of one cane, you should __?__.

3. If you know how much a Christmas tree costs and haven't enough money to pay for it, to find how much more you need, you should __?__.

4. If you know how much money you have and how much a book will cost, to find how much money you will have left after you buy the book, you should __?__.

5. If you know the cost of one toy, to find the cost of five toys at the same price, you should __?__.

6. If you know how much one toy airplane costs, to find how many of the airplanes you can buy with the money you have, you should __?__.

7. If you know how many inches long you should cut one bookmark, to find how many bookmarks you can make from a yard of ribbon, you should __?__.

8. If you know how much one book costs and how much another one costs, to find how much more one costs than the other, you should __?__.

9. If you know how many weeks it is until Christmas, to find out how many days that is, you should __?__.

10. If you know the cost of a picnic and how many persons will share the expense, to find how much each should pay, you should __?__.

11. If you know how many cards there are in a card game and how many boys are playing, to find how many cards can be dealt out to each boy, you should __?__.

12. To change feet to inches, you should __?__.

13. To change quarts to gallons, you should __?__.

14. To change pounds to ounces, you should __?__.

15. To change inches to yards, you should __?__.

16. To change quarters to dollars, you should __?__.

Put on your thinking cap

▶ Oral review

1. How many hours are there between 9 A.M. and 3 P.M.?

2. Paul has a dozen acorns. He wishes to give Ed half of them. How many acorns should he give him?

3. How much should you pay for a quarter of a pound of candy if it is marked 60¢ a pound?

4. Find $\frac{1}{2}$ of 4; of 10; of 14; of 18; of 22; of 24.

5. How would a clerk make change from a half dollar if the customer spent 32¢?

6. Would you estimate the change from a 5-dollar bill after spending $1.98 to be about $4, $3, or $2?

7. $2 \times 4 = \underline{\ ?\ }$ $2 \times 40 = \underline{\ ?\ }$ $2 \times 400 = \underline{\ ?\ }$

8. $6 \times 3 = \underline{\ ?\ }$ $6 \times 30 = \underline{\ ?\ }$ $6 \times 300 = \underline{\ ?\ }$

9. $7 \times 4 = \underline{\ ?\ }$ $7 \times 40 = \underline{\ ?\ }$ $7 \times 400 = \underline{\ ?\ }$

▶ Written review

1. If the materials to make 6 doll's beds cost $1.38, what will be the cost of each bed?

2. What part of this circle is colored?

3. Find the cost of 75 three-cent stamps.

4. 5 hours equals $\underline{\ ?\ }$ minutes.

5. Copy these numbers and put the commas in the proper places:

79659   82340   95000   64052

6. Is this division right or wrong? If you think it is wrong, work it correctly.

$$\begin{array}{r} 8 \\ 6\overline{)58} \\ 48 \\ \hline 10 \end{array}$$

7. If one cap costs $.78, what will two dozen caps cost?

8. If seven girls share a box of twenty-five sourballs, how many sourballs can each girl have? How many will be left over?

9. Which is larger: 6×9, or 56? 7×6, or 40? 8×6, or 50?

142

Problem Test 3

1. Bob bought a pair of dungarees for $2.49, a red Western shirt for $3.95, and a cowboy hat for $1.98. How much did his new clothes cost?

2. Don's mother bought him a baseball outfit. It cost $6.95. She paid for it with a 10-dollar bill. How much change did she get?

3. Six boys dug up 96 fishing worms. If they share the worms equally, how many will each boy get?

4. Peter has saved a dollar. If he buys a bicycle lock for 59¢, how much will he have left?

5. The 28 girls in a club want to order ties that cost 21¢ each. How much money should they send for the 28 ties?

6. The Brown children made 105 cookies. The cookies must last a week. How many cookies can the children have each day?

7. If 28 boys give 5¢ apiece toward a gift for their Scout leader, how much can they spend for the gift?

8. How much can you save by buying a gallon can of "Shiny White" instead of 4 one-quart cans?

9. Find the cost of $\frac{1}{4}$ yd. of red calico at 36¢ a yard.

10. How much would it cost to buy 5-cent ice-cream cones for 36 boys?

The Miracle Polish for Walls and Woodwork

SHINY WHITE

ONLY $2.39 Quart
Gallon Can $7.98

Write your score on your Problem Test Record.

143

Self-Help Test 3

Add and check:

1. $4.52
   6.87
   9.05 (15)

2. 697
   805
   967
   374 (83)

3. $7.98
   5.00
   6.49
   .75 (83)

4. 86
   543
   96
   647
   59 (128)

5. Find the difference between $76.85 and $49.47. (112)

6. 703
   × 6 (44)

7. $8.79
   × 6 (44)

8. 789
   × 7 (44)

9. $.65
   × 47 (130–131)

Self-Help Test 4

Divide and check:

1. 7)54 (125–126)

2. 6)96 (107–109)

3. 6)164 (107–109)

4. 7)357 (135)

5. 2)846 (76–77)

6. 7)574 (127)

7. Hal wants a new cowboy outfit. The jeans cost $3.29, the boots $4.98, the jacket $2.79, and a belt $.97. How much will the outfit cost? (83)

8. Six Scouts would like to have compasses. At $1.55 each, how much will the compasses cost? (44)

9. How much will Jean pay for a dozen pencils at 5¢ each? (138)

10. Would you estimate the cost of 6 pairs of skates at $3.98 a pair to be about $18 or $24? (140)

11. If 6 brushes cost $2.82, what is the price of each brush? (133)

12. If 7 boys together buy a football that costs $3.50, how much should each boy pay? (133)

13. The 8:55 bus did not come until 12 minutes after nine. It was __?__ minutes late. (1–2)

14. Draw lines on a rectangle to show that $\frac{1}{2}$ of $\frac{1}{4}$ is $\frac{1}{8}$. (56)

15. Write the numbers from 9,996 to 10,003. (30–32)

144

Now *is* the time to test yourself

Copy the numbers correctly. Work carefully. Check your answers. Be sure each answer is sensible.

1. Multiply 605 by 7. **2.** Find $\frac{1}{7}$ of 427. **3.** Multiply 28 by 10.

4. Multiply 67 by 34. **5.** Divide 560 by 7. **6.** 2 yd. = __?__ in.

7. A set of 7 victrola records costs $2.60. Would you estimate the cost of each record to be nearer 30¢, 40¢, or 50¢?

8. Betty is making "clown dolls." She needs a dozen bells for them. The bells cost 5¢ apiece. She has 50¢. Has she enough money?

9. See if you can prove that $1\frac{1}{2}$ yd. = 54 in.

10. Herbert stayed at his grandmother's a part of last summer's vacation. He was there three weeks and five days.

How many days all together did Herbert spend at his grandmother's?

Just for fun

1. What is the smallest number of boys who can walk like this: two boys in front of a boy, two boys behind a boy, and a boy between two boys?

2. Which is more: a half-dozen dozen or six dozen dozen?

3. Larry had 15 rabbits. All but 10 ran away. How many did he have left?

4. Which is correct: 9 and 7 *are* 15, or 9 and 7 *is* 15?

5. Here is a quick trick Joe uses when he needs to multiply a number by 5:

To find 5×120, he thinks, "$10 \times 120 = 1200$, so $5 \times 120 = \frac{1}{2}$ of 1200, or 600."

Explain why his trick works. Then use it to multiply each of these numbers by 5:

48   86   68   140   248   184   460   604

The facts of eights

1. Tom is selling apples at his roadside stand. He is making a multiplication table of eights to show how much he should charge for any number of pounds up to 10 pounds.

Copy what he has written. Then finish the table.

To find 8×8, Tom thinks, "$4 \times 8 = 32$, so 8×8 is *twice as many*, or 64." Discuss good ways of finding the answer to each fact in the table of eights.

2. How much should Tom charge for 6 pounds of apples? 7 pounds? 5? 9? 4? 8? 3? 2?

3. Find these answers. Use your table if you need to.

3×8	6×8	9×8	1×8	4 eights + 1
5×8	7×8	4×8	8×8	5 eights + 2

4. A lady asked Tom for 40 cents' worth of apples. How many pounds should he give her? To solve problems like this, turn your multiplication table of eights into a division table. The table is started for you.➝

$$8 \div 8 = 1$$
$$16 \div 8 = 2$$
$$24 \div 8 = 3$$

5. How many pounds of apples should Tom give for:

24¢?   32¢?   64¢?   72¢?   48¢?   56¢?   16¢?

6. Make a dot drawing to show this Number Family:

$8 \times 5 = 40$ $5 \times 8 = 40$ $40 \div 5 = 8$ $40 \div 8 = 5$

7. Tell the other members of the Number Family of each of these:

3×8 8×4 $48 \div 8$ $56 \div 7$ 8×9

Learning to remember the eights

1. How does $5 \times 8 = 40$ help you to find 6×8? 4×8?

2. How does $8 \times 8 = 64$ help you to find 7×8? 9×8?

3. How does $3 \times 8 = 24$ help you to find 6×8? 9×8?

Multiply. Practice until you can say every answer. Use the table below if you need to.

4.
$$\begin{array}{cccccc} 2 & 5 & 4 & 7 & 8 & 1 \\ \underline{8} & \underline{8} & \underline{8} & \underline{8} & \underline{2} & \underline{8} \end{array}$$

5.
$$\begin{array}{cccccc} 6 & 8 & 3 & 8 & 8 & 8 \\ \underline{8} & \underline{7} & \underline{8} & \underline{9} & \underline{1} & \underline{3} \end{array}$$

6.
$$\begin{array}{cccccc} 8 & 9 & 8 & 8 & 8 & 10 \\ \underline{4} & \underline{8} & \underline{6} & \underline{8} & \underline{5} & \underline{8} \end{array}$$

7. Add 1 to each answer in Exs. 4–6; add 2; add 3.

8. Copy Exs. 4–6 and write the answers.

9. Make Help-Yourself Cards for any facts you failed in Ex. 8. Study the cards; then do Ex. 8 again.

10. Out of clay Betsy made a hen and 8 chicks. If she makes 4 sets like that, how many hens will she make? how many chicks?

11. Tom did 8 rows of examples. There were 7 examples in each row. How many examples did he do in all?

12. George studied 6 columns of spelling words. There were 8 words in each. How many words did he study all together?

13. 9 rows of coins with 8 coins in each row is __?__ coins.

14. In Jim's checker box there are 3 layers of checkers, with 8 checkers in a layer. In all, he has __?__ checkers.

Multiplication Facts of Eights

$$\begin{array}{ccccccccc}
8 & 8 & 8 & 8 & 8 & 8 & 8 & 8 & 8 \\
\underline{1} & \underline{2} & \underline{3} & \underline{4} & \underline{5} & \underline{6} & \underline{7} & \underline{8} & \underline{9} \\
8 & 16 & 24 & 32 & 40 & 48 & 56 & 64 & 72
\end{array}$$

$$\begin{array}{ccccccccc}
1 & 2 & 3 & 4 & 5 & 6 & 7 & 8 & 9 \\
\underline{8} & \underline{8} & \underline{8} & \underline{8} & \underline{8} & \underline{8} & \underline{8} & \underline{8} & \underline{8} \\
8 & 16 & 24 & 32 & 40 & 48 & 56 & 64 & 72
\end{array}$$

Practice in multiplying

1. Patricia can get a one-pound box of prunes for $.35 or a five-pound box for $1.57.

How much will 5 one-pound boxes cost?

How much can Patricia save by buying a five-pound box instead of 5 one-pound boxes?

2. Barbara can get an eight-pound bar of modeling clay for $2.00. A one-pound bar costs $.55. How much will 8 one-pound bars cost?

How much can Barbara save by buying an eight-pound bar instead of 8 one-pound bars?

Multiply and check:

	a	b	c	d	e	f
3.	68 6	43 8	54 7	82 8	90 3	78 5
4.	$.38 7	$.53 6	$.89 2	$.70 3	$.16 8	$.93 4
5.	701 6	621 4	530 3	400 7	904 2	800 5
6.	$8.50 6	$9.09 3	$6.29 4	$7.34 5	$4.68 7	$7.00 6
7.	27 36	84 47	38 85	91 26	60 18	88 69
8.	$.78 56	$.49 38	$.85 28	$.38 48	$.24 89	$.70 87

Do these examples orally:

	a	b	c
9.	$4 \times 8 = \underline{\ ?\ }$	$\underline{\ ?\ } \times 8 = 16$	$8 \times \underline{\ ?\ } = 64$
10.	$5 \times \underline{\ ?\ } = 40$	$\underline{\ ?\ } \times 8 = 0$	$3 \times 8 = \underline{\ ?\ }$
11.	$\underline{\ ?\ } \times 8 = 56$	$8 \times \underline{\ ?\ } = 72$	$\underline{\ ?\ } \times 6 = 48.$

Division facts of eights

Betty carves flowers out of soap. She can make 8 flowers from 1 bar of soap. How many bars will she need for 24 flowers?

Betty thought, "If I can get 8 flowers from 1 bar of soap, to make 24 flowers I will need as many bars of soap as there are 8's in 24. $24 \div 8 = 3$. I'll need 3 bars of soap."

1. Count by 8's from 8 to 80.

2. Tell how many 8's there are in each of these numbers:

32	48	8	64	56
72	40	16	24	80

Tell the answers in Exs. 3–6. Then write the examples with the answers.

3. $8)\overline{16}$ $4)\overline{32}$ $8)\overline{72}$ $8)\overline{48}$

4. $3)\overline{24}$ $8)\overline{40}$ $7)\overline{56}$ $8)\overline{64}$

5. $6)\overline{48}$ $1)\overline{8}$ $8)\overline{56}$ $5)\overline{40}$

6. $8)\overline{24}$ $9)\overline{72}$ $2)\overline{16}$ $8)\overline{32}$

7. Do Exs. 3–6 again this way: If $16 \div 8 = 2$, then $16 \div 2 = 8$.

8. Make a rule for finding $\frac{1}{8}$ of a number.

9. Make and study Help-Yourself cards for facts you failed in Exs. 3–6. Then do Exs. 3–6 again.

Division Facts of Eights

1	2	3	4	5	6	7	8	9
$8)\overline{8}$	$8)\overline{16}$	$8)\overline{24}$	$8)\overline{32}$	$8)\overline{40}$	$8)\overline{48}$	$8)\overline{56}$	$8)\overline{64}$	$8)\overline{72}$

8	8	8	8	8	8	8	8	8
$1)\overline{8}$	$2)\overline{16}$	$3)\overline{24}$	$4)\overline{32}$	$5)\overline{40}$	$6)\overline{48}$	$7)\overline{56}$	$8)\overline{64}$	$9)\overline{72}$

Uneven division facts of eights

1. While playing ball, 8 boys broke a window. A new pane costs 35¢. To find each boy's share of the cost, Stewart used this table:⟶

How much would each boy's share of the cost have been if the glass had cost 8¢? 16¢? 24¢? 32¢? 40¢? 48¢? 56¢? 64¢? 72¢?

2. 8, 16, 24, 32, 40, 48, 56, 64, and 72 are Dividing-by-Eight Helping Numbers. To find $\frac{1}{8}$ of 35, Ed looked for his largest Helping Number smaller than 35. It is 32. He saw that $32 \div 8 = 4$; so $35 \div 8 = 4$ and __?__ over.

Dividing-by-Eight Helping-Number Chart

1	2	3	4	5	6	7	8
9	10	11	12	13	14	15	16
17	18	19	20	21	22	23	24
25	26	27	28	29	30	31	32
33	34	35	36	37	38	39	40
41	42	43	44	45	46	47	48
49	50	51	52	53	54	55	56
57	58	59	60	61	62	63	64
65	66	67	68	69	70	71	72

3. Explain the division in the box. It shows that each of the 8 boys (Ex. 1) should pay 4¢, and that __?__ of them should each pay an extra cent. Prove they will then have 35¢ to pay for the glass.

```
    4 r3
8)35
    32
     3
```

Divide each number below by 8. First find your Helping Number.

	a	b	c	d	e	f	g	h	i	j
4.	69	67	70	58	54	24	34	15	75	78
5.	28	9	38	76	47	77	46	65	17	63
6.	19	29	10	39	73	48	74	45	62	18
7.	50	20	30	11	40	68	49	79	44	27
8.	55	51	21	31	12	41	61	43	26	37
9.	59	56	52	22	32	13	42	25	36	64

10. What is the largest remainder you can have when you divide by 8? Why?

Dividing large numbers by eight

The 416 pupils in the Emerson School are to have a Folk-Dance Festival.   In the Circle Dance they need 8 pupils for each circle.   How many circles can they make out of 416 pupils?   To find out, do this division: 8)416

▶To divide 416 by 8, use the Hint System. Think, "41 ÷ 8 is a little more than _?_, so 416 ÷ 8 is a little more than _?_."   Write the 5 in _?_'s place.

▶Explain how to finish the division.

▶The division shows that 416 children can be divided into _?_ circles with 8 children in each circle. What does the check show?

```
        52      Check
    8)416        52
        40       × 8
        ──       ───
        16       416
        16
        ──
```

Copy, divide, and check:

	a	b	c	d	e	f
1.	8)95	8)176	8)250	8)344	8)$4.16	8)$6.16
2.	8)560	8)104	8)184	8)272	8)$3.52	8)$2.24
3.	8)243	8)376	8)128	8)200	8)$2.88	8)$3.60
4.	8)312	8)594	8)384	8)144	8)$2.16	8)$3.04
5.	8)164	8)697	8)752	8)392	8)$1.52	8)$5.12

151

Oral division practice

Do these examples without a pencil:

a	b	c	d	e	f
1. 2)46	3)93	4)80	3)69	2)68	4)48
2. 5)155	7)210	6)426	5)300	4)368	6)306
3. 8)80	3)69	2)100	8)640	8)320	4)200

	a	b	c	d	e
4.	$\frac{1}{8}$ of 16	$\frac{1}{7}$ of 35	$\frac{1}{4}$ of 36	$\frac{1}{8}$ of 64	$\frac{1}{3}$ of 27
5.	$\frac{1}{6}$ of 36	$\frac{1}{8}$ of 40	$\frac{1}{7}$ of 42	$\frac{1}{6}$ of 30	$\frac{1}{8}$ of 72

6.

72 ÷ 8	40 ÷ 8	48 ÷ 8	56 ÷ 8	32 ÷ 8
9 × 8	5 × 8	6 × 8	7 × 8	4 × 8
72 ÷ 9	40 ÷ 5	48 ÷ 6	56 ÷ 7	32 ÷ 4
8 × 9	8 × 5	8 × 6	8 × 7	8 × 4

Written division practice

Copy, divide, and check:

a	b	c	d	e	f
1. 7)$1.05	8)$2.72	6)$4.98	8)$5.20	4)$3.92	5)$4.70
2. 8)488	7)163	3)221	5)355	8)505	6)376
3. 7)450	6)367	4)243	8)178	3)262	4)367
4. 6)378	5)352	8)257	7)638	6)434	8)408

5. Martha has 96 cookies to sell at a cooky sale. How many bags does she need if she puts 8 cookies in each bag?

6. How many yards are there in 96 feet?

7. 126 days = ___?___ weeks.

8. George knows how to make a pinwheel out of 8 drinking straws. He has a package of 100 straws. How many pinwheels can he make?

152

Be your own teacher

You have never been taught how to solve these problems. Good thinkers can solve them anyway. See how many different ways your class can find to solve each problem.

1. Sam's father said to the man at the service station, "Eight gallons of gasoline, please."

Sam looked at the gasoline marker on the dashboard of their car. It showed the tank was $\frac{1}{4}$ full.

After the 8 gallons of gasoline were put in, the marker showed the tank was $\frac{3}{4}$ full.

Sam figured the gasoline tank in their car holds __?__ gallons.

2. Jean measured and found she needed 54 inches of cord for a drawstring in a laundry bag.

The cord sold at 12¢ a yard. She said, "The cord for my bag will cost 18¢." Was she right?

3. Bill wants a bicycle that costs $54.75. If he saves 10¢ a day for a year, he will have __?__. That will not be enough.

If he saves 20¢ a day, he will have __?__. That will be too much.

How much ought he to save each day, if he is to get the bicycle?

4. For a wall Ben needs 6 lb. of cement. He has $3\frac{1}{2}$ lb. How much more cement should he get?

5. Numbers that cannot be divided evenly by any numbers except themselves are called *prime numbers*. 1, 3, and 5 are prime numbers. How many others are there in the numbers up to 100?

A 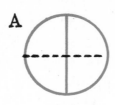 B

C 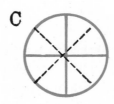 D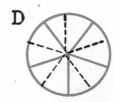

6. Tom studied these pictures. Was he right when he thought:
- Picture A shows $\frac{1}{2}$ of $\frac{1}{2}$ = $\frac{1}{4}$?
- Picture B shows $\frac{1}{2}$ of $\frac{1}{3}$ = $\frac{1}{6}$?
- Picture C shows $\frac{1}{2}$ of $\frac{1}{4}$ = $\frac{1}{8}$?
- Picture D shows $\frac{1}{2}$ of $\frac{1}{5}$ = $\frac{1}{10}$?

7. Tom made up a rule that shows him how to find $\frac{1}{2}$ of a fraction without drawing a picture. Can you figure out what his rule was? If so, find $\frac{1}{2}$ of $\frac{1}{8}$; $\frac{1}{2}$ of $\frac{1}{16}$; $\frac{1}{2}$ of $\frac{1}{10}$.

To the Teacher: See Note 1 on page 310.

Children's everyday problems

1. Sue has 17 little glass animals, for which she paid 15¢ apiece. How much did she spend for them?

2. Tom has saved $3 to build a doghouse. If he spends $1.75 for wood, paint, and nails, how much money will he have left?

3. Herbert bought a box containing 8 magic tricks for $2.48. How much did each trick cost?

4. Betty wants 4 large bars of soap for carving. At 2 bars for 15¢ how much will 4 bars cost?

5. How much will 3 dance records cost at $1.49 each?

6. Dan is planning to get a new radio. The one he wants is shown in the picture. How much money will Dan need if the clerk allows him $1.50 for his old radio?

7. Donald paid $3.08 for a camera and $.34 for a roll of film. How much change did he receive from four dollars?

8. Sally borrowed a book from the library on January 13. It will be due in 2 weeks. On what date must it be returned?

9. Janet has 63 wild flowers to paste in a loose-leaf notebook.

If she pastes 3 flowers on each page, how many pages will she need?

10. June is making a birthday card for her mother. The card is $5\frac{1}{2}$ in. long and $4\frac{1}{2}$ in wide.

Draw a rectangle the size of the card June is making.

11. What should Ruth pay for $\frac{1}{2}$ yard of lace at 32¢ a yard?

The temperature

On Joy's birthday, the thermometer outside looked like this one. What was the temperature? Was it a cold day?

A thermometer tells you how warm or cold it is. It measures the temperature in *degrees*.

When it is warm, the mercury in the glass tube of a thermometer is high. When it is cold, the mercury is low.

The sign ° means degrees. 22 degrees is written 22°.

1. What is the temperature when the mercury reaches each line on the thermometer from 0° to 100°?

2. Show on the thermometer where the mercury would be when the temperature is 70°; 40°; 43°; 54°; 67°; 78°.

3. *Water freezes at 32°.* Does the temperature ever go to 32° where you live? to 0°? below zero?

4. Do you know how high the temperature goes where you live?

5. When the temperature falls to 20°, it is __?__° below freezing.

6. When the temperature is 35°, what kind of clothes do you wear to school?

7. *Water boils at 212°.* Is that hot enough to give you a bad burn?

8. *A comfortable room temperature is 68°.* When the temperature is 59°, the room is __?__° too cold.

9. When the outdoor temperature is 50°, could you ice-skate outdoors? swim in the lake? play soccer?

10. Which of the things in Ex. 9 could you do when the temperature is 85°? 20°?

11. Keep a record of the outdoor temperature every day at 9:00 A.M. for a month.

12. Tell all the different ways you and your family use thermometers.

Problems without numbers

1. If you know how many weeks it is before your birthday, how can you find how many days it is?

2. If you know how many days it is before your birthday, how can you find how many weeks it is?

3. If you know how many animals you can carve from one bar of soap, how can you find how many animals you can carve from three bars of soap?

4. If you know how many animals you can carve from one bar of soap, how can you find how many bars of soap you will need to make 20 animals?

5. If you know the cost of one bar of soap, how can you find the cost of five bars of soap?

6. If you know how much money you have and how much you are going to spend, how can you find how much money you will have left?

7. If you know the number of pages in a stamp book and the number of stamps on each page, how can you find the number of stamps in the book?
Be careful. This is tricky.

8. If you know how much a 5-pound bag of sugar costs, how can you find the cost per pound?

9. If you know the cost of a roll of film for a camera and the cost of developing and printing the pictures, how can you find the cost of the pictures?

10. If you get 5 good pictures from a roll of film and you know the total cost of the film, the printing, and the developing, how can you find the cost of each picture?

11. If you know how many cookies you need for a party and how many cookies there are in a package, how can you find how many packages of cookies to buy?

12. If you know how many pages of spelling words you are to study for a test and how many words there are on each page, how can you find how many words you must study in all?

13. Harry said the answer to Ex. 12 is "multiply." Bill said it is "add."
Give an illustration to prove that Harry might be wrong; that Bill is right, but that there might be a better way.

A page of review

▶ **Addition**　　**1.** Take the addition test on page 11.

2. Copy, add, and check:

a	b	c	d	e	f
56	147	265	$3.10	$10.00	$12.52
183	92	400	2.75	4.50	8.75
300	305	90	.89	.75	.04
165	64	48	.46	2.69	6.39

▶ **Subtraction**　　**1.** Take the subtraction test on page 21.

2. Subtract $3.72 from $10; from $20; from $30.

3. Copy, subtract, and check:

a	b	c	d	e	f
6930	8346	5702	$77.00	$84.08	$69.10
3578	5289	2479	42.73	1.79	43.64

▶ **Multiplication**　　*Copy and multiply.　Check your work.*

	a	b	c	d	e	f
1.	34	90	87	$.75	$.68	$.89
	87	68	46	38	52	73
2.	802	600	310	$7.50	$6.80	$8.09
	7	8	9	8	4	6

▶ **Division**　　*Copy, divide, and check:*

	a	b	c	d	e	f
1.	4)97	8)490	3)163	8)753	6)366	5)316
2.	7)106	6)446	3)291	4)275	8)670	7)503
3.	6)$3.90	8)$5.92	7)$3.01	5)$4.25	6)$4.32	8)$7.44

Multiplication facts of nines

1. The Junior Baseball Team bought nine 9-cent caps.   Whose way of finding the cost of the 9 caps do you like best?

Roy	Bob	Bill
$3 \times 9¢ = 27¢$	$8 \times 9¢ = 72¢$	$10 \times 9¢ = 90¢$
$3 \times 9¢ = 27¢$	$+ 9¢$	$- 9¢$
$3 \times 9¢ = 27¢$	$9 \times 9¢ = 81¢$	$9 \times 9¢ = 81¢$
$9 \times 9¢ = 81¢$		

2. Can you think of any other ways of finding 9×9?

3. Find the cost of 2 nine-cent caps; 3; 4; 5; 6; 7; 8.

Multiply.   Practice until you can say every answer.

4.	9	6	9	9	9	2
	3	9	7	8	5	9

5.	9	4	10	7	9	5
	1	9	9	9	4	9

6.	9	9	1	9	3	8
	6	9	9	2	9	9

7. Add 1 to each answer in Exs. 4–6; add 2; add 3.

8. Copy Exs. 4–6 and write the answers.

9. Make and study Help-Yourself Cards for any facts you failed in Ex. 8.   Then do Ex. 8 again.

10. Nine players make a baseball team.   How many players are needed for 2 teams? 3? 6? 4? 7? 5? 9? 8?

11. How many days are there in 9 weeks?

Multiplication Facts of Nines

9	9	9	9	9	9	9	9	9
1	2	3	4	5	6	7	8	9
9	18	27	36	45	54	63	72	81

1	2	3	4	5	6	7	8	9
9	9	9	9	9	9	9	9	9
9	18	27	36	45	54	63	72	81

Practice in multiplying

1. The manager of the Junior Baseball Team needs to know the cost of 9 pairs of baseball shoes at $2.89 a pair. How much will they cost?

2. Find the cost of 9 baseball suits at $3.69 each.

3. How much will 9 balls cost at 82¢ each?

4. Find the cost of 9 baseball caps at $.79 each.

5. The Pineville baseball team went to New Hope to play. The bus fare was $.48 each way. How much was the round-trip fare for 1 player? for 9 players?

6. How much will 9 baseball club pins cost at $.59 each?

Multiply and check by going over your work:

	a	b	c	d
7.	849 by 8	37 by 69	$.20 by 48	$8.00 by 9
8.	394 by 6	89 by 94	$.75 by 39	$4.50 by 8
9.	457 by 9	63 by 19	$.49 by 78	$3.05 by 9

What are the missing numbers?

	a	b	c
10.	$9 \times 9 = \underline{\ ?\ }$	$\underline{\ ?\ } \times 9 = 0$	$7 \times \underline{\ ?\ } = 63$
11.	$6 \times \underline{\ ?\ } = 54$	$9 \times \underline{\ ?\ } = 9$	$\underline{\ ?\ } \times 9 = 81$

Multiply and check by going over your work:

	a	b	c	d	e	f	g
12.	87 49	39 45	68 32	95 67	30 98	52 71	74 86
13.	498 9	526 8	418 9	823 7	567 9	264 8	329 9
14.	$8.75 9	$6.03 9	$8.00 8	$3.75 7	$4.69 6	$8.89 9	$5.50 8

Division facts of nines

1. The 9 members of Junior Radio Club spent 83¢ for materials to fix an old radio. The division at the right shows that each member should pay __?__ ¢, and that 2 of the members will each have to pay an extra __?__.

$$\begin{array}{r} 9 \\ 9\overline{)83} \\ 81 \\ \hline 2 \end{array}$$

2. This Dividing-by-Nine Helping-Number Chart shows that in 18 there are __?__ 9's; in 45 there are __?__ 9's; in 72 there are __?__ 9's.

3. How could the members of the Junior Radio Club (Ex. 1) use the chart to solve their problem?

4. How many 9's are there in 54? 55? 63? 62? 81? 80? 82?

5. Use the chart to help you make a division table of nines.

Dividing-by-Nine Helping-Number Chart

1	2	3	4	5	6	7	8	9
10	11	12	13	14	15	16	17	18
19	20	21	22	23	24	25	26	27
28	29	30	31	32	33	34	35	36
37	38	39	40	41	42	43	44	45
46	47	48	49	50	51	52	53	54
55	56	57	58	59	60	61	62	63
64	65	66	67	68	69	70	71	72
73	74	75	76	77	78	79	80	81
82	83	84	85	86	87	88	89	90

Divide:

6. 9)36   5)45   6)54   9)81

7. 7)63   9)27   4)36   9)63

8. 9)45   9)9   9)18   3)27

9. Copy Exs. 6–8 and write the answers.

10. Make Help-Yourself Cards for any facts you missed in Ex. 9. Study the cards. Do Ex. 9 again.

Division Facts of Nines

1	2	3	4	5	6	7	8	9
9)9	9)18	9)27	9)36	9)45	9)54	9)63	9)72	9)81

9	9	9	9	9	9	9	9	9
1)9	2)18	3)27	4)36	5)45	6)54	7)63	8)72	9)81

Helps in dividing by nine

1.
  6 × 9
  9 × 6
  54 ÷ 9
  54 ÷ 6

2.
  5 × 9
  9 × 5
  45 ÷ 9
  45 ÷ 5

3.
  8 × 9
  9 × 8
  72 ÷ 9
  72 ÷ 8

4.
  7 × 9
  9 × 7
  63 ÷ 9
  63 ÷ 7

5.
  4 × 9
  9 × 4
  36 ÷ 9
  36 ÷ 4

6. How many baseball teams can you form with 72 players? 36 players? 63? 90? 45? 54? 27? 81? 18?

7. Oliver needed to divide 67 by 9.

He found 67 on the chart on page 160 and thought, "I must find my Helping Number. It is 63. 63 ÷ 9 is __?__. So 67 ÷ 9 is __?__, and __?__ over."

8. What is the largest remainder you can have when you are dividing by 9?

9. Name all the numbers from 9 to 90 that can be divided by 9 without a remainder.

Which of these numbers can be divided by 9 without a remainder?

10. 45   20   27   54   30

11. 18   47   64   48   56

Tell what your Helping Number is in dividing each of these numbers by 9. Then divide each number by 9.

	a	b	c	d	e	f	g	h	i	j	k
12.	68	66	69	56	51	27	38	16	75	78	60
13.	31	10	42	76	77	52	46	64	19	62	82
14.	21	53	11	41	73	54	72	40	65	20	24
15.	47	22	33	12	45	67	55	79	49	30	70
16.	57	48	25	34	13	43	63	44	29	14	61
17.	84	23	39	81	59	37	28	87	50	58	88

18. What is wrong with this division? ⟶

```
Wrong
    8
9)84
   72
   12
```

19. Work the division in Ex. 18 correctly.

20. Charlie needs 40 thumbtacks. How many of these cards of tacks will he need to buy?

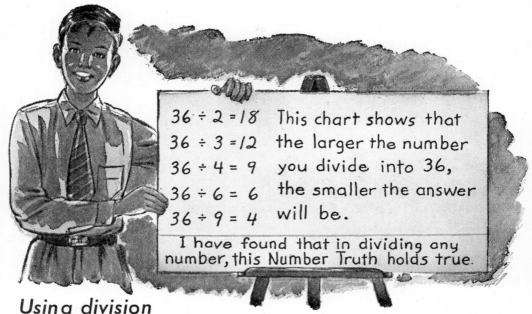

$36 \div 2 = 18$ This chart shows that
$36 \div 3 = 12$ the larger the number
$36 \div 4 = 9$ you divide into 36,
$36 \div 6 = 6$ the smaller the answer
$36 \div 9 = 4$ will be.

I have found that in dividing any number, this Number Truth holds true.

Using division

Whenever any pupil in Miss Allison's class discovers a "Number Truth," he puts it on a chart and shows the class. Above is a Number Truth that Jack discovered.

1. Divide 12 by 6; by 4; 3; 2. Does Jack's Number Truth hold true?

2. Divide 24 by 8; by 6; 4; 3; 2. Does Jack's Number Truth hold true?

Here are two everyday uses of this truth. Can you think of others?

● The more boys who share the cost of a football, the less each person pays.

● If you have a box of candy, the more pieces you eat each day, the fewer days the candy will last.

3. Make a rule for finding $\frac{1}{9}$ of a number.

4. If 9 boys share these costs, how much should each pay?

64¢   71¢   74¢   76¢   85¢

Find $\frac{1}{9}$ of each of these numbers:

5.	12	73	52	46	16
6.	84	48	79	29	78
7.	34	45	54	72	64

8. How many 8-cent lights for a Christmas tree can you buy for a half-dollar? How much money will you have left over?

9. What is wrong with this division?⟶

Do the division correctly.

```
 Wrong
   7
9)74
  63
  11
```

162

Dividing large numbers by nine

Each of the 158 fourth-grade children in the Hamilton School has made a drawing of his favorite wild flower. Look at the picture. The pupils are mounting their drawings on colored cardboard. How many drawings are they putting on each piece of cardboard?

How many sheets of cardboard do they need for their 158 drawings?

To find out, they divided 158 by 9. Explain their division in the box. Will 17 sheets of cardboard be enough to hold all their drawings?

$$
\begin{array}{r}
17\text{ r}5 \\
9)\overline{158} \\
9 \\
\hline
68 \\
63 \\
\hline
5
\end{array}
\qquad
\begin{array}{r}
\text{Check} \\
17 \\
\times 9 \\
\hline
153 \\
+5 \\
\hline
158
\end{array}
$$

Practice in division

1. Joe is manager of the Midget Baseball Team. He can buy 9 baseballs for $7.83. How much is that for each ball?

2. Each player wants a shirt. Joe can get 9 shirts for $9.90. How much will each shirt cost?

3. Joe can also buy 9 pairs of socks for $3.51. If each player pays for his own socks, how much will each have to pay?

4. The 9 Midgets spent $4.49 on a baseball trip. Was each one's share about 40¢, 50¢, or 60¢?

Find:

	a	b	c	d	e
5.	$\frac{1}{9}$ of 18	$\frac{1}{9}$ of 45	$\frac{1}{9}$ of 90	$\frac{1}{9}$ of 36	$\frac{1}{9}$ of 72
6.	$\frac{1}{9}$ of 63	$\frac{1}{9}$ of 81	$\frac{1}{9}$ of 54	$\frac{1}{9}$ of 27	$\frac{1}{9}$ of 9

Divide each of these numbers by 9, and check:

	a	b	c	d	e	f	g	h	i
7.	279	478	639	109	408	384	747	600	668
8.	753	396	855	208	287	828	738	550	539

	a	b	c
9.	$18 \div 9 = \underline{\ ?\ }$	$72 \div \underline{\ ?\ } = 8$	$63 \div 9 = \underline{\ ?\ }$
10.	$45 \div \underline{\ ?\ } = 5$	$36 \div 9 = \underline{\ ?\ }$	$27 \div \underline{\ ?\ } = 3$
11.	$\underline{\ ?\ } \div 9 = 9$	$\underline{\ ?\ } \div 9 = 6$	$\underline{\ ?\ } \div 9 = 1$

Copy, divide, and check:

	a	b	c	d	e
12.	3)73	4)94	3)57	3)79	2)75
13.	7)217	6)494	8)418	5)465	4)365
14.	6)248	8)329	4)367	7)509	6)428
15.	9)$6.66	8)$7.36	6)$4.92	7)$5.88	5)$2.80

A page of practice

1. Multiply each of the numbers in the box by 4; by 6; 7; 8; 9. Write down all the facts you do not answer quickly. Find those facts in your Help-Yourself Cards. Plan ways to learn them.

2	7	5	10	4
6	1	8	3	9

Name the 3 other facts in the number family of each of these:

	a	b	c	d
2.	$6 \times 8 = 48$	$9 \times 8 = 72$	$7 \times 9 = 63$	$6 \times 7 = 42$
3.	$7 \times 4 = 28$	$3 \times 9 = 27$	$9 \times 4 = 36$	$5 \times 8 = 40$
4.	$9 \times 5 = 45$	$8 \times 7 = 56$	$4 \times 6 = 24$	$7 \times 3 = 21$

5. Jimmie made the kite drawing below. How long is the kite? How wide?

6. How far is the crosspiece from the top? from the bottom?

7. Can you make a kite, using Jimmie's pattern?

8. Have you a pattern of anything else your class could make? If so, bring it to school.

HOW A KITE FLIES

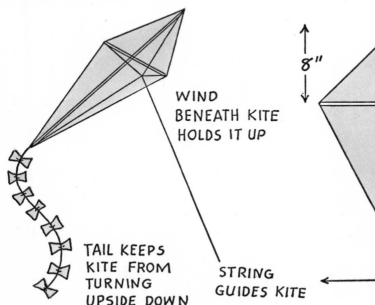

WIND BENEATH KITE HOLDS IT UP

TAIL KEEPS KITE FROM TURNING UPSIDE DOWN

STRING GUIDES KITE

KITE PATTERN

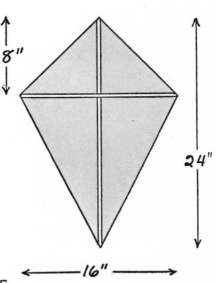

8"

24"

16"

UNIT

23

Three-place quotients
Test on division facts
Review

Dividing dollars and cents

① Six boys in a camera club paid $8.52 for materials. Jim said that each should pay more than one dollar and less than 2 dollars. Was he right? How do you know?

▶ Then he said, "If each pays $1.00, we will collect $6.00 and will still need to collect __?__." Explain the division in Box A.

▶ Next Jim had to figure out how to collect $2.52. He decided to have each member pay $.40. That would bring in __?__. There would still be __?__ to be paid. Explain the division in Box B.

▶ Finally he had to figure how to collect the $.12. To collect $.12 each of the members had to pay __?__. Explain the division in Box C.

▶ In all, each boy paid $1.00 + $.40 + $.02, or $__?__.

```
A     $1.00
   6)$8.52
      6.00
      $2.52

B     $ .40
   6)$2.52
      2.40
      $ .12

C     $.02
   6)$.12
      .12
       0
```

② Jim's class thought his solution to 6)$8.52 was clear, but too long.

▶ The pupils voted to solve the problem as shown in Box D. Explain their division. How is it like Jim's work? How is it different?

▶ The check shows that if each of the 6 members pays __?__, the club will collect __?__.

```
D     $1.42      Check
   6)$8.52       $1.42
     6 ↓↓          × 6
     2 5         $8.52
     2 4↓
       12
       12
```

Divide and check:

	a	b	c	d	e
1.	3)$5.35	4)$7.05	3)$7.30	2)$5.73	9)$11.29
2.	8)$11.50	8)$9.86	6)$7.92	7)$9.44	7)$15.15
3.	9)$10.99	7)$8.65	4)$9.74	8)$9.98	9)$12.89
4.	9)$20.47	9)$7.41	5)$7.79	9)$14.33	8)$25.75
5.	7)$32.53	9)$48.74	8)$2.32	6)$3.29	6)$19.05

166

$$\frac{1}{7} \text{ of } 2800 = 400$$
$$\frac{1}{7} \text{ of } 35 = \frac{5}{}$$
$$\text{so } \frac{1}{7} \text{ of } 2835 = 405$$

Three-figure answers in division

1. Explain how Jim found $\frac{1}{7}$ of 2835 in the picture above.

Use Jim's method above to find:

2. $\frac{1}{6}$ of 1812 $\frac{1}{7}$ of 2114

3. $\frac{1}{8}$ of 3240 $\frac{1}{9}$ of 3609

4. Bill needs to divide 2754 by 9. How can he tell the answer is about 300, rather than about 3, or about 30?

5. Explain each division below. Then check the work. Is the answer sensible?

```
   907        735        306
6)5442     7)5145     9)2754
  54         49         27
   42         24         54
   42         21         54
              35
              35
```

Estimate each answer. Start this way: $3708 \div 9 = $ more than 400; $5818 \div 7 = $ more than 800; and so on.

	a	b	c	d	e	f
6.	9)3708	7)5818	8)7245	8)5667	6)248	8)6445
7.	6)4562	4)2878	7)3529	8)3227	3)278	8)7293
8.	7)6399	5)4592	8)5043	7)2139	9)846	5)4074

9. Now copy, divide, and check Exs. 6–8.

Test on division facts

Practice saying the answers to these division facts. Then try to write the answers on folded paper in 7 minutes.

Make and study Help-Yourself Cards for any facts you do not know. See page 309. Then take the test again. Practice until you can write every answer correctly.

1. $3\overline{)18}$ $5\overline{)25}$ $7\overline{)49}$ $1\overline{)5}$ $2\overline{)16}$ $1\overline{)2}$ $2\overline{)10}$ $9\overline{)54}$ $1\overline{)6}$

2. $4\overline{)28}$ $5\overline{)30}$ $4\overline{)12}$ $3\overline{)24}$ $1\overline{)9}$ $2\overline{)14}$ $3\overline{)3}$ $5\overline{)40}$ $3\overline{)9}$

3. $8\overline{)40}$ $5\overline{)10}$ $1\overline{)8}$ $2\overline{)8}$ $5\overline{)45}$ $4\overline{)24}$ $2\overline{)18}$ $2\overline{)12}$ $2\overline{)4}$

4. $6\overline{)24}$ $5\overline{)20}$ $3\overline{)15}$ $4\overline{)20}$ $1\overline{)1}$ $3\overline{)21}$ $4\overline{)32}$ $5\overline{)15}$ $4\overline{)4}$

5. $3\overline{)12}$ $6\overline{)6}$ $1\overline{)4}$ $4\overline{)8}$ $4\overline{)16}$ $1\overline{)7}$ $6\overline{)18}$ $5\overline{)35}$ $2\overline{)2}$

6. $7\overline{)14}$ $7\overline{)35}$ $8\overline{)16}$ $6\overline{)30}$ $8\overline{)24}$ $9\overline{)18}$ $6\overline{)36}$ $9\overline{)9}$ $2\overline{)6}$

7. $9\overline{)27}$ $9\overline{)45}$ $7\overline{)7}$ $3\overline{)27}$ $6\overline{)12}$ $7\overline{)21}$ $9\overline{)36}$ $8\overline{)8}$ $1\overline{)3}$

8. $7\overline{)56}$ $8\overline{)32}$ $4\overline{)36}$ $8\overline{)72}$ $9\overline{)81}$ $6\overline{)54}$ $7\overline{)42}$ $8\overline{)64}$ $3\overline{)6}$

9. $8\overline{)56}$ $7\overline{)63}$ $6\overline{)48}$ $9\overline{)63}$ $6\overline{)42}$ $8\overline{)48}$ $7\overline{)28}$ $9\overline{)72}$ $5\overline{)5}$

---

1. Turn to page 11. Think of those addition examples as multiplication examples. Say the answers. Then try to write them on folded paper in 6 minutes.

Make Help-Yourself Cards for any facts you missed. Then do the multiplication examples again.

2. If a friend cannot remember the answers to these facts, how would you help him learn them?

$6\overline{)54}$ 6×7 $9\overline{)63}$ 9×9

3. $4 \times 8 = 32$, so $8 \times 8 = $ _?_ .

4. $30 \div 3 = 10$, so $30 \div 6 = $ _?_ .

Keeping up your good work

Add and check. Use folded paper.

	a	b	c	d	e	f	g
1.	6	86	39	408	69	327	573
	9	65	40	37	23	506	820
	5	70	8	592	487	893	475
	2	29	67	764	645	640	908

Find the sum of:

2. $7.58, $9.23, $36.40, and $8.   **3.** $32.64, $5.98, $76.05, and $3.49.

Subtract and check. Use folded paper.

	a	b	c	d	e	f
4.	9674	7856	6947	5786	8679	9502
	6243	4324	3610	256	4025	6874
5.	7963	6327	9741	8630	6800	7900
	4229	2186	297	3917	1592	2583
6.	$45.68	$59.50	$75.00	$84.04	$93.24	$79.05
	28.79	3.90	69.49	59.39	38.96	9.87

Multiply. Check by going over your work.

	a	b	c	d	e	f
7.	36	57	48	92	61	35
	82	46	73	65	78	86
8.	618	432	$7.75	$6.09	$9.50	$7.63
	7	9	8	7	9	8

Divide and check:

	a	b	c	d	e	f
9.	9)192	8)256	7)287	9)289	8)417	7)504
10.	9)7256	7)3643	9)4528	8)4093	7)5952	8)6206

169

The hobby show

1. A fourth-grade Hobby Club gave a Hobby Show. Herbert's hobby is doing magic tricks. He made the Number Trick poster shown in the picture below. Can you do the tricks on it?

NUMBER TRICKS

Tell this answer in half a minute

$9 \times 8 \times 7 \times 6 \times 0 = ?$

What numbers are missing?

$$4\boxed{?}2 \times 9 = 3618$$

$$23\boxed{?} \times 8 = 1880$$

$$256 \times \boxed{?} = 2304$$

$$6\overline{)2\boxed{?}0} = 35$$

$$8\overline{)48\boxed{?}8} = 601$$

$$\boxed{?}\overline{)837} = 93$$

A Tricky Trick
1. Write down a number.
2. Add 9 to it.
3. Multiply the answer by 2.
4. Subtract 4.
5. Divide the remainder by 2.
6. Subtract the number you started with.
7. Your answer should be 7. Is it?

2. Joe's hobby is collecting pictures of the Presidents of the United States.

Who is President of the United States now? Find out how many Presidents we have had.

At the hobby show Joe had pictures of 19 Presidents. How many more pictures does he need to complete his collection?

3. Peter's hobby is coin collecting. He had 90 pennies in his penny coin-collection-card and 35 nickels in his nickel coin-collection-card.

How many coins did he show all together?

4. Eve's hobby is cooking. For the show she baked an orange cake.

After the show she cut the cake as shown, and shared it with her best friends.

What part of the cake did each one get?

5. Janet showed her pressed-wild-flower collection. She showed 29 spring flowers, 33 summer flowers, 13 fall flowers, and 2 winter flowers.

What was the total number of flowers?

6. Tom's hobby is carpentry. He made a shoeshine box. He said the wood cost $.29 and the paint $.15. How much did the box cost in all?

7. Henry showed 179 foreign stamps and 246 United States stamps. How many stamps was that?

8. William likes to work with electricity. He showed 5 switches he made. He said the materials for them cost 35¢. How much did each switch cost?

9. Ruth's hobby is sewing. She dressed 3 families of dolls for the show. There were 6 dolls in each family.

How many dolls did she dress all together?

10. John's hobby is making model airplanes. The kit he wants costs $5.00. He has $3.67. How much more money does he need?

11. A good hobby should be interesting to you, give you pleasure, and teach you something.

What is your hobby? Is it a good one for you? Why?

12. When you work on your hobby, what needs for arithmetic do you have?

Oral practice

1. At 6¢ each, find the cost of 4 airmail stamps; 7 airmail stamps; 9; 5; 8; 6.

2. At 9¢ each, find the cost of 7 magnets; 9 magnets; 6; 8; 5; 4; 3.

3. Soap-bubble pipes are marked 8¢ each. How much should you pay for 6 pipes? 8 pipes? 9? 7?

4. How many days are there in 8 weeks? 9 weeks? 7? 6?

	a	*b*	*c*
5.	$\frac{1}{4}$ of 168 = __?__	$\frac{1}{3}$ of 240 = __?__	$\frac{1}{2}$ of 184 = __?__
6.	$\frac{1}{2}$ of 140 = __?__	$\frac{1}{2}$ of 446 = __?__	$\frac{1}{4}$ of 808 = __?__
7.	75 ÷ 8 = __?__	79 ÷ 8 = __?__	84 ÷ 9 = __?__
8.	57 ÷ 9 = __?__	69 ÷ 7 = __?__	52 ÷ 8 = __?__
9.	1 yd. = __?__ in.	1 yd. = __?__ ft.	1 ft. = __?__ in.
10.	1 qt. = __?__ pt.	1 hr. = __?__ min.	1 gal. = __?__ qt.
11.	$\frac{1}{2}$ yd. = __?__ in.	$\frac{1}{2}$ ft. = __?__ in.	1 min. = __?__ sec.
12.	5 + 6 + 7 = __?__	6 + 9 + 8 = __?__	7 + 8 + 9 = __?__
13.	8 + 9 + 4 = __?__	9 + 6 + 7 = __?__	6 + 8 + 8 = __?__

14. Are these the correct answers to the multiplication facts of 9, starting with 9 × 9?

$$81 \quad 72 \quad 63 \quad 54 \quad 45 \quad 36 \quad 27 \quad 18 \quad 9$$

15. Add the 2 figures of each number in Ex. 14. 8 + 1 = __?__; 7 + 2 = __?__; 6 + 3 = __?__; and so on. The sum of each pair of figures is __?__.

16. Read all the tens figures in the numbers in Ex. 14; read all the units figures. What discoveries do you make?

Written practice

1. Take the addition test on page 11.

Add and check:

a	b	c	d	e
2. $46.38	$47.64	$47.86	$89.75	$47.82
9.84	8.09	4.69	93.84	3.95
20.89	76.54	.87	7.69	6.24

3. Take the division test on page 168.

Divide and check:

a	b	c	d	e
4. 8)$16.96	9)$27.36	7)$39.20	6)$42.72	9)$83.70
5. 7)2837	8)4897	6)5647	9)3627	8)5697

6. Take the subtraction test on page 21.

Subtract and check:

a	b	c	d	e	f
7. 875	345	620	875	$7.00	$4.82
482	280	199	795	6.35	.95
8. 428	905	462	803	$5.00	$3.95
219	674	175	428	2.56	1.08

9. Turn to page 11 and do the examples as multiplications.

Multiply and check by going over your work:

a	b	c	d	e	f
10. 346	257	809	416	680	759
8	9	7	6	9	8
11. $.54	$.39	$.61	$.50	$.47	$.89
78	67	98	72	89	37

Problem Test 4

1. George has earned three dollars. He plans to buy a bicycle pump for $1.69. How much money will he have left?

2. Betty can carve 8 animals from a large bar of soap. How many animals can she carve from 2 bars of soap?

3. There are 31 days in January. 31 days = _?_ weeks and _?_ days extra.

4. Eight fourth-grade girls are going to take tennis lessons. Tennis shoes cost $2.49 a pair. How much will shoes for eight girls cost?

5. How much will Sue have to pay for a dozen linoleum blocks for block printing at 6¢ each?

6. The 28 pupils in Miss Allison's room are going to make napkin rings. Plain rings for them to decorate cost 12¢ apiece. What will 28 rings cost?

7. How much would it cost to buy a basketball for $2.10, a soccer ball for $1.98, a softball for $1.20, and a volleyball for $2.25?

8. How many quarts of milk would be needed to serve a glass of milk to each of 12 children?

9. The four Brown children are going to buy a door chime for their mother's birthday. The chime costs $2.48. What will be each one's share?

10. The thermometer in the house shows 68°, and the thermometer outside shows 32°. Can you tell how much colder it is outside than in the house?

Write your score on your Problem Test Record.

Put on your thinking cap

▶ Oral review

1. What would one-half dozen oranges cost at 40¢ a dozen?

2. How many 5-cent oranges can be bought for 40¢?

3. How much change should you get from a half dollar if you buy a dozen oranges for 40¢?

4. Four boys are to share the cost of a dozen oranges at 40¢ a dozen. How much should each boy pay? How many oranges will each boy get?

5. What would 4 dozen oranges cost at 40¢ a dozen?

6. Is the sum of 498 and 205 about 500, 600, or 700?

7. Is the difference between 902 and 395 about 600, about 500, or about 400?

8. Is 8×89 closer to 600, 700, or 800?

9. Is the answer to $9\overline{)4527}$ about 400, 500, or 600?

▶ Written review

1. Write the next five numbers after 79,998.

2. 14 yards = ___?___ inches.

3. Four mothers are to share the cost of refreshments for a mothers' meeting. How much should each one pay if the expenses are $2.40?

4. On Tuesday the temperature was 52° and on Wednesday it was 43°. Which day was colder?

5. Howard filled a gallon pail half full of milk for his calf. How many quarts of milk was that?

6. Charlie's school begins at 9:00 A.M. If Charlie allows 15 minutes to walk to school, at what time should he leave home?

7. What will you have to pay for 15 three-cent stamps?

8. One bicycle is marked $38.95 and another $43.45. What is the difference in the prices?

9. Sally needs 70 inches of ribbon. She says she will buy 2 yards. Will that be enough?

10. 28 days = ___?___ weeks.

175

Self-Help Test 5

1. 1 minute = _?_ seconds; 1 hour = _?_ minutes. **(4)**

2. 1 foot = _?_ inches; 1 yard = _?_ feet. **(49)**

3. 1 quart = _?_ pints; 1 gallon = _?_ quarts. **(115)**

4. 97,640 is read: _?_ thousand, _?_ hundred _?_. **(32)**

5.
```
   876
    43
   277
 + 473  (83)
```

6.
```
  $49.64
   93.27
    8.76
 + 87.63  (83)
```

7.
```
   9873
 − 8964  (112)
```

8. $86.43 − $57.95 **(112)**

9.
```
 906
 × 5  (44)
```

10.
```
 $6.57
 × 6  (44)
```

11.
```
 $.76
 × 54  (130–131)
```

12.
```
 798
 × 8  (44)
```

Self-Help Test 6

Divide and check:

1. 6)51 **(98–99)**

2. 7)245 **(127)**

3. 8)192 **(151)**

4. 7)567 **(135)**

5. 6)540 **(103)**

6. 8)729 **(135)**

7. 8)$40.96 **(166)**

8. 7)4263 **(167)**

9. 9)$48.60 **(166)**

10. Six boys bought a ping-pong set for $8.70. If they share the cost equally, how much should each boy pay? **(166)**

11. In a school assembly hall there are 32 rows of seats with 18 seats in each row.

How many pupils can be seated in the assembly hall at once? **(130)**

12. If the material for making 7 knitted wash cloths costs $1.47, how much does the material for one wash cloth cost? **(133)**

13. Find the cost of 25 apples at 5¢ each. **(138)**

14. Write the next five numbers after 29,996. **(32)**

Now is the time to test yourself

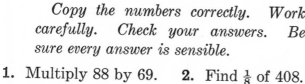

Copy the numbers correctly. Work carefully. Check your answers. Be sure every answer is sensible.

1. Multiply 88 by 69. **2.** Find $\frac{1}{8}$ of 408. **3.** Multiply 367 by 9.

4. Divide 7208 by 8. **5.** Divide 108 by 9. **6.** Divide $18.84 by 6.

7. If you know how many balloons there are in 1 package, how can you find how many balloons there are in 8 packages?

8. When the thermometer rises from 68° to 72°, how much warmer is it?

9. The five members of the camera club need new supplies that cost $6.75. What will be each one's share of the cost?

10. Henry bought 9 airmail stamps at 6¢ each. How much did they cost in all?

Just for fun

1. Write any 3-figure number in which you use three different figures. Try 375, for example.
- Write the same number backward.
- Now subtract the smaller of the two numbers from the larger.
- Next write your answer backward and add it to your answer. The sum is 1089.
- Choose another number for this trick. Be sure to use three *different* figures. You almost always get 1089 for your answer.

```
Sample
  573
- 375
  198
+ 891
 1089
```

Can you find the missing numbers in these examples?

2.
```
 475
 823
 ???
 536
2038
```

3.
```
1586
- ???
 937
```

4.
```
  75
  ??
 450
 375
4200
```

5.
```
    9? r2
?)754
   72
   34
   3?
    2
```

6.
```
1623
+ ???
2549
```

Measures of time

Adams School chose February 22nd as the date for its circus.

Sally wondered how many weeks the school had to get ready.

• She said, "This is January 25th. There are 31 days in January. 31 − 25 = 6.

• "Six days in January and 22 in February make 28 days. 28 days is 4 weeks."

1. Show on the calendar in the picture that from Jan. 25 to Feb. 22 is 4 weeks.

2. Learn this rhyme:
Thirty days have September,
April, June, and November.

All the *other* months have 31 days, except February.

February has 28 days except in leap year, when it has 29 days. Leap year comes every four years.

3. These years were leap years: 1936, 1940, 1944, 1948. Divide each of these numbers by 4.

The date of a leap year can be divided by 4 without a remainder.

Tell the leap years from 1948 to 1960.

4. Name the months in order and tell how many days there are in each. Check your answers by looking at your classroom calendar.

5. In February there are either _?_ days or _?_ days.

6. In September there are _?_ weeks and _?_ days.

7. In March there are _?_ weeks and _?_ days.

8. How many months are there in 1 year? 2? 3?

9. This is how three boys proved there are 365 days in a year.   Explain each way.   Whose way do you like best?

Arthur		Tom		
Jan. 31	July 31	30	31	120
Feb. 28	Aug. 31	30	31	217
March 31	Sept. 30	30	31	28
April 30	Oct. 31	30	31	365
May 31	Nov. 30	120	31	
June 30	Dec. 31		31	
181	+ 184 = 365		31	
			217	

Paul

30	31	120
×4	×7	217
120	217	+28
		365

LEARN THESE FACTS

60 seconds (sec.) = 1 minute
60 minutes (min.) = 1 hour
24 hours (hr.) = 1 day
7 days (da.) = 1 week
52 weeks (wk.) = 1 year (yr.)
365 days = 1 year
366 days = 1 leap year
12 months (mo.) = 1 year

Tell the missing numbers:

	a	b	c
10.	1 min. = ? sec.	1 da. = ? hr.	2 yr. = ? wk.
11.	½ min. = ? sec.	3 wk. = ? da.	1 yr. = ? days
12.	½ hr. = ? min.	1 yr. = ? wk.	366 da. = 1 ? year
13.	¼ hr. = ? min.	½ yr. = ? wk.	24 mo. = ? years

Problem study

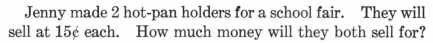

Jenny made 2 hot-pan holders for a school fair. They will sell at 15¢ each. How much money will they both sell for?

● *The problem asks* how much money both the hot-pan holders will sell for.

● *The problem tells* that Jenny made 2 holders and that they will sell at 15¢ each.

● *So I must find* 2 times the price of one holder; that is, 2 times 15¢. $2 \times 15¢ = $ __?__ .

Before you work each problem, read it carefully and tell:

● *What the problem asks*
● *What the problem tells*
● *What you must find*

1. Dan has 80 tickets to make for the school fair. After he has made 57 of them, how many more will he have to make?

2. The Poster Committee paid $.84 for cardboard to make 7 posters. Each poster cost __?__ .

3. The Ticket Committee spent 60¢. The Poster Committee spent 84¢. How much did both committees spend?

4. The posters cost $.84. If the six girls on the Committee share the cost of the posters equally, each should pay __?__ .

5. The Decoration Committee can cut 4 red-paper streamers out of a roll of paper. For 24 streamers they will need __?__ rolls of paper.

6. Find the cost of a half-dozen rolls of colored paper. The paper sells at 96¢ a dozen rolls.

7. The Decoration Committee need 2 thumbtacks to put up each of the 24 streamers. How many thumbtacks do they need in all?

8. The Food-Table Committee plan to sell 100 glasses of fruit punch at the fair. How many quarts of punch will they need to make?

9. The Ticket Committee were given 75¢ to pay their expenses. They spent only 60¢. How much did they have left to turn back to the class?

10. Fifteen girls have each promised to bring a cake to the fair. If each cake is cut into 16 servings, how many servings will they have all together?

180

Review practice

1. Find the cost of a pair of bicycle tires at $2.19 each.

2. Harry paid $6.00 for a set of 4 boxing gloves. He said, "These gloves cost _?_ apiece."

3. The bus fare from Fairmont to Chicago is $1.69. How much will it cost June to go from Fairmont to Chicago and back?
   If Ann and Ethel go with June, the fare for all will be _?_.

4. David and his sister want a George Washington costume and a Martha Washington costume to wear in a play.
   The costumes cost $3.98 each. How much will both cost?

5. George paid $2.70 for a box of 6 tennis balls. The balls cost _?_ apiece.

6. How many 8-inch lengths can you cut from 96 in. of cord?

Multiply. Check by going over your work.

	a	b	c	d	e	f
7.	$.23 59	$.50 76	$.93 87	$.59 68	$5.00 9	$4.72 8
8.	$8.13 7	$6.29 9	$7.50 8	$3.89 6	$6.35 6	$8.10 8
9.	$7.56 7	$7.05 8	$8.88 7	$9.29 9	$7.49 4	$5.67 5
10.	$9.46 8	$9.87 9	$6.98 7	$8.74 8	$9.05 8	$7.69 9

Divide and check:

11. $9\overline{)657}$ $6\overline{)792}$ $8\overline{)696}$ $9\overline{)783}$ $7\overline{)\$9.94}$ $8\overline{)\$5.12}$

12. $6\overline{)2550}$ $9\overline{)576}$ $7\overline{)5068}$ $7\overline{)875}$ $8\overline{)\$7.60}$ $6\overline{)\$5.76}$

13. $9\overline{)3687}$ $8\overline{)2963}$ $6\overline{)4987}$ $7\overline{)983}$ $7\overline{)\$14.28}$ $8\overline{)\$7.76}$

14. $5\overline{)985}$ $6\overline{)379}$ $7\overline{)894}$ $9\overline{)3984}$ $8\overline{)\$6.88}$ $9\overline{)\$6.85}$

Making tickets for the fair

1. Dan bought sheets of cardboard 27 inches long and 18 inches wide to make tickets for the school fair.

On the blackboard draw a rectangle the size of a sheet of the cardboard.

2. Dan made the tickets 3 inches long and 2 inches wide. Draw lines on your blackboard drawing to show where the cardboard was cut.

How many 3-inch lengths are there in 27 inches? How many tickets are there in one row?

How many 2-inch widths are there in 18 inches? How many rows of tickets are there?

3. How many tickets did Dan get from 1 sheet of cardboard, if he got 9 rows of tickets, with 9 tickets in a row?

4. 36 boys and 28 girls are to sell tickets. Dan made 5 tickets for each to sell, or ___?__ tickets all together.

5. Was 1 sheet of cardboard enough to make 320 tickets? Were 2 sheets enough? 3 sheets? 4?

6. One sheet of cardboard cost 15¢. How much did 4 sheets cost?

7. Have you ever made tickets for a show or a fair? If so, what arithmetic did you use?

Dan's ticket record

1. If each ticket seller sold 5 tickets at 5¢ each, how much money should each turn in?

2. At the end of the first week Dan's record of tickets sold showed 18 pupils had each turned in $.25.

How much money should he have had in his ticket-money box?

3. The table at the bottom of the page shows the coins Dan had in his money box at the end of each week.

At the end of the first week he had 1 dollar and 2 half dollars. What other coins did he have?

He should have had $4.50 at the end of the first week. Did he?

4. At the end of the second week Dan's record showed 37 pupils had each turned in $.25. How much money should he have had in his money box then?

From the table find out if he had the correct amount of money in the box at the end of the second week.

5. At the end of the third week Dan's record showed 59 pupils had each turned in $.25. How much money should he have had in his money box then?

From the table find out if he had the correct amount of money at the end of the third week.

6. At the end of the fourth week Dan's record showed 72 pupils had each turned in $.25. How much money should he have had in his money box then?

From the table find out if he had the correct amount of money at the end of the fourth week.

7. Dan used these quick tricks to find the value of the money in his box. Explain each trick.

12 half dollars = $\frac{1}{2}$ of $12 = $6
14 quarters = $\frac{1}{4}$ of $14 = $3.50
12 dimes = 12 × $.10 = $1.20
52 nickels = $\frac{1}{2}$ of $5.20 = $2.60

8. Use a quick trick to find the value of 16 half dollars.

MONEY IN THE TICKET-MONEY BOX	DOLLARS	HALF DOLLARS	QUARTERS	DIMES	NICKELS	CENTS
End of First Week	1	2	4	4	21	5
End of Second Week	2	5	7	7	43	15
End of Third Week	3	10	12	9	52	25
End of Fourth Week	4	12	14	12	60	30

Time-rate-work

1. Dan timed himself when he stamped the school name on the tickets he made. He found that he could stamp 8 tickets in 1 minute.

How many tickets could he stamp in 5 minutes? 7 min.? 9 min.?

2. We say that Dan's *rate of work* was *8 tickets per minute.* At that rate, how many tickets could he stamp in 4 min.? 6 min.?

3. If Dan could stamp the tickets at the rate of 7 tickets per minute, how many tickets could he stamp in 4 min.? 6 min.? 8 min.?

4. Does the *amount of work* Dan does depend upon *the number of minutes he works* and upon *his rate of work per minute?* Explain.

5. Ellen can make clothespin dolls at the rate of 4 dolls per hour. At that rate how many can she make in 2 hours? in ½ hour? in 3 hours?

6. Charlie decided to make garden stakes. He can make them at the rate of 5 per hour. How many stakes can he make in 3 hours? 8 hours?

7. If Charlie can make 5 stakes an hour, how long will it take him to make 10 stakes? 15? 20?

8. If Dan can stamp 8 tickets a minute, how long will it take him to stamp 16 tickets? 24? 40? 80?

9. Does the *number of minutes* needed to do some work depend on *the amount of work to be done* and upon *the rate of work per minute?* Explain.

10. Dick and Peter were addressing cards for the school to send to the members of the Parent-Teacher Association.

Dick addressed 20 cards in 5 minutes. Peter addressed 24 cards in 8 minutes. Can you figure out which of the boys is the faster worker?

Dick addressed cards at the rate of __?__ cards per minute. Peter addressed cards at the rate of __?__ cards per minute.

11. At camp it took Ellen 6 minutes to pare 12 potatoes. It took Molly 4 minutes to pare 12 potatoes. It took Grace 3 minutes to pare 12 potatoes.

Who was the fastest worker?

How many potatoes per minute did Ellen pare? Molly? Grace?

12. Does your *rate of work* depend on *the amount of work you do* and *how long it takes you to do it?*

How many feet does this train travel in 5 minutes?

Time-rate-distance

Henry ran a guessing contest on how many feet his train would travel in 5 minutes.

1. Paul estimated that the train's *rate of travel* was *40 feet per minute.* Then he figured that in 5 minutes the train would travel 5 × 40 feet, or __?__ feet.

2. Ann estimated that the train traveled 60 feet per minute, or __?__ feet in 5 minutes.

3. Fay estimated that the train traveled at the rate of 20 feet per minute, or __?__ feet in 5 min.

4. Henry's train traveled 25 feet per minute, or __?__ feet in 5 min.

5. Who made the best guess: Paul, Ann, or Fay? (See Exs. 1–3.)

6. If the train had traveled at the rate of 40 feet per minute, what distance would it have traveled in 4 min.? in 6 min.? in 9 min.?

7. At the rate of 30 feet per min., could you travel 270 feet in 9 min.? 150 feet in 5 min.?

8. If a turtle crawls 8 in. in 1 min., how far can it go in 5 min.?

9. Time yourself to see how far you can run in a minute.

Can you run twice as far in 2 minutes? 15 times as far in 15 minutes? Why not?

10. Make up a time-rate-distance problem about traveling in an automobile, in an airplane, and on a bicycle.

185

Making salted peanuts

Eve and Jan had 5 lb. of peanuts to salt.   Here is their recipe.

SALTED PEANUTS

5 lb. shelled, unroasted peanuts
2 lb. cooking fat or oil   salt

Pour 1 pt. boiling water over $\frac{1}{2}$ lb. nuts. Let stand 3 min. Drain. Cover nuts with cold water. Remove red skins from nuts. Dry the nuts.

Heat 2 lb. fat in a French fryer until hot enough to brown a cube of bread quickly. Put $\frac{1}{2}$ lb. nuts in basket of fryer and lower slowly into hot fat. Fry 4 min. Lift basket from fat. Pour nuts on brown wrapping paper to drain. Salt at once.

1. The girls did only $\frac{1}{2}$ lb. of nuts in each batch.

How many batches of nuts did they have in 1 lb.? in 4 lb.? 5 lb.?

2. If they did 10 batches of nuts and had to fry each batch 4 minutes, how long did it take to fry all the nuts?

3. At 37¢ a lb., the 5 lb. of peanuts cost __?__. At 26¢ a lb., the 2 lb. of fat cost __?__ ¢.

The girls paid 10¢ for salt. Show that the total cost of the nuts, fat, and salt was $2.47.

4. The girls sold the leftover fat and salt for 20¢; so the salted nuts cost them __?__.

5. The girls put the nuts into paper bags. Each bag held $\frac{1}{4}$ lb. How many bags of nuts should they get from 1 lb.? 2 lb.? 5 lb.?

6. When the girls finished, they had only 19 bags of salted nuts. They had eaten __?__ bag of nuts.

7. At 30¢ a bag, how much would they receive for 19 bags? The girls figured they would make $3.43 on the nuts.   Explain.

Keep up your good work

Multiply.   Check by doing each example again.

	a	*b*	*c*	*d*
1.	9 times 406	6 times 847	34 times 78	27 times 27
2.	7 times 805	7 times 769	71 times 69	65 times 76
3.	8 times 907	8 times 685	62 times 95	46 times 84

Divide.   Check each example.

	a	*b*	*c*	*d*	*e*
4.	9)7357	7)4987	8)6962	7)$46.90	8)$8.56
5.	8)5732	6)5479	7)5954	8)$50.40	9)$9.54
6.	7)6549	8)7298	9)8557	6)$59.40	7)$7.56

Find these sums.   Check each example.

7. $6.19 + $4 + $7.50 + $2.75 + $3.98

8. $7.25 + $.10 + $4.69 + $8.08 + $3

9. $8.49 + $.05 + $.11 + $9.90 + $7.75

10. $9.50 + $4.25 + $7.75 + $8.89 + $9.95

In each of these pairs of numbers subtract one number from the other.   Check each answer.

	a		*b*		*c*		*d*	
11.	357	879	267	709	2934	8979	3500	2784
12.	984	781	704	368	7650	3864	2999	4110
13.	693	800	1873	940	8500	4920	5006	2090

Which is more:

14. 7 × 56, or 400?   6 × 39, or 240?   7 × 83, or 540?

15. 8 × 45, or 320?   8 × 79, or 600?   6 × 93, or 530?

UNIT

26

Estimating answers
Using measures of
length, weight, liquid

Practice in estimating answers

1. Betty needed to know how much to pay for 3 balloons at 29¢ each. She estimated the cost to be 3 × 30¢, or __?__ ¢. How far off was that from the exact cost?

2. Sue wanted to buy 2 yards of material at 39¢ a yard for a costume. She estimated the cost to be 2 × 40¢, or __?__ ¢. How far off was her estimate?

3. Estimate the cost of 8 costumes at 38¢ each. See how far off your estimate is.

4. Jean had a dollar to buy a 78-cent costume. She estimated that she would have 20 cents left. Was her estimate close?

5. Peter needed two of the cowboy hats in the picture for prizes at a party. He estimated that they would cost 2 × 80¢, or __?__. How far off was his estimate?

6. Roy estimated the cost of 8 yards of material, at 18¢ a yard, to be 8 × 20¢, or $__?__. How far off was his estimate?

7. Ann paid 87¢ for enough material to make 3 witches' capes.
She estimated the cost of each cape to be ⅓ of 90¢, or __?__ ¢. How far off was her estimate?

8. Bill estimated the cost of 4 pirates' hats at 89¢ each to be $3.60. How close was his estimate to the exact cost?

9. Estimate the cost of each of the following. Then find how far off each estimate is.

3 sweaters at $3.98 each
4 caps at 24¢ each
5 pairs of skates at $4.98 a pair
8 records at 49¢ each
4 bicycle tires at $2.98 each

Cowboy Hats
79¢ EACH

10. Donald had a dollar. He bought a 69¢ record. Estimate how much he had left.

Is your estimate within 1¢ of the exact amount?

11. Estimate the cost of a 38-cent belt and a 49-cent pair of socks. Was your estimate within 3¢ of the exact cost?

12. Estimate the cost of 4 puzzles at 59¢ each.

13. If you read 8 pages of a book in 5 minutes, estimate how long it will take you to read 50 pages.

14. Joe estimated the sum of these numbers by thinking, "40 and 10 are 50, and 50 more are 100, and 30 more are __?__, and 10 more are __?__."

```
  39
   8
  51
  28
+ 12
```

How far off was his estimate?

Estimate the sum of each of the following. Then find how far off each of your estimates is from the exact sum.

	a	b	c	d	e	f
15.	38	48	69	121	398	497
	9	8	9	69	201	101
	42	53	64	32	102	298
	27	28	27	8	97	9
	11	13	12	21	104	31
16.	47	74	38	139	497	149
	29	88	39	72	289	19
	9	60	53	89	33	302
	31	9	62	30	301	28
	53	47	99	101	74	401

17. Joe likes to estimate the answers to subtractions. He says it keeps him from making foolish mistakes. In this example he thought: $200 - 40 =$ __?__. How far off was his estimate from the exact answer?

```
 197
- 38
```

18. Estimate these answers. How far off is each estimate?

a	b	c	d	e	f
198	369	498	803	1604	1398
− 49	− 78	− 179	− 504	− 906	− 199

8 X 58 IS more than 8 x 50.
8 X 58 IS less than 8 x 60.
But 8 x 58 IS nearer to 480 than to 400.

Estimating answers

1. Look at the picture to see what Tom thinks when he estimates the answer to 8 × 58.

Why does he think the answer is more than 8 × 50? less than 8 × 60? nearer to 480 than to 400?

2. Tom estimates 9 × 72 to be more than 9 × 70 and less than 9 × 80. He says the answer is nearer to _?_ than to _?_.

3. To estimate 7 × 198, Tom thinks, "7 × 200 is _?_; so the answer is a little _?_ than _?_."

4. To estimate 8 × 297, Tom thinks, "8 × 300 is _?_; so the answer is a little _?_ than _?_."

5. Would you estimate 8 × 298 to be closer to 1600 or to 2400?

6. Would you estimate 8 × 68 to be more or less than 500? Why?

Use Tom's method to estimate the answers to these multiplications. Then find the exact answer for each.

	a	b	c
7.	7 × 98	8 × 198	6 × 307
8.	8 × 79	9 × 203	7 × 296
9.	9 × 59	7 × 104	8 × 207
10.	8 × 92	7 × 805	9 × 798

11. Tom likes to estimate the answers to divisions. He would estimate the answer to 7)4912 by thinking $\frac{1}{7}$ of 49 hundred is _?_ hundred. How far off is his estimate?

12. To estimate 7)4893, Tom thinks, "4893 is close to 4900. $\frac{1}{7}$ of 49 hundred is _?_ hundred." How far off is his estimate?

Estimate the answers to these divisions. Then find how far off each estimate is.

	a	b	c
13.	8)5672	9)3672	8)6424
14.	8)7193	9)4491	7)3498
15.	8)6385	9)8091	7)6314
16.	6)4830	8)7192	9)2678

Estimating heights and lengths

At the school circus Jerry guessed a person's height. Then he measured the person.

If his guess was within an inch of the correct height, the person paid him a penny. If his guess was off by an inch or more, he paid the person a penny.

1. Jerry guessed the height of 115 persons. He made 102 correct guesses. How many wrong guesses did he make?

How much did Jerry earn for the circus?

2. Jerry has just guessed Roger's height. Look at the picture and tell if Jerry has to pay Roger a penny.

3. Guess the height of some classmates. Find their heights by measuring. Tell each pupil's height in inches and also in feet and inches.

4. Tom is 47 in. tall. Carl is 1 yd. 13 in. tall. Who is taller?

5. Paula said, "My father is 6 ft. tall. My 4-year-old brother is half as tall as my father." Could Paula possibly be right?

6. Guess the width of the teacher's desk. Measure to see how good your guess was.

7. Guess how many feet long the room is; how many inches long your pencil is. Measure to see how good your guesses were.

Using measures

At the circus Tom guessed a person's weight. Then he weighed the person.

If his guess was within two pounds of the correct weight, the person paid him a penny. If he made a mistake of two pounds or more, he paid the person a penny.

1. Tom guessed the weight of 123 persons. He made 99 correct guesses, and __?__ wrong guesses. How much did Tom earn for the circus?

2. Guess the weights of some classmates. Check by weighing.

3. Guess the weight of a book; a chair; a dictionary. Check by weighing.

4. John says this picture puzzle shows the name of a State. Figure out what State it is.

5. How many boys and girls, each weighing 100 lb., would it take to weigh a ton?

6. Find the sum of the weights of all the boys and girls in your class to see if all together you weigh a ton.

7. Name some place that is a mile from your school. How long does it take to walk the mile? to ride it on your bicycle?

MEASURES OF WEIGHT

16 ounces (oz.) = 1 pound (lb.)
2000 pounds (lb.) = 1 ton (T.)

MEASURES OF LIQUID

2 pints (pt.) = 1 quart
4 quarts (qt.) = 1 gallon (gal.)

MEASURES OF LENGTH

12 inches (in.) = 1 foot (ft.)
3 feet (ft.) = 1 yard (yd.)
36 inches = 1 yard
5280 feet = 1 mile (mi.)

Practice with measures

1. Peggy has two 1-gallon Thermos jugs. How many quarts of lemonade will they hold?

2. At a candy counter they have three 4-ounce weights and two 2-ounce weights.

Which weights should they use to weigh 1 lb. of candy? $\frac{1}{2}$ lb.? $\frac{1}{4}$ lb.?

3. Harry and Fred dressed up as Jumbo, the elephant, at the school circus.

Jumbo wore a sign saying he weighed 2 tons. How many pounds is that?

4. Helen needed 90 inches of paper edging for closet shelves. The kind of edging she bought came in 3-yard packages. Was one package enough?

On the blackboard draw a line 3 yards long. Mark off the 90 inches Helen needed for the shelves.

5. Driving along in his father's car, David saw the following signs. How would you estimate the distance mentioned in each sign?

- Railroad crossing 100 ft. ahead
- Dangerous crossroad — 50 yd.
- Hot dog stand — $\frac{1}{4}$ mi.
- Sharp curve — 200 ft.
- Pinehurst — 5 mi.

6. Frank saw this sign on a bridge:

CLEARANCE - 18 FEET
WEIGHT ALLOWED - 2 TONS

Do you know what the sign means? Estimate a height of 18 ft.

7. Would a truck whose weight when empty is 2200 pounds be allowed to cross the bridge (Ex. 6) carrying a ton of coal?

Practice these until you can tell every missing number:

a	b	c
8. 1 qt. = __?__ pt.	1 gal. = __?__ qt.	$\frac{1}{2}$ mi. = __?__ ft.
9. 1 ft. = __?__ in.	1 mi. = __?__ ft.	3 gal. = __?__ pt.
10. 1 lb. = __?__ oz.	$\frac{1}{4}$ lb. = __?__ oz.	$\frac{1}{2}$ lb. = __?__ oz.
11. 1 yd. = __?__ in.	$\frac{1}{4}$ yd. = __?__ in.	2 ft. = __?__ in.
12. 1 yd. = __?__ ft.	$\frac{1}{2}$ T. = __?__ lb.	$\frac{1}{4}$ mi. = __?__ ft.

UNIT
27

Two-step problems
Problems in grouping
Review practice

Thinking about two-step problems

1. At a bazaar Martha sold caramels at 60¢ a pound.

John bought $\frac{1}{2}$ pound of caramels and a 10-cent box of popcorn.

How much did Martha charge John in all?

Martha thought, "*My first step* is to find the cost of the caramels. That is $\frac{1}{2}$ of 60¢, or 30¢.

"*My second step* is to add the cost of the caramels to the cost of the popcorn.

"That is 30¢ + 10¢, or __?__¢."

2. At 16¢ a quart, what will 3 gal. of cider cost for a Halloween party?

The first step is to find the number of quarts in 3 gallons.

1 gal. = 4 qt. 3 gal. = 3 × 4 qt., or __?__ qt.

The second step is to find the cost of 12 quarts of cider at 16¢ a quart. 12 × 16¢ = __?__¢ = $1.92.

3. The children in Miss Allen's fourth-grade class bought a dozen apples for 25 cents and sold them for 3 cents each. How much did they make on the apples?

The first step is to find how much they got for the apples.

That is 12 × 3¢, or 36¢.

The second step is to subtract the cost of the apples from the amount they got for them.

That is 36¢ − 25¢, or __?__¢.

4. The children bought popcorn balls at 6 for 25¢ and sold them for 8¢ each. How much did they make on the 6 popcorn balls?

The first step is to find how much they sold the 6 popcorn balls for. 6 × 8¢ = __?__¢.

The second step is to find the difference between the cost and the selling price. 48¢ − 25¢ = __?__¢.

Solving two-step problems

Tell the first step in solving each of these problems; then tell the second step. Find the answers.

1. David had 50¢ when he went downtown. He spent 18¢ for candy, 5¢ for punch, and 9¢ for a puzzle. How much money did he have left?

2. At the bakery cupcakes sold for 30¢ a dozen. Find the cost of a half-dozen cupcakes and a 35-cent pie.

3. Anne Marie bought 2 lb. of candy and a 50-cent cake. The candy cost 60¢ a lb. How much did the candy and the cake cost?

4. To cover a picnic table, Janet bought 9 ft. of paper at 10¢ a yd. The paper cost ___?___.

5. How much change should Dan give from a quarter after selling 6 pinwheels at 3¢ each?

6. Betty made 2 lb. of popcorn. How many 4-ounce packages of popcorn can she make from the 2 lb.?

7. The candy-table committee at a carnival bought 200 paper bags. The price of the bags was 50 for 20¢. Did 200 bags cost 40¢, 60¢, or 80¢?

8. Roy treated Betsy to a bottle of soft drink. Look at the picture.
Roy gave Bill a quarter. How much change did he get?

Where is the mistake?

Find the four mistakes in the multiplications in Exs. 1–2.

	a	b	c	d	e
1.	987	807	$8.09	$5.48	$6.78
	7	6	9	7	9
	6909	4842	$72.81	$37.36	$60.02
2.	69	70	86	78	58
	54	58	43	36	49
	276	560	258	458	522
	345	350	344	234	232
	3726	4060	3798	2798	2842

Copy, add, and check:

	a	b	c	d	e
3.	$8.76	$7.86	$8.09	$7.89	$9.56
	7.95	8.06	7.86	.98	8.79
	.89	.98	6.75	6.78	7.97
	6.78	7.89	.78	5.67	.89
	7.67	8.78	6.09	4.56	8.67

Copy and multiply. Check by doing each example again.
Don't forget the dollar sign and the cents point in each answer.

	a	b	c	d	e
4.	$7.68	$8.79	$9.87	$6.57	$6.58
	8	9	7	6	9
5.	$9.80	$8.97	$7.89	$6.97	$7.89
	9	8	7	8	9

Divide and check:

6.	6)3457	8)6472	6)789	9)$10.89	5)$14.00
7.	8)923	9)3564	7)964	8)$25.60	6)$24.36
8.	7)2345	5)2950	8)3762	7)$12.74	8)$19.76

196

Everyday problems

1. Five boys bought a 10-cent package of rubber bands. There were 35 bands in the package. What was each boy's share of the cost? of the bands?

2. Tom had 25¢ when he went to the park. He had 9¢ left when he went home. How much had he spent?

3. Find the cost of a quarter of a pound of salted peanuts at 80¢ a pound.

4. Find the cost of a 6-cent air-mail stamp and six 3-cent stamps.

5. Paul has $7.87. How much more does he need to buy a gas engine for his model plane at $8.49?

6. How much will 18 five-cent Christmas-tree balls cost?

7. How much change will you get from a half dollar if you buy 3 oranges at 6¢ each?

8. Harry gathered 7 dozen eggs. How many eggs was that?

If he packs them in boxes like the one shown in the picture, how many boxes will he need?

9. Joe's father is a dairy farmer. Today he took five 10-gallon cans of milk to the dairy. How many quarts of milk is that?

10. Arthur weighs 69 pounds. The school nurse says he should weigh 73 pounds. How many pounds underweight is he?

11. Miss Strong has 4 packages of book covers. There are 24 covers in each package. Has she enough covers to give 3 to each of the 29 pupils in her class?

12. Bill likes to drink his milk through a straw. He has a package of 100 straws.

If he uses 3 straws a day, how many straws will he use in a week?

Will the 100 straws last for 2 weeks? 3 weeks? 4 weeks? 5 weeks?

13. Arthur wants a 29-cent mechanical pencil and a package of black leads, blue leads, and red leads. The leads cost 5¢ a package.

How much will the pencil and the leads cost?

14. If a package of 8 picnic plates costs 15¢, find the cost of 2 dozen plates.

197

Selling groups of things

1. Look at the picture to see how much Barbara charges for balloons at a school carnival.

Dennis asked for 4 balloons. Barbara thought, "2 balloons cost 5¢; so 4 balloons, which are 2 times 2 balloons, will cost 2 times 5¢, or __?__ cents." Was Barbara right? Look at these balloons.

2. At 2 for 5¢, how much would 6 balloons cost? 8 balloons? 10 balloons? 12 balloons?

3. At 2 for 5¢, how many balloons can Jean buy for 10¢? 15¢? 20¢? 25¢? 30¢? 35¢? 40¢?

4. Jim asked for a quarter's worth of balloons. How many balloons did he buy?

5. John asked for 1 balloon. He gave Barbara a nickel. Barbara gave him 2¢ change. How much did she charge for 1 balloon? Why do you think she charged 3¢?

6. At 2 for 5¢, what should Martha charge for a half-dozen jumping jacks? Draw a picture.

7. Look at the picture again. How much does Alice charge for popcorn balls? How much did Jean have to pay for half a dozen?

5¢   5¢   5¢

8. At 3 for 5¢, how much would 9 popcorn balls cost? 12? 15? 21? 30? 18? 24? 27?

9. How did you find the cost of each number of popcorn balls in Ex. 8?

Alice said, "I first find the number of 3's there are in the number of popcorn balls I am selling. Then I charge that number of nickels." Is that correct?

10. At 3 for 5¢, how many popcorn balls can you get for 10¢? 15¢? 20¢?

11. How did you find the number of popcorn balls in Ex. 10?

Alice said, "I find the number of nickels there are in the number of cents. Then I multiply 3 popcorn balls by that number." Is Alice correct?

12. Look at the picture. How much should Tom charge for 6 whistles? 9? 15? 12? 18? 21? 27? 30? 24?

13. How many whistles can you get for 20¢? 30¢? 50¢? 40¢? 70¢? 60¢? 80¢? $1.00?

Review and practice

Multiply, and check by going over your work:

	a	b	c	d	e	f
1.	89	78	67	76	87	86
	97	69	89	87	78	68
2.	470	906	876	987	896	709
	8	9	7	6	7	8
3.	896	986	869	796	976	789
	6	7	8	9	8	7
4.	$8.78	$8.87	$9.78	$8.09	$7.98	$7.07
	6	7	8	9	8	9

Watch out for the zeros in these subtractions:

	a	b	c	d	e
5.	$1.00	$20.00	$30.00	$40.00	$50.05
	.27	12.94	29.85	19.96	49.99
6.	$89.76	$99.67	$75.67	$98.73	$76.84
	59.67	58.69	24.78	27.74	10.85

7. Estimate to see if the sum of 207, 694, and 1218 is nearer 2000 or 2100.

8. Is the sum of $7.98, $26.05, $4.07, and $6.98 nearer $45 or $46?

9. Estimate the difference between $45.96 and $10.15.

Copy in columns, add, and check:

10. 346, 289, 75, and 406

11. 283, 94, 47, 9, and 573

12. $9.62, $2.84, $.79, and $5.63

Copy, subtract, and check:

13. $45.89 − $29.75

14. $50 − $17.83

15. $60 − $19.98

Subtract the smaller number from the larger in Ex. 16; in Ex. 17.

16. 2095   3874

17. 1472   975

18. Find $245 + 623 - 354 + 211$.

19. Find $1000 - 742 + 98 + 107$.

Meaning and equivalence
of halves, fourths, eighths;
of halves, thirds, sixths

UNIT
28

Thinking about halves

1. Joy had 4 cakes to sell at a food sale. She said, "I am cutting these into halves. Many people will want only a half cake.

"If somebody wants a whole cake I'll sell them __?__ halves."

2. How many half cakes did Joy make out of 4 whole cakes?

3. Eight halves is written $\frac{8}{2}$. In $\frac{8}{2}$ the 8 tells us how many pieces or parts there are. The 2 tells into how many equal parts each cake is cut.

The name of each of these parts is a __?__.

4. Cover one of the cakes. Write the fraction that tells how many halves you can now see.

5. In the first 10 minutes of the food sale, Joy sold three halves of the cakes.

Joy said, "I've sold a cake and a half ($1\frac{1}{2}$ cakes) already." Do you agree with Joy?

6. Use the picture of the cakes below to prove these Number Truths:

$$\frac{2}{2} = 1 \qquad \frac{3}{2} = 1\frac{1}{2} \qquad \frac{4}{2} = 2 \qquad \frac{5}{2} = 2\frac{1}{2}$$

7. Use the picture to discover a Number Truth about $\frac{6}{2}$; about $\frac{7}{2}$; about $\frac{8}{2}$.

8. To find these answers, cover parts of the cakes below.

How many halves remained after Joy had sold 1 cake? $1\frac{1}{2}$ cakes? 2 cakes? $2\frac{1}{2}$? 3? $3\frac{1}{2}$?

Thinking about fourths

1. In each whole circle above there are __?__ fourths.

Use the circles to help you tell the missing numbers below:

2. $\frac{2}{4} = \frac{?}{2}$ $\frac{2}{2} = \frac{?}{4}$ $2\frac{1}{4} = \frac{?}{4}$ $\frac{7}{4} = ?$

3. $2 = \frac{?}{4}$ $\frac{5}{4} = ?$ $2\frac{1}{2} = \frac{?}{4}$ $\frac{12}{4} = ?$

4. Count the number of fourths in the 3 circles above. Point to the fourths as you count. Begin this way: $\frac{1}{4}, \frac{2}{4}, \frac{3}{4}, \frac{4}{4}$, and so on.

5. Ex. 4 shows that $3 = \frac{?}{4}$.

6. Count the number of halves in the circles above. Your counting shows that $3 = \frac{?}{2}$.

7. Count from 1 to 3 by fourths.

8. Count from 1 to 3 by halves.

9. Bob and Bill counted the parts of circles above this way:

Bob: $\frac{1}{4}$ $\frac{2}{4}$ $\frac{3}{4}$ $\frac{4}{4}$ $\frac{5}{4}$ $\frac{6}{4}$
     $\frac{7}{4}$ $\frac{8}{4}$ $\frac{9}{4}$ $\frac{10}{4}$ $\frac{11}{4}$ $\frac{12}{4}$

Bill: $\frac{1}{4}$ $\frac{1}{2}$ $\frac{3}{4}$ 1 $1\frac{1}{4}$ $1\frac{1}{2}$
     $1\frac{3}{4}$ 2 $2\frac{1}{4}$ $2\frac{1}{2}$ $2\frac{3}{4}$ 3

Prove that both boys counted correctly.

202

10. Here are two groups of fourths. Show how counting may be used to add the two groups.

11. Here are two groups of halves. Add the two groups by counting. How many whole circles can you make out of all these halves?

12. If you cover $\frac{1}{2}$ circle in Ex. 1, how many circles can you see? $3 - \frac{1}{2} = $ __?__

13. If you cover $1\frac{1}{4}$ circles in Ex. 1, how many circles can you see? $3 - 1\frac{1}{4} = $ __?__

14. Begin at 3. Count backward by halves.

15. Begin at 3. Count backward by fourths.

16. How many dollars can you get for 4 quarters? 5 quarters? 6? 7? 8? 9? 10? 11? 12?

What does this prove about fourths?

Selling parts of things

1. Patsy baked a small cake for the food sale. This picture shows that she cut it into six equal parts. What is each of the six equal parts of the cake called?

Look at the cake. One half of the cake is how many sixths? Does $\frac{1}{2} = \frac{3}{6}$?

2. David wanted to buy two sixths of the cake. Joan said, "That will be $\frac{1}{3}$ of the cake, won't it?" Was Joan right? Does $\frac{1}{3} = \frac{2}{6}$?

3. Two thirds of the cake is the same as ___?___ sixths of the cake. $\frac{2}{3} = \frac{?}{6}$.

4. Alice cut a pie as in this picture. Why do you think one of the equal parts is called one eighth of the pie? How do you write "one eighth" in figures?

5. How many eighths are there in $\frac{1}{2}$ of Alice's pie? in $\frac{1}{4}$ of the pie? in $\frac{3}{4}$ of the pie?

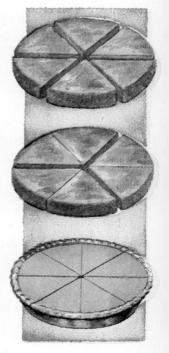

6. 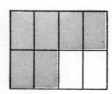 The colored parts of these 2 rectangles show that $\frac{3}{4} = \frac{?}{8}$.

The white parts of the rectangles show that $\frac{1}{4} = \frac{?}{8}$.

7.  The colored parts of the 2 lower rectangles show that $\frac{1}{3} = \frac{?}{6}$.

The white parts of the rectangles show that $\frac{2}{3} = \frac{?}{6}$.

8. Look at your ruler. $\frac{1}{2}$ in. $= \frac{?}{4}$ in.; $\frac{1}{4}$ in. $= \frac{?}{8}$ in.; $\frac{3}{4}$ in. $= \frac{?}{8}$ in.

9. Tom and Harry counted the parts of this circle this way:

Tom: $\frac{1}{6}$ $\frac{2}{6}$ $\frac{3}{6}$ $\frac{4}{6}$ $\frac{5}{6}$ $\frac{6}{6}$

Harry: $\frac{1}{6}$ $\frac{1}{3}$ $\frac{1}{2}$ $\frac{2}{3}$ $\frac{5}{6}$ 1

Prove that both boys counted correctly.

Equal parts

1. Tom drew bars A, B, C, and D to show that 1 whole = 2 halves, or _?_ fourths, or _?_ eighths.

2. Look at Bar B and Bar C. You see that $\frac{1}{2} = \frac{?}{4}$.

3. What can you tell by looking at Bar B and Bar D? by looking at Bar C and Bar D?

4. Tom drew bars E, F, and G to show that 1 whole = _?_ thirds, or _?_ sixths.

5. Which bars show that:

$\frac{1}{3} = \frac{2}{6}$? $\frac{2}{3} = \frac{4}{6}$? $\frac{5}{6}$ is smaller than 1?

Make drawings to show that:

6. $\frac{1}{2}$ of a cake = $\frac{4}{8}$ of a cake.

7. $\frac{1}{4}$ of a cake = $\frac{2}{8}$ of a cake.

8. $\frac{3}{4}$ of a cake = $\frac{6}{8}$ of a cake.

Use drawings to prove that the statements in Exs. 9–12 are true.

9. A whole pie is 8 eighths; so $\frac{1}{2}$ pie is $\frac{1}{2}$ of 8 eighths, or 4 eighths.

10. A whole pie is 8 eighths; so $\frac{1}{4}$ pie is $\frac{1}{4}$ of 8 eighths, or 2 eighths.

11. A whole pie is 6 sixths; so $\frac{1}{2}$ pie is $\frac{1}{2}$ of 6 sixths, or 3 sixths.

12. A whole pie is 6 sixths; so $\frac{1}{3}$ pie is $\frac{1}{3}$ of 6 sixths, or 2 sixths.

13. Is one third of a pie more than $\frac{1}{2}$ of it?

14. Is one fourth of a pie less than $\frac{1}{2}$ of it?

15. Is $\frac{1}{2}$ yard equal to 12 inches?

16. Is it a fair trade to give $\frac{2}{4}$ dollar for $\frac{1}{2}$ dollar?

17. Can one-half yard of ribbon be cut into two pieces each $\frac{1}{4}$ yd. long?

18. Is one-fourth hour half as long as $\frac{1}{2}$ hour?

Thinking about fractional parts

1. Fold a piece of paper to show that $\frac{1}{2}$ of it equals $\frac{2}{4}$ of it.

2. Fold a piece of paper to show that $\frac{1}{3}$ of it equals $\frac{2}{6}$ of it.

3. What part of this cake has been eaten? In $\frac{3}{8}$ what does the 8 tell? What does the 3 tell?

4. What part of the cake is left? In $\frac{5}{8}$ what does the 8 tell? What does the 5 tell?

5. How many quarters of a dollar are there in a half dollar? How many quarters of an hour are there in a half hour?

You may use the charts below to help you find the missing numbers in Exs. 6–8.

6. $\frac{1}{4} = \frac{?}{8}$ $\qquad$ $\frac{3}{4} = \frac{?}{8}$ $\qquad$ $\frac{1}{2} = \frac{?}{8}$ $\qquad$ $\frac{1}{2} = \frac{?}{4}$

7. $1 = \frac{?}{2}$ $\qquad$ $1 = \frac{?}{4}$ $\qquad$ $1 = \frac{?}{8}$ $\qquad$ $\frac{2}{4} = \frac{?}{8}$

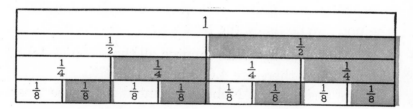

8. $1 = \frac{?}{3}$ $\qquad$ $\frac{1}{3} = \frac{?}{6}$ $\qquad$ $\frac{1}{2} = \frac{?}{6}$ $\qquad$ $\frac{2}{3} = \frac{?}{6}$

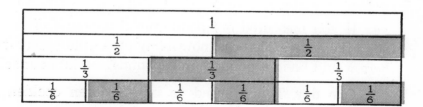

9. Bob and Ralph each wanted to divide a circle into sixths. Bob started by cutting his circle into halves. Ralph cut his into thirds. What did each do then?

BOB $\qquad$ RALPH

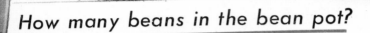

How Many Beans in the Bean Pot?
Each Guess 1¢
Fine Prize for the Best Guesser

Charlie	90,000	William	16,666
Mark	16,500	Joe	9,090
Donald	32,305	Jean	2,150
Molly	9,000	Eve	75,000
Janet	7,500	Joseph	100,000
Sally	4,250	Dan	19,999
Barbara	12,000	Jimmy	18,005

How many beans in the bean pot?

1. How many beans did Charlie guess were in the bean pot? Mark? Donald? each of the other pupils?

2. John announced that there were about 4,000 beans in the pot. Who made the best guess? the poorest?

3. Mark asked, "Who counted all those beans, John? How do you know there are 4,000 beans there?"

John answered, "Nobody counted all those beans. We weighed out a half pound of beans and counted them. There were 401 beans. Then we put 5 pounds of beans in the pot."

Explain how John figured there were about 4,000 beans.

4. If you measured out a quarter of a pound of peas and found there were 250 peas, how many peas would you estimate there would be in a pound? in 5 pounds? in 10 pounds?

5. One day Tom wanted to buy 3 dozen cookies. The cookies were sold by the pound, not by the dozen, so Tom didn't know how many cookies to ask for.

He said to the clerk, "Please weigh out $\frac{1}{4}$ lb. of cookies."

She did. There were 9 cookies in that $\frac{1}{4}$ lb., so Tom figured that to get 36 cookies he should buy __?__ lb. of cookies.

Counting to 100,000

1. Look at the picture above. How many bean pots are there in the top row? How many beans in each pot?

Count the beans in the top row by 10's. How many are there? 10 times 10 = __?__ .

2. How many bean pots are there in the second row across? How many beans are there in each pot?

Count the beans in the second row by 100's. How many are there? 10 times 100 = __?__ .

3. How many bean pots are there in the third row across? How many beans are there in each pot?

Count the beans in the third row by 1,000's. How many are there? 10 times 1,000 equals __?__ .

4. How many bean pots are there in the bottom row? How many beans in each pot?

Count the beans in the bottom row by 10,000's. How many are there? 10 × 10,000 equals __?__ .

5. How many beans will you have in all if you have 2 pots from the bottom row, 2 pots from the row above it, 2 pots from the second row, and 2 pots from the top row?

6. How many beans are there in all if you have 4 pots from the bottom row and 3 pots from the second row?

7. Make up some questions about how many beans you would have if you had certain numbers of pots from certain rows.

Hundreds of thousands

1. Sam needed to write one hundred thousand.

He thought, "I'll add 1 to 99,999. That will show me how to write one hundred thousand." Do you agree?

$$\begin{array}{r} 99,999 \\ 1 \\ \hline 100,000 \end{array}$$

2. Here are some Number Truths about 100,000. How many others can you add to the list?

- 100,000 is 100 times 1,000
- 100,000 is 90,000 + 10,000
- 100,000 is 10 times 10,000

3. What is the largest 5-place number? What is the smallest 6-place number?

Count:

4. From 450 to 1,150 by 100's; by 50's.

5. From 375 to 675 by 25's.

6. From 2,450 to 8,450 by 1,000's.

7. From 20,000 to 120,000 by 10,000's; by 20,000's.

8. From 100,000 to 100,010.

9. 325,403 is read "325 thousand, 403." Add 2,000 to 200,000. Read your answer.

10. Add: 100,000 + 20,000 + 3,000 + 400 + 50 + 6.

In the numbers below, tell how many hundred-thousands there are in each; how many ten-thousands; how many thousands; hundreds; tens; ones.

	a	*b*	*c*	*d*	*e*
11.	125,000	500,005	875,896	504,806	480,156
12.	179,000	180,087	777,777	278,900	386,060
13.	104,404	804,067	508,976	700,070	606,060
14.	563,270	470,006	600,006	806,062	900,074

15. Read the numbers above. Then your teacher will dictate them for you to write.

Remember that when she says "thousand," you must write a comma. Always write three more figures after the comma.

16. Copy these numbers. Place a comma in each. Then read them.

275467   34568   204035   7865

17. Prove that you understand the large numbers you find in your geography and science books.

Number, please!

Tell the missing numbers:

1. $6 \times \underline{\ ?\ } = 54 \qquad \underline{\ ?\ } \times 8 = 40$

2. $3 \times 7 = \underline{\ ?\ } \qquad 81 \div \underline{\ ?\ } = 9$

3. $\underline{\ ?\ } \div 7 = 9 \qquad 54 \div \underline{\ ?\ } = 6$

4. $4 + 9 = \underline{\ ?\ } \qquad 24 + 9 = \underline{\ ?\ }$

5. $84 + 9 = \underline{\ ?\ } \qquad 114 + 9 = \underline{\ ?\ }$

6. $45\cent = \underline{\ ?\ }$ nickels

7. $4 \times 600 = \underline{\ ?\ } \qquad 4 \times 601 = \underline{\ ?\ }$

8. $280 \div 7 = \underline{\ ?\ } \qquad 287 \div 7 = \underline{\ ?\ }$

9. 2, 9, 16, $\underline{\ ?\ }$, 30, $\underline{\ ?\ }$, 44

10. 3, 11, 19, $\underline{\ ?\ }$, 35, $\underline{\ ?\ }$, 51

11. 4, 13, 22, $\underline{\ ?\ }$, 40, $\underline{\ ?\ }$, $\underline{\ ?\ }$

12. 605, 705, $\underline{\ ?\ }$, 905, $\underline{\ ?\ }$

13. $4\frac{1}{4}$, $4\frac{1}{2}$, $\underline{\ ?\ }$, $\underline{\ ?\ }$, $5\frac{1}{4}$, $\underline{\ ?\ }$

14. 10, $9\frac{1}{2}$, $\underline{\ ?\ }$, $\underline{\ ?\ }$, 8, $\underline{\ ?\ }$, 7

15. 700 is $\underline{\ ?\ }$ larger than 693.

16. The difference between 500 and 488 is $\underline{\ ?\ }$.

17. The total of $17 + 18 + 6 + 10$ is $\underline{\ ?\ }$.

18. $20 \times 7 = 140$ shows you that $140 \div 7 = \underline{\ ?\ }$.

19. When you count by 10's, the next number after 990 is $\underline{\ ?\ }$.

20. When you count by 100's, the next number after 990 is $\underline{\ ?\ }$.

21. When you count by 100's, the next number after 9,900 is $\underline{\ ?\ }$.

22. When you count by 1,000's, the next number after 9,900 is $\underline{\ ?\ }$.

23. 1 ft. 8 in. = $\underline{\ ?\ }$ in.

24. 2 lb. 1 oz. = $\underline{\ ?\ }$ oz.

25. 1 yd. 2 ft. = $\underline{\ ?\ }$ ft.

26. 16 in. = 1 ft. $\underline{\ ?\ }$ in.

27. 80 min. = 1 hr. $\underline{\ ?\ }$ min.

28. In the month of July there are $\underline{\ ?\ }$ wk. $\underline{\ ?\ }$ da.

29. At 2 for $5\cent$, a dozen Christmas-tree balls will cost $\underline{\ ?\ }\cent$.

30. At 3 for $5\cent$, you can get $\underline{\ ?\ }$ large rubber bands for $20\cent$.

31. From 8:45 A.M. to 10:00 A.M. is $\underline{\ ?\ }$ hr. and $\underline{\ ?\ }$ min.

32. $20 \times 14 = 2 \times 14 \times \underline{\ ?\ }$.

33. $30 \times 12 = 3 \times 12 \times \underline{\ ?\ }$.

34. $4 \times \$2.98$ amounts to almost $\underline{\ ?\ }$ dollars.

35. $\frac{1}{7}$ of 490 = $\underline{\ ?\ }$.

36. $\frac{1}{8}$ of 6400 = $\underline{\ ?\ }$.

FROZEN FOODS SALE TODAY

	Regular Price	SALE PRICE		Regular Price	SALE PRICE
Peaches	35¢ box	29¢	Ice cream	35¢ pint	33¢
Peas	26¢ box	23¢	Orange juice	28¢ can	26¢
Strawberries	34¢ box	28¢	Chopped steak	49¢ ½-lb. box	47¢

The grocer's sale

How much can Mary Ann save by buying at sale prices:

1. 2 packages of peaches?

2. 3 packages of peas?

3. 2 packages of strawberries?

4. 2 quarts of ice cream?

5. 2 cans of orange juice?

6. 1 pound of chopped steak?

How much will it cost to buy the following at sale prices:

7. 6 cans of orange juice?

8. 6 packages of peas and 1 pound of chopped steak?

9. 2 packages of peaches?

10. 2 quarts of ice cream and a package of strawberries?

11. At the sale, Mary Ann gave the clerk a dollar to pay for a quart and a pint of ice cream. How much change did she receive?

12. Thomas has 75¢. Has he enough to buy 2 boxes of peaches and a package of peas? If not, how much more does he need?

13. If you had a dollar, what would you buy at the sale?

14. What would you buy if you had $1.50?

15. Cut out some sale notices from your newspaper. Make up problems for your class to solve.

Using arithmetic

1. Joan has just arrived at the zoo. Look at the picture to see what time it is.

How long will she have to wait before she can get in? Use a toy clock to prove your answer.

2. Billy arrived at the zoo at 10 minutes of 4. He stayed until the zoo closed. Use a toy clock to show how long he was there.

3. On March 10, the Globe Movie Theater closed for 2 weeks. It reopened on March ___?___.

4. Find the cost of 28 six-cent candy bars.

5. Estimate the cost of one arrow if a set of 4 arrows costs $3.99.

6. George has 12 addition examples to do. He can do 4 of them in 5 minutes. How long will it take him to finish the examples?

What part of each of these circles is colored?

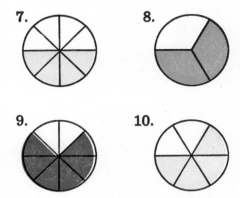

7.   **8.**

9.   **10.**

11. Find the cost of 3 yards of material at 59¢ a yard and a 10-cent spool of thread.

211

How to solve problems

Tell whether to add, subtract, multiply, or divide to find the missing numbers. Then tell the missing number in each problem. Do not use a pencil.

1. The show opened at two o'clock and closed at five o'clock. It lasted _?_ hours.

2. Dan has 12 quarters in the ticket-money box. He said, "I have _?_ dollars in quarters."

3. Paul weighed 76 lb. and Sam weighed 69 lb. Paul weighed _?_ lb. more than Sam.

4. Barbara spent 4¢ for punch, 5¢ for balloons, and 10¢ for popcorn balls. In all, she spent _?_ ¢.

5. Eve guessed that there were 75,000 beans in a bean pot and Joseph guessed 100,000 beans. Joseph's guess was _?_ thousand larger than Eve's.

6. At 2¢ each, Sally can get _?_ rolls for a quarter.

7. When Jimmie went to the park, he had 50¢. When he went home, he had 10¢. He had spent _?_ cents.

8. William guessed the heights of 6 people in 10 minutes. At that rate, he could make _?_ guesses in half an hour.

9. The pen for Bobby's rabbits is 9 ft. long. That is the same as _?_ yd. long.

10. In Dorothy's pan of fudge there were 12 pieces. She sold $\frac{1}{3}$ of the fudge, or _?_ pieces.

11. A quarter of a dollar is _?_ more than 20¢.

12. A 2-gallon punch bowl will hold _?_ quarts.

13. At a cost of 2 for 5¢, you can get _?_ balloons for a quarter.

14. If 4 yards of material are needed for one costume, from 36 yards _?_ costumes can be made.

15. Barbara weighs 54 pounds and Eve weighs 61 pounds. Barbara is _?_ pounds lighter than Eve.

16. At 5¢ a ticket, 9 tickets will cost _?_ cents.

17. You wish to make an 18-inch strip of cardboard into tickets 2 inches long. From the strip you can make _?_ tickets.

212

Put on your thinking cap

▶ Oral review

1. Which is larger, $\frac{1}{6}$ or $\frac{1}{4}$?

2. Joy says $\frac{1}{2}$ of a cake is twice as big as $\frac{1}{4}$ of a cake. Prove it.

3. If Jan. 12 is on Friday, the next Friday will be Jan. __?__.

4. Which of these equal 1 yr.? 12 mo.   90 da.   365 da.   52 wk.

5. What number means 31 thousands, 7 hundreds, and 9 tens?

6. Betty spent 15¢. She got __?__ ¢ change from a quarter.

7. Jane says her birthday is February 30. Is she right? Why?

8. Is $\frac{2}{3}$ of a pie more than $\frac{2}{6}$ of a pie? Do you need a picture?

9. A sign said, "Roller skates $675." Is this sensible?

10. Estimate the cost of shoes for $3.98 and a hat for $1.49.

11. Tell the missing numbers:

1 gal. = __?__ qt.   1 yd. = __?__ in.
1 hr. = __?__ min.   1 ft. = __?__ in.

▶ Written review

1. Copy, add, and check:

a	b	c	d	e
784	980	789	$9.56	$8.57
96	89	96	8.97	7.86
679	798	40	.70	6.70
897	879	897	5.89	.90

2. Subtract and check:

$10.00	$20.00	$40.50	$10.98	$76.00
2.98	8.76	4.05	2.99	7.06

3. Multiply, and check by going over your work:

86	78	97	$6.05	$8.70
97	89	68	8	9

4. Divide and check:

6)2440   7)5850   8)7230   9)5580   8)7584

213

Problem Test 5

1. Diana had $5.79 in the School Bank. Today she deposited $.35. How much has she in the bank now?

2. A class wants 3 pounds of potato chips for a picnic. The chips come in $\frac{1}{4}$-lb. cellophane bags. How many bags should the class buy to get 1 lb.? 3 lb.?

3. Lollipops sell at 3 for 5¢. How many can you get for a dime? Draw a picture of the problem.

4. Eight boys want to share the cost of a football. Its price is $4.64. How much should each boy pay?

5. If Barbara takes care of Mrs. Brown's baby from 9:00 A.M. to 1:00 P.M., at 25¢ an hour, how much will she earn?

6. Jean measured and found she needed 106 inches of binding for a pair of curtains. She bought 3 yards of binding. Prove that she bought enough.

7. Tom's grandmother sent him a box of salt-water taffy. There were 4 layers of candy in the box. In each layer there were 2 rows of candies, with 12 pieces in a row. How many pieces of candy were there in 1 layer? in the box?

8. How much change will you get from a dollar after buying a 49-cent notebook and a 15-cent pack of notebook paper?

9. John's United States Savings Stamps book holds 75 twenty-five-cent stamps. How much money will he have saved when his book is full?

10. Bill is earning money to buy a bicycle for $49.00. He now has $33.79. How much more must he earn?

Write your score on your Problem Test Record.

Estimating answers in division

1. Study the multiplications below. Then tell a rule for finding 10 times a number; 100 times a number.

$10 \times 6 = 60$ $100 \times 5 = 500$
$10 \times 8 = 80$ $100 \times 7 = 700$

2. Does $100 \times 4 = 40$, or 400, or 4000? Does $435 \div 4$ equal more than 100?

3. Which is more: 10×8 or 78? Are there as many as 10 eights in 78?

4. Which is more: 100×6 or 585? Are there as many as 100 sixes in 585? Does $585 \div 6 =$ more than 100 or less than 100?

5. $927 \div 9$ is more than __?__.

Which examples have answers that are smaller than 10?
Which have answers larger than 100?   Now give the answers
without using pencil and paper.

	a	b	c	d	e
6.	7)64	7)69	7)75	7)700	7)728
7.	8)58	8)69	8)89	8)800	8)808
8.	9)65	9)88	9)96	9)900	9)936
9.	8)78	8)87	9)901	7)707	8)880
10.	6)68	7)79	8)806	9)909	9)6300
11.	4)456	5)1045	6)1260	7)770	8)708

Tell which examples have answers that are smaller than 100.
Then copy Exs. 12–15, divide, and check.

12. 4)395	5)498	6)630	7)701	8)7200
13. 3)297	4)408	5)514	6)600	7)700
14. 7)856	8)7264	9)6740	8)7212	9)8475
15. 8)5840	9)8875	8)7864	9)909	7)5607

215

1. Find the sum of $75.24 + $9.63 + $7 + $.75 + $9.36. (187)

2. Find the difference between $55.98 and $56.75. (112)

3. 705,009 is read __?__ thousand, __?__. (208)

4. Would you estimate the cost of 3 pairs of woolen socks at $1.98 each to be about $3, $5, or $6? (188)

5. Find 7 times 604. (44)   6. Find 65 times 78. (130–131)

7. How many days are there in a year? in a leap year? (178–179)

8. If a motor scooter travels 35 miles an hour, how far will it go in 3 hours? (185)

9. Does the colored part of this circle show that $\frac{1}{3} = \frac{2}{6}$ or that $\frac{1}{2} = \frac{3}{6}$? (203–204)

10. At 2 for 15¢, how much will 6 candles cost? (198–199)

Self-Help Test 8

Divide and check:

1. 9)87 (161)   2. 8)96 (151)   3. 9)585 (163–164)

4. 8)675 (151)   5. 9)810 (135)   6. 4)484 (76–77)

7. 6)$42.96 (166)   8. 9)$36.54 (167)   9. 8)$76.00 (166)

10. Six boys found a box containing 150 pennies. If they share them equally, how many should each take? (107–109)

11. Find the cost of 75 six-cent airmail stamps. (138)

12. Find the cost of $\frac{1}{2}$ doz. eggs at 58¢ a dozen and a 25-cent box of frozen spinach. (194)

13. How much will 24 pink rambler rosebushes cost at $.39 each? (130–131)

216

Now is the time to test yourself

*Work carefully. Check your answers.
Be sure that all answers are sensible.*

1. If enough material to make 5 model airplanes costs $6.25, would you estimate the cost of 1 plane to be less than a dollar or more than a dollar?

2. Multiply $7.08 by 9.

3. Write in figures: seven hundred thousand, eight.

4. If a jeep travels 35 miles in 1 hour, how many miles will it travel in 4 hours?

5. How many days are there in March?

6. Joan bought peanuts for 5¢ and a whistle for 10¢. How much change should she get from a quarter?

7. How many pony-ride tickets can you get for a half dollar, if they are selling at three for a quarter?

8. Dancing Dora, an elephant, weighs 2,239 pounds. How much more than a ton is that?

9. Copy and complete the following:

1 minute = __?__ seconds
1 year   = __?__ months
1 week   = __?__ days
1 year   = __?__ weeks
1 day   = __?__ hours
1 year   = __?__ days

10. Do the colored parts of these bars show that $\frac{1}{2}$ is less than $\frac{5}{8}$?

Just for fun

Can you find the missing numbers in these divisions?

```
       9?4                4??               6??               ?7?
1.  9)????        2.  8)?6??        3.  7)????        4.  6)???6
       ??                ??                ??                54
       66                ?6                39                4?
       ??                ??                ??                ??
       ??                ?4                ?9                3?
       ??                ??                ??                ??
```

217

SPECIAL SALE
ELECTRIC TRAIN
$29.95

Buying an electric train

1. The four Barnes boys want to buy this electric train. How much does it cost?

2. Ted Barnes has $6.74, Bob has $11.63, Bill has $4.98, and Jerry has $5.39. All together, have they enough to buy the train? If not, how much more do they need?

3. If they buy the train, they will also need at least 10 sections of track at 25¢ a section. To buy the train and track, how much more money do they need?

4. Ted said, "If the four of us earn a dollar each, we'll have enough to buy the train and track." Do you agree?

5. If you know how far an electric train travels in 1 minute, how can you find how far it travels in 5 minutes?

6. If an electric train takes $\frac{1}{2}$ minute to make a trip around its track, how long will it take to make 2 trips around? 3? 4?

7. If any of the pupils in your class have electric trains, ask them what arithmetic problems they have had in buying parts for them.

8. Maybe some pupil can bring to class a list of prices of things needed for an electric train. Then you can make up some electric-train problems.

Vacation problems

1. Steven has a half dollar to spend at the carnival. If he spends 15¢ for a ride on the roller coaster, he will have __?__ ¢ left.

2. If Joan buys a pair of saddle shoes for $3.98 and a sweater for $4.98, all together she will have to spend about __?__ dollars.

3. If you know your bus leaves at 3:10 P.M. and you wish to allow a half hour to get to the station and buy your ticket, you should leave home at __?__.

4. If six boys are going to share equally a package containing four dozen fishhooks, each boy should get __?__ hooks.

5. If the hooks in Ex. 4 cost $.98, each of the 6 boys should pay __?__ ¢ and __?__ boys should each pay 1¢ extra.

6. If you know the camp fee for one week, to find the fee for six weeks, you should __?__.

7. If you know how much you weigh when you go to camp and how much you weigh when you come home, to find how much you have gained, you should __?__.

8. Joe rode a pony 3 miles in 30 minutes. He rode at the rate of __?__ miles an hour.

9. The campers at Camp Joy go to bed at 9 P.M. and get up at 7 A.M. They are in bed __?__ hours every night.

10. If flashlight bulbs cost 2 for 15¢, 6 bulbs will cost __?__ ¢.

11. George went to camp on July 9. He is to stay 2 weeks. He will come home on July __?__.

12. At Camp Dark Water there are 8 cabins. There are 16 campers living in each of the cabins. There are __?__ campers all together.

13. If 2 boys share equally the cost of a beach ball marked $1.78, each boy should pay __?__.

14. Martha wants a bathing suit marked $2.29 and a pair of water wings that cost $1.87. Martha needs __?__.

15. In going to his grandfather's farm, Leon flew 425 miles on a plane. Then he rode 37 miles on a bus and 9 miles more in his grandfather's truck.

In all, he traveled __?__ miles.

Be your own teacher

You have not yet been taught how to solve these problems. Good thinkers, however, will be able to solve many of them. See how many you can solve.

You may need to draw pictures to help you find the answers.

1. George went shopping for his mother. He bought $1\frac{1}{2}$ pounds of cheese at 64 cents a pound. How much did the cheese cost?

2. Which is larger, $\frac{2}{3}$ or $\frac{3}{4}$? Draw a picture.

3. A refreshment committee planned to serve $\frac{1}{4}$ of a pie to each person who came to a party. The committee had 8 pies. How many persons could be served?

4. The cost of a picnic was $2.10. There were 15 pupils to share the cost. How much should each pupil pay?

Hint: Would 10 cents apiece be enough? Would 20 cents apiece be too much?

5. At $2.40 a gallon, how much would $1\frac{1}{2}$ quarts of ice cream cost?

6. At a school luncheon each pupil was served $\frac{1}{2}$ of a grapefruit. Thirty-two pupils were there.

Grapefruit were selling at 2 for 25 cents. How much did the grapefruit for the luncheon cost?

7. One day Mary got 84 eggs from her chickens. Eggs were selling for 60 cents a dozen. Can you tell how much money she should have been paid for the eggs?

8. Jane had difficulty with the division $21\overline{)86}$. She asked Alice for help.

Alice said, "We haven't learned how to divide by two-place numbers yet, but I think I can figure it out. I can guess and check." Can you?

9. Pat wants to buy a new plastic hose so that he can water his garden.

How much will he have to pay for a 50-foot length of hose if the price is 5 feet for $1.39?

10. Tony paid $5.00 for a 100-foot roll of Wild West Cowboy Rope. Jean wants to buy 25 feet of the rope.

How much should Tony charge for 25 feet of rope? He doesn't want to gain or lose anything by the sale.

To the Teacher: See Note 1 on page 310.

Right or wrong?

Tell why you answer "right" or "wrong" to each of these statements:

1. You can cut more 2-inch pieces than 3-inch pieces from a yard of string.

2. Your weight is closer to 1,000 ounces than to 100 ounces.

3. An hour spent in playing games is shorter than an hour spent in the dentist's chair.

4. The sum of 4 numbers is always larger than the sum of 3 numbers.

5. $\frac{1}{4}$ of a pie is more than $\frac{1}{3}$ of it.

6. 8×398 is a little more than 3200.

7. $60.00 minus $39.75 is a little more than $20.00.

8. April, June, September, and November are the only months that have 30 days.

9. $\frac{1}{5}$ of $994 is close to $200.

10. There are more feet than inches in the length of your classroom.

11. 300,030 is read "three hundred thousand, thirty."

12. The year 1960 will be a leap year.

13. From 11:45 A.M. to 1:15 P.M. is 90 minutes.

14. $7 \times 9 = 63$; $7 \times 90 = 630$; and $7 \times 900 = 6,300$.

15. $\frac{1}{6}$ of 4,196 is almost 700.

16. To change any number of dollars to dimes, divide by 10.

17. 1 mile is 5,280 feet or 1,760 yards.

18. Nine times 2 is a two-place number, so nine times 3 is a three-place number.

19. The sum of $48 + 12$ is as many as the sum of $58 + 2$.

20. The answer to $50 - 12$ is the same as the answer to $40 - 2$.

21. 3 ones and 4 tens are 34.

22. Adding 10 to a number and subtracting 3 is the same as adding 7.

23. Subtracting 10 from a number and adding 3 is the same as subtracting 7.

24. Multiplying a number by 8 and dividing by 2 is the same as multiplying by 4.

UNIT

32

*Multiplying by numbers
ending in zeros
A 2-place number times
a 3-place number*

Multiplying by 100 and 1,000

1. 2 times 100 equals 200, so 100 times 2 equals __?__ .

2. 15 times 100 equals 1500, so 100 times 15 equals __?__ .

3. Tell these answers:

100 twos	100×2
100 eights	100×8
100 twelves	100×12
100 twenty-fives	100×25

4. How are all the answers in Ex. 3 alike?

To find 100 times a number, put __?__ zeros after the number.

5. Tell these answers:

1,000 threes	$1,000 \times 3$
1,000 sevens	$1,000 \times 7$
1,000 fifteens	$1,000 \times 15$
1,000 thirty-twos	$1,000 \times 32$

6. How are all the answers in Ex. 5 alike?

To find 1,000 times a number, put __?__ zeros after the number.

7. Multiply each of these by 100; by 1,000:

5	10	14	18	20
25	31	40	54	49

8. Jane wants to find 200×15. She knows that $2 \times 15 = 30$. What should she do next?

9. Make a rule for multiplying a number by 200; by 500; by 300.

Multiply the numbers in Ex. 7 by 200; by 500.

10. Make a rule for multiplying a number by 3,000; by 2,000.

Multiply the numbers in Ex. 7 by 2,000; by 3,000.

11. To find 30×36, Jane first found $3 \times 36 = 108$. Then she found $10 \times 108 = $ __?__ .

She wrote the multiplication this way: ➤
In her work where is the 3×36? the 10×108?

$$\begin{array}{r} 36 \\ \times\ 30 \\ \hline 1080 \end{array}$$

12. To find 200×46, Jane wrote the multiplication this way: ⟶
Where is the 2×46? the 100×92?

$$\begin{array}{r} 46 \\ \times\ 200 \\ \hline 9200 \end{array}$$

13. If Bob learns how to spell 12 words every day in April, how many words will he learn to spell during the month?

14. There are 300 pupils in the Franklin School. How many pencils are needed to give each pupil 8 pencils during the school year?

15. Twelve 2-dollar bills are worth __?__ cents.

Multiplying large numbers

Explain these multiplications. Then copy them without the answers and multiply. See if your work is correct.

	a	b	c	d	e
1.	28	$.54	25	18	75
	× 30	× 40	× 200	× 400	× 3,000
	840	$21.60	5000	7200	225,000

Copy and multiply. Check by going over your work.

2.	74	$.25	$.87	28	46
	30	50	400	900	3000

3.	65	$.45	$.75	76	73
	20	60	300	400	4000

4.	24	$.72	$.89	95	85
	50	80	200	800	5000

5. Don and Fred want to set out 12 rows of cabbage plants. There are to be 125 plants in each row. They need to find out how many cabbage plants to buy.

▶ Don thought:
$$10 \times 125 \text{ plants} = 1250 \text{ plants}$$
$$2 \times 125 \text{ plants} = \underline{+ 250 \text{ plants}}$$
$$\text{So } 12 \times 125 \text{ plants} = 1500 \text{ plants}$$

▶ Fred thought:
$$2 \times 125 \text{ plants} = 250 \text{ plants}$$
$$10 \times 125 \text{ plants} = \underline{+ 1250 \text{ plants}}$$
$$\text{So } 12 \times 125 \text{ plants} = 1500 \text{ plants}$$

▶ Miss Allison said most people would find 12×125 in the way shown in this box:—————————➤
Explain her written work. How is it like Fred's way? How does it differ from Fred's way?

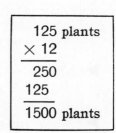

125 plants
× 12
250
125
1500 plants

6. How would Fred do these multiplications? How would Miss Allison? 12×124 15×345 23×460

Practice in multiplying

Study these multiplications. Copy them without the work.
Do them yourself. Compare your work with the work in the book.

1.	2.	3.	4.
187	309	$2.29	$4.50
16	74	26	53
1122	1236	1374	1350
187	2163	458	2250
2992	22,866	$59.54	$238.50

Multiply, and check by doing each example again:

	a	b	c	d	e
5.	708	459	908	678	$5.90
	29	68	45	73	98
6.	790	809	567	675	$7.56
	78	39	89	98	89
7.	348	846	657	589	$4.78
	79	69	98	76	89

Just for fun

▶ You can be a magician if you practice on this multiplication trick. Be sure you know why the trick works.

You say: Somebody give me a 2-place number — any 2-place number. In half a minute I'll tell you what 99 times the number equals.
A boy or girl in the audience calls out: 45
You say: O.K. 45. (You think: $100 \times 45 = 4500$; $4500 - 40 = 4460$; $4460 - 5 = 4455$.)
You say: 99×45 equals 4455. Who wants to check me? (When they do the multiplication in the box to check you, they will find you are right.)

$$\begin{array}{r} 45 \\ \times\ 99 \end{array}$$

▶ Multiply these numbers by 99 until you are a perfect magician:

34   87   92   96   65   43   83   18   56   27

▶ Make up a trick for multiplying any 3-place number by 99.

More practice in multiplying

Ted said that he could do the multiplications in Exs. 1–3 in his head. Can you? Be sure each answer is sensible.

	a	b	c	d	e	f
1.	24	62	71	$.25	$.50	$.86
	3	3	4	4	3	3
2.	325	400	504	$4.03	$2.40	$4.50
	3	6	7	8	5	8
3.	69	59	78	$.78	$1.65	$2.25
	4	8	6	6	5	8

4. To find 7×197 Ted thought, "$7 \times 200 = 1400$; $7 \times 3 = 21$; so $7 \times 197 = 1400 - 21 =$ _?_." Explain.

5. Use Ted's method to do these multiplications:

198	297	499	$6.03	$7.99	$8.03
6	7	8	8	4	9

Copy and multiply:

	a	b	c	d	e	f
6.	34	12	45	48	64	25
	200	300	700	500	300	400
7.	723	846	789	$9.68	$8.96	$9.95
	91	82	62	95	45	19
8.	199	199	199	$1.99	$1.99	$199
	2	20	200	2	20	20
9.	167	428	932	$4.65	$3.68	$4.79
	89	56	87	74	79	39
10.	463	29	245	$1.75	$2.83	$.74
	60	600	800	90	70	90

Buying Savings Stamps

1. Roy has four 10-cent U.S. Savings Stamps in his album.

He has 8 more stamps he wants to paste in. In all, he has __?__ stamps. They are worth __?__.

2. Jean saves 25-cent stamps. She has 14 stamps in her album. They are worth __?__.

3. How many 25-cent stamps can you buy for $1.00? for $5.00?

4. How much will Roy save in a year if he buys a 10-cent stamp every week? if he buys a 25-cent stamp every week?

5. Five 25-cent stamps and eight 10-cent stamps are worth __?__.

Multiply, and check by doing each example again:

	a	b	c	d	e	f
6.	86 79	70 67	49 81	$.40 68	$.69 13	$.78 67
7.	56 900	84 70	89 60	$.42 80	$.39 60	$.79 70
8.	874 91	923 86	618 17	$4.25 67	$6.43 98	$9.86 79
9.	690 76	807 43	408 79	$8.07 86	$9.09 98	$6.50 87

SPELLING RECORD

	Bob	Joe	Ted	Ann	Jean
Mon.	18	18	16	17	15
Tues.	16	19	15	20	a
Wed.	19	20	17	a	a
Thurs.	20	18	20	13	13
Fri.	17	20	12	18	17
Total	90	?	?	?	?
Average	18	?	?	?	?

Finding averages

Miss Gardner's class kept a spelling record during the first week in March. Part of the record is shown above.

1. Miss Allison gave the class 20 words each day. On Monday, Bob spelled 18 words correctly. How many did he spell correctly on each of the other days of the week?

2. How many words did Bob spell correctly during the 5 days?

He divided the 90 by 5 and got 18 as the *average* number of words he spelled correctly each day. This means he is just as good a speller as a pupil who spelled 18 words correctly each day.

To find the average of several numbers, add them and divide the sum by the number of numbers.

3. How many words did each of the other children spell correctly during the 5 days?

4. What was the average number of words a day each of the other children spelled correctly?

Ann was absent on __?__, so to find her average score you divide the total score by __?__.

How will you find Jean's average score?

5. Which of the children was the best speller? the poorest?

227

Practice in finding averages

In each of the following examples estimate the average. Then work the example to see how nearly right you were.

In the first example could the average be as large as 25? as small as 16? Do you think it lies somewhere between 15 and 25? Is it about 21?

a	b	c
1. 25, 16, 22	15, 30, 27, 41, 37	100, 113, 98, 125
2. 31, 26, 19, 24	32, 26, 17, 29	5, 12, 14, 8, 16
3. 9, 8, 5, 6, 7	4, 5, 7, 8, 3, 6, 2	10, 17, 23, 27, 35, 14
4. 83, 160, 72	75, 64, 81, 94, 86	90, 89, 95, 84, 97

5. Miss Allison's pupils found out the prices of foods in their neighborhood.

Five pupils brought in these prices of a pound of butter: 64¢, 70¢, 68¢, 72¢, and 61¢. The average price was __?__ ¢ a pound.

6. Four pupils reported the price of bacon, by the pound, to be 56¢, 60¢, 58¢, and 66¢. The average price was __?__ ¢ a pound.

7. Six pupils found that the price of a loaf of bread was 22¢, 17¢, 9¢, 16¢, 20¢, and 12¢. The average price was __?__ ¢ a loaf.

8. Jane said, "The 22-cent bread is __?__ ¢ *above average* in price and the 9-cent bread is __?__ ¢ *below average.*"

9. Can you think of any reasons why they found so many different prices of a loaf of bread?

When they investigated, they found the 22-cent loaves were made from special flour and the 9-cent loaves were day-old bread.

10. Roy is 9 years old. His mother said, "Roy is very tall for his age."

Make a statement about Roy's height, using the word "average."

11. Find the average height of a group of 4 boys whose heights are 50 in., 52 in., 54 in., and 48 in.

12. How many boys in Ex. 11 are taller than the average height of the group? shorter than the average height?

Practice in division

Tell the answers without using your pencil:

	a	b	c	d	e
1.	$\frac{1}{2}$ of 6	$\frac{1}{2}$ of 24	$\frac{1}{2}$ of 246	$\frac{1}{2}$ of 178	$\frac{1}{4}$ of 176
2.	$\frac{1}{3}$ of 18	$\frac{1}{3}$ of 96	$\frac{1}{3}$ of 396	$\frac{1}{4}$ of 376	$\frac{1}{5}$ of 320
3.	$\frac{1}{4}$ of 12	$\frac{1}{4}$ of 48	$\frac{1}{4}$ of 992	$\frac{1}{5}$ of 475	$\frac{1}{9}$ of 72
4.	$\frac{1}{5}$ of 45	$\frac{1}{5}$ of 105	$\frac{1}{2}$ of 404	$\frac{1}{3}$ of 258	$\frac{1}{5}$ of 1505
5.	$\frac{1}{6}$ of 48	$\frac{1}{6}$ of 30	$\frac{1}{3}$ of 906	$\frac{1}{6}$ of 444	$\frac{1}{8}$ of 656
6.	$\frac{1}{7}$ of 63	$\frac{1}{7}$ of 49	$\frac{1}{4}$ of 804	$\frac{1}{7}$ of 504	$\frac{1}{9}$ of 639
7.	$\frac{1}{8}$ of 64	$\frac{1}{8}$ of 72	$\frac{1}{4}$ of 160	$\frac{1}{8}$ of 504	$\frac{1}{9}$ of 504

8. $\frac{1}{6}$ of any number between 60 and 600 is between __?__ and __?__. It is a __?__-figure number.

10. $\frac{1}{8}$ of any number between 80 and 800 is between __?__ and __?__. It is a __?__-figure number.

9. Which of these divisions have 2-figure answers?

6)68   7)68   5)68   8)68   9)68

11. Which of these divisions have 2-figure answers?

5)54   5)504   4)54   7)54   3)54

Copy, divide, and check:

	a	b	c	d	e
12.	3)48	2)37	4)57	5)68	3)76
13.	9)477	8)504	7)666	6)475	4)284
14.	3)290	7)497	8)649	9)819	6)486
15.	6)300	6)304	7)635	8)726	9)634
16.	4)$9.72	8)$15.76	9)$14.31	7)$35.35	6)$49.02
17.	3)$19.47	4)$39.08	9)$74.70	6)$24.48	7)$63.49

Roman numerals to XII

1. The numbers on Ruth's clock are called *Roman numerals.* The clock is set at __?__ o'clock.

On clock faces *four* is written IIII. But the more common way of showing *four* in Roman numerals is IV.

2. Look at the table at the bottom of the page. What does the Roman numeral I mean? V? X? VI? VII? XI? XII?

3. Make a toy clock with Roman numerals on it. Show: 1 o'clock, 2 o'clock, and so on up to 12 o'clock.

4. Show: 1:30, 2:30, and so on up to 6:30.

5. Show: 7:15, 8:15, and so on up to 12:15.

6. Show: 1:45, 2:45, and so on up to 6:45.

7. Show: 4:30; 4:35; 4:40; 4:45; 4:50; 4:55; 5:00.

8. Where have you seen Roman numerals besides on a clock face?

9. John said, "I know a Roman numeral number trick. I can show that half of 9 is 4." This is how he did it: →

Use John's trick to show that one half of 11 is 6; that one half of 12 is 7.

IX

1	2	3	4	5	6	7	8	9	10	11	12
I	II	III	IV	V	VI	VII	VIII	IX	X	XI	XII

Roman numerals to XXX

The boys at Camp Deerfield decided that the bunks on the big sleeping porch should be numbered.

Pete offered to make Roman numerals from strips of wood about 2½ inches long. Here are the numbers he made for the 30 bunks. Read them.

I	II	III	IV	V	VI	VII	VIII	IX	X
XI	XII	XIII	XIV	XV	XVI	XVII	XVIII	XIX	XX
XXI	XXII	XXIII	XXIV	XXV	XXVI	XXVII	XXVIII	XXIX	XXX

1. In the numbers above find 4; 6; 8; 9; 12; 15; 19; 23; 27; 29.

2. X means ⸛?⸛; VI means ⸛?⸛; so XVI means ⸛?⸛.

3. X means ⸛?⸛; IX means ⸛?⸛; so XIX means ⸛?⸛.

4. XX means ⸛?⸛; IV means ⸛?⸛; so XXIV means ⸛?⸛.

5. XX means ⸛?⸛; X means ⸛?⸛; so XXX means ⸛?⸛.

6. XX means ⸛?⸛; VII means ⸛?⸛; so XXVII means ⸛?⸛.

7. Without looking at Pete's numbers above try to tell how many strips of wood he needed to make the Roman numeral for 6; for 9; 11; 17; 24; 29.

8. Peter says he has a Roman numeral trick. He can take 1 from 4 and leave 5. Can you show how he does it?

Can you take 1 from 9 and make 10?

9. Maybe you can make up other Roman numeral tricks.

10. Make a list of all the places where you have seen Roman numerals used.

11. Try to find out how some of the American Indians wrote their numbers.

12. Would you like to read a book about ways people have used to count and write numbers?

If so, you will enjoy reading *The Wonderful Wonders of One-Two-Three* by David Eugene Smith. It may be in your school library.

Who can tell the answers?

Tell the missing numbers in Exs. 1–6.

	a	b	c	d	e	f	g	h	i	j
1.	10	14	18	22	26	30	?	?	?	46
2.	4	11	18	25	32	?	?	?	?	67
3.	39	139	239	339	?	?	?	?	?	939
4.	$\frac{1}{2}$	1	$1\frac{1}{2}$	2	$2\frac{1}{2}$	3	$3\frac{1}{2}$	?	?	5
5.	$\frac{1}{4}$	$\frac{1}{2}$	$\frac{3}{4}$	1	$1\frac{1}{4}$	?	?	?	?	$2\frac{1}{2}$
6.	$\frac{1}{3}$	$\frac{2}{3}$	1	$1\frac{1}{3}$	?	?	?	?	?	$3\frac{1}{3}$

7. Add 6 to each of the numbers below; add 7; 8; 9.

    29   56   74   91   38   83   47   65

8. Divide each of these numbers by 6:

    44   40   51   58   33   29   69   30

9. Divide each of these numbers by 7:

    37   60   65   54   47   30   40   30

10. Divide each of these numbers by 8:

    67   50   75   60   42   39   70   59

11. Divide each of these numbers by 9:

    43   67   78   58   86   32   71   60

12. Find an item in the blue block to match each item in the white block:

$\frac{1}{2}$ pound 3 gallons a mile $\frac{1}{4}$ ton 5 minutes	5280 feet 8 ounces 300 seconds 12 quarts 500 pounds

13. Make up some other matching games about measures.

232

Some oral practice

1. Multiply each of these numbers by 8 and add 7:

4   7   0   9   6   3   5   8   2

2. Multiply each of the numbers in Ex. 1 by 9 and add 8.

3. Multiply each of the numbers in Ex. 1 by 7 and add 6..

4. Tell 10 numbers that can be divided by 6 without a remainder. Begin with 60 and go on up.

5. The average of 30¢, 40¢, and 20¢ is _?_ ¢.

6. Count by 9's to 91, beginning with 1.

7. Multiply each of these numbers by 10; by 40; by 100:

15   25   40   50   80   100

8. $\frac{1}{4}$ of a pound is _?_ ounces.
$\frac{1}{4}$ of a yard is _?_ inches.
$\frac{1}{4}$ of an hour is _?_ minutes.
$\frac{1}{4}$ of a dollar is _?_ cents.

Can you find anything wrong with these divisions?

9. 7)31 → 4 r3   7)32 → 4 r4   7)33 → 4 r5

10. 7)34 → 4 r6   7)35 → 4 r7   7)36 → 4 r8

11. Sam did these divisions:

2)1000 → 500   4)1000 → 250   8)1000 → 125

If the 1000 stays the same and the number he divides it by gets larger, then the answer gets _?_ .

12. What multiplication is missing from this table?

$$10 \times 9 = 90$$
$$20 \times 9 = 180$$
$$40 \times 9 = 360$$

13. How many 9's does it take to make 369? 360? 351?

14. At 36 cents a yard, how much should you pay for a 1-inch piece of ribbon? a 10-inch piece?

15. Is 46×1200 more than 12×4500? How can you tell?

16. Does $2724 \div 3$ equal 98, or 908, or 980?

17. Do you know an easy way to find 25×36?

18. If you write nine 60's in a column and add, the sum is _?_ .

19. Turn to page 11. Think of the examples as multiplications. Say the answers.

20. Tell the answers to the division test on page 168.

What is missing in the problem?

1. Martha wants to find how much new curtains for her room will cost.

She already knows the muslin costs 49¢ a yard. What else must she know?

2. Bob wants to know how much it will cost to paint the walls of his room.

He knows how many quarts of paint he will need. What else must he know?

3. Sam wants to know how much it will cost to put new electric cord on some lamps.

He knows the price of the cord is 3 feet for 10¢. What else must he know?

4. Hal is going to put a knocker on his bedroom door. The knocker is to be an equal distance from each side of the door.

What must he know in order to place the knocker correctly?

5. Janet wants to know how much material to buy for new cushion covers. She knows how many cushions she wants to cover. What else must she know?

6. Catherine plans to put red ball fringe around the top of some wastebaskets. She knows how much fringe she needs for one basket and how much the fringe costs per yard.

To find the cost of the fringe for all the baskets, what else must she know?

7. You are helping to fix up your bedroom. Exactly what do you need to know to answer this question: Will it be cheaper to buy ready-made curtains or to make them?

8. The pupils in Miss Fry's class know how many sheets of notebook paper they have.

To find out how many science notebooks they can make out of the paper, what else must they know?

9. Susan wants to know how many boxes of cookies to buy for a party. She knows how many cookies she wants.

What else must Susan know in order to buy enough cookies?

234

Practice with fractions

1. Using your ruler, draw a line 1 inch long. Now draw lines of these lengths: $\frac{1}{2}$ in.; $\frac{1}{4}$ in.; $\frac{1}{8}$ in.; $\frac{3}{4}$ in.; $\frac{3}{8}$ in.; $\frac{7}{8}$ in.; $\frac{5}{8}$ in.

2. Which is longer, $\frac{3}{8}$ in. or $\frac{1}{4}$ in.? $\frac{3}{8}$ in. or $\frac{3}{4}$ in.? $\frac{5}{8}$ in. or $\frac{1}{2}$ in.? $\frac{5}{8}$ in. or $\frac{3}{4}$ in.?

3. How many inches are there in $\frac{1}{2}$ yd.? in $\frac{1}{4}$ yd.? Which is longer, $\frac{1}{2}$ yd. or $\frac{1}{4}$ yd.?

4. How many ounces are there in $\frac{1}{8}$ lb.? in $\frac{1}{4}$ lb.? Which is more, $\frac{1}{8}$ lb. or $\frac{1}{4}$ lb.?

5. How many ounces are there in $\frac{1}{4}$ lb.? in $\frac{1}{2}$ lb.? Which is more, $\frac{1}{2}$ lb. or $\frac{1}{4}$ lb.?

6. How many inches are there in $\frac{1}{2}$ ft.? in $\frac{1}{3}$ ft.? Which is longer, $\frac{1}{2}$ ft. or $\frac{1}{3}$ ft.?

7. How much longer than 1 in. is this line?

1 in. $\frac{7}{8}$ in.

8. Draw a line $\frac{5}{8}$ in. long; $1\frac{5}{8}$ in. long; $2\frac{5}{8}$ in. long; $3\frac{5}{8}$ in. long; $4\frac{5}{8}$ in. long.

9. Draw a line $\frac{3}{4}$ in. long; $1\frac{3}{4}$ in. long; $2\frac{1}{2}$ in. long.

10. How many minutes are there in $\frac{1}{2}$ hr.? in $\frac{1}{4}$ hr.? Which is longer, $\frac{1}{2}$ hr. or $\frac{1}{4}$ hr.?

11. How many cents are there in $\frac{1}{2}$ dollar? in $\frac{1}{4}$ dollar? Which is more, $\frac{1}{2}$ dollar or $\frac{1}{4}$ dollar?

12. How many servings of $\frac{1}{2}$ a cantaloupe can you make from 2 cantaloupes? from 3 cantaloupes? 4? 5? 6?

Your ruler will help you tell the missing numbers below:

	a	b	c	d
13.	$1 = \frac{?}{4}$	$2 = \frac{?}{4}$	$\frac{1}{2} = \frac{?}{4}$	$\frac{4}{8} = \frac{?}{2}$
14.	$1 = \frac{?}{2}$	$2 = \frac{?}{2}$	$\frac{1}{2} = \frac{?}{8}$	$\frac{2}{8} = \frac{?}{4}$
15.	$1 = \frac{?}{8}$	$2 = \frac{?}{8}$	$\frac{1}{4} = \frac{?}{8}$	$\frac{3}{4} = \frac{?}{8}$
16.	$1\frac{1}{4} = \frac{?}{4}$	$2\frac{1}{8} = \frac{?}{8}$	$2\frac{1}{2} = \frac{?}{2}$	$3\frac{1}{2} = \frac{?}{2}$
17.	$1\frac{1}{2} = \frac{?}{2}$	$2\frac{1}{4} = \frac{?}{4}$	$2\frac{3}{4} = \frac{?}{4}$	$3\frac{1}{4} = \frac{?}{4}$

Yes or no?

1. Is a distance of 5000 ft. more than a mile?

2. Would $2\frac{1}{8}$ yd. of ribbon cost more than $2\frac{1}{2}$ yd. of the same kind of ribbon?

3. Would 4 whole pears be enough to fill a can that holds 8 half pears?

4. If 5 boys share a cantaloupe equally, is each boy's share more than $\frac{1}{4}$ of a cantaloupe?

5. Would your pencil weigh less than a pound?

6. Does your family eat breakfast in the P.M.?

7. Is 9 quarters more than 2 dollars?

8. Could a person have a birthday on September 31?

9. Are $2\frac{1}{2}$ cakes more than $\frac{5}{2}$ cake?

10. Does $2\frac{1}{4}$ dozen equal $12 + 12 + 3$?

11. Does 5×38 equal 5×40 minus 5×2?

12. Does 5×42 equal 5×40 plus 5×2?

13. Does $1\frac{1}{8}$ lb. $= 16$ oz. $+ 2$ oz.?

14. Is 12×15 half as many as 12×30?

15. When ice cream sells for $2 a gallon, would a quart cost $1?

16. Is $\frac{1}{4}$ of a yard shorter than $\frac{1}{3}$ of a yard?

17. Does $1\frac{1}{2}$ tons equal 2000 lb. $+ 1000$ lb.?

18. Would you measure your weight in ounces?

19. Could anyone have only one birthday in four years?

20. Does 8 in. $= \frac{1}{4}$ yd.?

21. Is 7 in. more than $\frac{1}{2}$ ft.?

22. Is 16 in. more than $\frac{1}{2}$ yd.?

23. Is 72¢ more than 3 quarters?

24. Is the missing number $3\frac{1}{2}$?

| 2 | $2\frac{1}{2}$ | 3 | ? | 4 |

25. Does 1 ft. 8 in. $= 20$ in.?

26. Does 1 lb. 5 oz. $= 20$ oz.?

27. If you know that $39 \times 6 = 234$, do you know that $234 \div 6 = 39$?

28. If the 8 o'clock bus arrives at 7:52, is it late?

a
perfect
score

1. Bert wants to buy a bicycle basket, a headlight, and a bicycle seat. Look at the poster. Then find how much money he will need.

2. Find the cost of 3 gallons of paint at $3.98 a gallon.

3. Find the cost of 6 pairs of socks at 3 pairs for $.79.

SALE
BICYCLE SUPPLIES
——o——

Baskets $ 1.19
Headlights   .77
Seats   .98
Pedals (pair)   .79

4. Billy wrote the answers to 100 addition facts in 4 minutes. He wrote the answers at the rate of __?__ a minute.

5. John wants to buy a football. It costs $1.77. He has $.89. How much more does he need?

6. If 6 boys bought a tennis net for $6.96 and shared the cost equally, each boy paid __?__.

7. How many dollar bills can you get for 20 quarters?

8. How much will you have left out of 5 dollars if you spend $2.37?

9. Last year Bob caught 17 fish. This year he caught 35. Show that he caught over twice as many this year as he caught last year.

10. Find the total cost of 2 loaves of bread at 19¢ a loaf and a pound of butter at 68¢ a pound.

———————

Write your score on your Problem Test Record.

Put on your thinking cap

▶ Oral review

1. How many 3-cent stamps can you buy for 30¢?

2. The average of 6, 11, and 16 is __?__.

3. How many days will there be in the month of February in 1958?

4. What is the largest 2-place number that can be divided by 5 without any remainder?

5. Multiply each of these numbers by 10; by 100:

8   15   26   40   57   99

6. Bill needs 12 screws to fix his wagon. The screws sell at 3 for a cent. How much will 12 cost?

7. Would you estimate the sum of 39 and 62 to be close to 100?

8. Read these numbers in order, from smallest to largest:

XXIV   XVI   IX   XIX

9. Tell the missing numbers:

$1\frac{1}{4}$ $1\frac{1}{2}$ $1\frac{3}{4}$ __?__ $2\frac{1}{4}$ __?__

10. $100{,}000 - 10{,}000 = $ __?__

11. Which is larger: $\frac{1}{2}$ of 6 or 6 halves?

12. Is $468 - 230$ about 150, 240, or 270?

13. There are 225 pages in Tom's book. He has read 110 pages. Has he read about $\frac{1}{2}$, $\frac{1}{3}$, or $\frac{1}{4}$ of the book?

14. What is the helping fact in each of these divisions?

$32 \div 7$	$32 \div 8$	$32 \div 9$
$32 \div 5$	$32 \div 6$	$32 \div 4$
$24 \div 7$	$34 \div 8$	$24 \div 9$

15. Use the Hint System to estimate these answers:

$324 \div 7$ $324 \div 8$ $324 \div 9$

16. Multiply each of these numbers by 9 and add 7:

2   5   0   6   9   4   8   7   3

17. Multiply each of the numbers in Ex. 16 by 8 and add 7.

18. Multiply each of the numbers in Ex. 16 by 7 and add 6.

19. In dividing by 7, what are the helping facts?

20. Divide each of these numbers by 7; by 8; by 9:

37   58   69   143   215   735

238

Put on your thinking cap

▶ **Written review**

1. Write in figures:
twenty-four thousand, six.

2. What is the cost of ½ a gallon of paint at $3.40 a gallon, and two brushes at $.69 each?

3. A camp brands its boats, rafts, and so on, with a design made from 9 tin strips. It has 500 strips. It can brand __?__ articles.

4. Find the difference between 4,404 and 4,044.

5. Donald has collected 189 stamps. Jerry has 203. How many more stamps has Jerry than Donald?

6. Joe said that if he saved ten cents a day for a year he would save nearly 40 dollars. Check to see if he is right.

7. Joe said his father is paid at his factory every two weeks. Can you figure out how many paydays Joe's father has in a year?

8. Multiply, and check by going over your work:

a	b	c	d	e
809	$.79	$8.76	24	78
89	68	67	200	3000

9. Divide and check:

7)5000   8)2448   6)3784   8)$76.96   7)$56.35

10. Subtract and check:

$100	$1000	$50.00	8000	5000
27	268	27.86	2457	48

11. Add and check:

456	867	970	$8.72	$9.86
687	98	8	6.97	8.79
798	76	47	.98	.89
869	787	897	.07	.68
496	869	86	7.98	6.96

239

Indian designs

Miss Lester's class is studying about Indians. The boys are painting Indian designs on a teepee they made.

1. How many *rectangles* can you find on the teepee? How many *circles? squares? triangles?*

2. Have you learned the names of these figures?

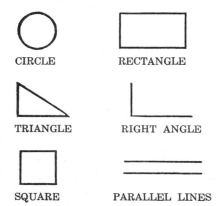

CIRCLE   RECTANGLE

TRIANGLE   RIGHT ANGLE

SQUARE   PARALLEL LINES

3. How many sides has a triangle? a rectangle? a square?

4. How many *right angles* are there in a rectangle? Is a right angle a square corner?

5. Do you see the two pairs of *parallel lines* in the rectangle?

6. A square is a rectangle whose sides are equal. How many right angles are there in a square?

Figures such as those shown in Ex. 2 are called *geometric figures.*

7. Ben says he has seen geometric figures in bridges, in buildings, and in furniture. Have you?

8. What kinds of geometric figures do you see in your classroom?

240

9. Harry says that this star is made of two triangles with equal sides. Do you think he is right?

10. What geometric figures do you see in this drawing of an end of a building? (Half of a circle is called a *semicircle*.)

11. Jane cut a square into two equal parts as shown. What shape was each of the parts?

12. Bob cut a square into two equal parts as shown. What shape was each of the parts?

13. Can you cut a rectangle into two equal rectangles? Prove they are equal by putting one on top of the other.

14. Can you cut a rectangle into two triangles? Place one triangle on the other. Are they equal?

15. Draw a rectangle that is 4 inches long and 3 inches wide.

16. Ann used geometric figures in drawing this dog. Can you draw a boy or an animal, using nothing but geometric figures?

17. Carl made these lists of geometric figures. Can you think of any things to add to the lists?

Circles	Triangles	Rectangles
1. plate	1. arrow point	1. sheet
2. coin	2. top part of kite	2. pillow slip
3. clock face	3. bottom part of kite	3. blanket
		4. birthday card

Squares	Parallel lines
1. napkin	1. railroad tracks
2. handkerchief	

A practice page

Tell in as many ways as you can what these measures mean.
For example, 1 qt. = 2 pt., 1 qt. = 4 cups, 1 qt. = $\frac{1}{4}$ gal.

1. 1 qt.   1 ft.   1 gal.   1 yd.   1 min. $\frac{1}{3}$ yd.   1 yr.

Tell the missing numbers:

	a	b	c
2.	1 lb. = __?__ oz.	$\frac{1}{2}$ ft. = __?__ in.	1 da. = __?__ hr.
3.	$\frac{1}{4}$ lb. = __?__ oz.	$\frac{1}{4}$ ft. = __?__ in.	1 mi. = __?__ ft.
4.	$\frac{1}{8}$ lb. = __?__ oz.	$\frac{1}{4}$ yd. = __?__ in.	1 wk. = __?__ da.
5.	$\frac{1}{2}$ lb. = __?__ oz.	$\frac{1}{2}$ yd. = __?__ in.	1 T. = __?__ lb.

Copy these numbers on the blackboard. Place a comma in each number. Then read it.

	a	b	c	d	e
6.	8763	26340	463278	6284	700562
7.	5008	53800	543824	32075	909080

8. Which is the largest number in Exs. 6 and 7? the smallest?

9. Tell what each zero in the numbers in Ex. 7 means. Tell what each 8 means; each 5.

Copy, divide, and check:

	a	b	c	d
10.	190 ÷ 9	$5.18 ÷ 7	$2.70 ÷ 9	$49.35 ÷ 7
11.	274 ÷ 6	$2.45 ÷ 7	$4.08 ÷ 8	$58.50 ÷ 9
12.	168 ÷ 8	$4.56 ÷ 8	$1.14 ÷ 6	$67.36 ÷ 8

Copy and multiply:

13. 32 and 76	506 and 14	609 and 7	72 and 30
14. 95 and 41	760 and 8	775 and 28	45 and 100

Problem study

If you have trouble with Problem 1 in Column A, do Problem 1 in Column B. Then go back and try Problem 1 in Column A again, and so on.

A

1. Edith wants a radio that costs $28.98. Her father has promised her that every time she earns some money he will give her an equal amount toward the price of the radio.

How much will Edith have to earn before she can buy the radio? Don't forget her father's promise.

2. Edith (Ex. 1) earned $.75. She also earned $2 for finding a lost dog. After her father keeps his promise, how much will she have?

3. The Emerson School wants to set up 6 swings. It can get a set of 3 ready-built swings for $36.75. How much would 6 ready-built swings cost?

All the materials to make 6 swings would cost $62.77. How much can the school save by making the swings?

4. The materials for a birdhouse cost $.75. The cement for a birdbath costs $1.05. If three boys share the total cost equally, how much should each boy pay?

B

1. (*a*) Dick earned 25¢. His father gave him 25¢. How much did he have then? What part of the 50¢ did Dick earn? What part did his father give him?

(*b*) Tom has $1.28. He earned $\frac{1}{2}$ of it. His father gave him $\frac{1}{2}$. How much did Tom earn? How much did his father give him?

2. Dick earned 10¢ and 35¢. In all, he earned __?__ ¢. After his father gives him an equal amount, how much money will Dick have?

3. (*a*) Eve wants to buy 6 hair bows. She can buy 2 bows ready to wear for 10¢. How much will 6 bows cost?

(*b*) Eve can get enough ribbon to make 6 bows for 15¢. How much can she save by making the bows herself instead of buying the ready-made ones?

4. Three boys bought a 10-cent bat and a 5-cent ball. In all, they spent __?__ ¢. If they share the cost equally, each boy will pay $\frac{1}{3}$ of 15¢, or __?__ ¢.

243

Review and practice

1. Polly needs 12 spools for 1 spool doll. For 10 dolls, she will need __?__ spools.

2. Susan knows how many yards of calico she needs for curtains for her room. What else must she know to find the cost of the curtains?

3. How much will 24 rulers cost at 5¢ each?

4. Mary needs 54 inches of ribbon. She is buying $1\frac{1}{2}$ yd. Will that be enough?

5. At the movie, Bill counted 24 rows of seats, with 18 seats in a row. How many persons could sit in the movie?

6. At $.79 a can, 3 cans of paint would cost about __?__.

7. Write the Roman numbers for these figures:

17   23   29   19   9

8. Write in figures: eleven thousand, one hundred six.

9. $990 +$ __?__ $= 1000$

10. $9,999 +$ __?__ $= 10,000$

11. $10 \times 100 =$ __?__

12. $10 \times 1000 =$ __?__

13. Joe walks 3 blocks in 5 minutes. At that rate it would take him __?__ minutes to walk 15 blocks.

14. $15 \times 12 = 10 \times 12$ plus $5 \times 12, =$ __?__

15. $9\overline{)963} = 9\overline{)900} + 9\overline{)63} =$ __?__

16. $5\overline{)2825} = 5\overline{)2500} + 5\overline{)300} + 5\overline{)25} =$ __?__

17. $12 \times 25 = 10 \times 25$ plus $2 \times$ __?__ $, =$ __?__

18. Does $28 \times 6 \div 6$ equal 28? Why?

19. $6\overline{)252} = 6\overline{)240} + 6\overline{)12} =$ __?__

20. $8\overline{)448} = 8\overline{)400} + 8\overline{)48} =$ __?__

21. Do you know some quick tricks for finding these answers mentally?

99×72 25×36
5×64 $83 \times 64 \times 0$

22. Does $875 + 69 - 69$ equal 875? Why?

Tell the missing numbers:

23. $4\frac{1}{2}$ 5   __?__   6   __?__   __?__

24. $5\frac{1}{4}$ $5\frac{1}{2}$ __?__   __?__ $6\frac{1}{4}$ __?__

25. 7 $6\frac{1}{2}$ __?__   __?__   5   __?__

244

Self-Help Test 9

1. Copy in columns, add, and check:
   $6.57 + $4.79 + $8 + $.75 + $2.43 + $6.75   (187)

2. 5,056 − 1,578 (112)   3. $92.65 − $67.53 (112)

Multiply. Check by going over your work.

4. 65   5. 157   6. $4.85   7. 65
   47 (130)   23 (223–224)   78 (223–224)   1000 (222)

8. 100×34 (222)   9. 20×75 (129)   10. 300×8 (222)

11. Find the average of 6, 8, 7, and 11.   (227–228)

12. Write the missing numbers: $3\frac{1}{4}$ $3\frac{1}{2}$ $3\frac{3}{4}$ _?_ _?_ $4\frac{1}{2}$.   (202)

13. Does 3618 ÷ 9 = 42, or 402, or 420?   (167)

14. Is $\frac{1}{7}$ of 506 more than 70 but less than 80?   (127)

Self-Help Test 10

Divide and check:

1. 8)67̄ (150)   2. 7)87̄ (127)   3. 8)776̄ (151)

4. 7)496̄ (135)   5. 8)640̄ (135)   6. 9)432̄ (163–164)

7. 6)$5.76̄ (133)   8. 9)$81.36̄ (167)   9. 8)$50.40̄ (166)

10. What numbers do these Roman numerals stand for?

XVI   XXIV   XIX   (231)

11. Draw a line $2\frac{5}{8}$ in. long. Use your ruler.   (235)

12. 296,500 is read _?_ thousand, _?_ hundred.   (208)

13. John bought a half-dozen batteries for $1.19. Would you estimate the cost of one battery to be about 10¢, 15¢, or 20¢?   (188)

14. At 3 for 5¢, how many California plums can you get for a quarter?   (198–199)

Now is the time to test yourself

Copy numbers correctly. Work carefully. Check your answers. Be sure each answer is sensible.

1. Which is larger, the fraction $\frac{1}{4}$ or the fraction $\frac{3}{8}$?————→

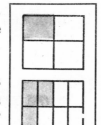

2. Dorothy knows she needs 5 buttons down the front of each blouse.

To find how many buttons to buy for the blouses her mother is making her, what else must she know?

3. Write the missing numbers:

$\frac{1}{3}$ $\frac{2}{3}$ 1 $1\frac{1}{3}$ _?_ _?_ _?_ _?_ 3

4. What numbers do the following stand for?

XXV   XIV   XVII   XIX

5. What is the average of 7, 8, 9, and 4?

6. Write the letter you see on the triangle; on the circle; on the line; on the square; on the rectangle. If you made no mistake, the letters will tell you so.

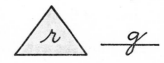

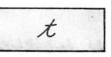

7. When both hands of a clock point to XII, what time is it?

8. Draw a line $4\frac{1}{4}$ inches long.

9. Find 100 times 83.

10. Multiply 689 by 78.

Just for fun

1. Can you take 1 away from 19 and have 20 left?

2. Can you make 6 out of 3 toothpicks? Don't bend or break the toothpicks.

3. Now make 9 out of 3 toothpicks.

4. Two fathers and two sons shared 3 apples equally. Each received a whole apple. Can you explain how they shared the apples?

5. Harry weighs 65 lb. standing on one foot. How much does he weigh standing on two feet?

Dividing money by money

1. Joe wants to buy a chain to tie his pet lamb to a stake. The chain costs 8¢ a foot. Joe has $2.00 to spend. He wonders how many feet of chain he will be able to get for $2.00.

Joe reasons this way:
- For 8 cents I can get 1 foot of chain.
- For 16 cents I will be able to buy __?__ feet.
- The number of feet I can get for 2 dollars, or 200 cents, is the number of times 8 cents is contained in 200 cents.
- I must divide __?__ by __?__ .
- How many times is 8 cents contained in 200 cents?
  (200 cents ÷ 8 cents = __?__ .)
- I can get __?__ feet of chain.

2. "Mary, will you get 2 dollars' worth of 3-cent stamps, please?"
"Yes, Mother, but how many 3-cent stamps can we get for $2?"
Can you tell?
- Mary knows that the number of stamps she can get is the same as the number of times __?__ cents is contained in 200 cents.
- Divide 200 by 3.
- Mary can get __?__ stamps and have __?__ cents left.

3. Make up a problem in which you need to divide 60¢ by 4¢; a problem in which you need to divide $1.25 by 5¢.

4. Make up a problem in which you need to divide 4 dollars by 8¢.

Tell what you think in doing these divisions. In the first example think: $1.60 = 160 cents; 160¢ ÷ 8¢ = __?__ .

	a	b	c	d	e
5.	8¢)$1.60	3¢)$2.10	8¢)$3.20	9¢)$5.40	4¢)$1.20
6.	4¢)$2.40	4¢)$3.24	8¢)$4.00	5¢)$1.50	8¢)$2.40
7.	5¢)$3.55	6¢)$4.80	6¢)$1.80	6¢)$2.40	9¢)$3.60
8.	5¢)$2.50	3¢)$1.50	7¢)$4.90	4¢)$2.84	8¢)$7.20
9.	4¢)$3.20	6¢)$1.20	9¢)$8.10	3¢)$1.89	8¢)$6.40

247

TOY SALE

PINWHEELS	6¢	BALLS 5¢
PLASTIC BOATS	8¢	BUBBLE PIPES 4¢
WHISTLES	2¢	PUZZLES 9¢
		JUMPING JACKS 7¢

Dividing money by money

1. How many of each kind of toy can Jane buy for $1.00 at the toy sale?

2. Jack has $1.50. He can buy __?__ puzzles; __?__ boats.

3. Bill has $1.25. Can he buy more jumping jacks or more balls for his money? Why?

4. Would you estimate that Teddy can get about 10, 20, or 30 puzzles for $2.00? Why?

5. If you know how many balls you can get for $1.00, do you know a quick trick for finding how many you can get for $2.00? for $3.00? for $5.00?

6. How many nickels can you get for $3.50?

7. Thelma saved 437 pennies in her penny bank. Using dollar sign and cents point, write the amount of money she saved.

8. Bill says he can get seventy-five 2-cent whistles for $1.50.

Do a division to prove that he is right.

Do a multiplication to prove that he is right.

9. If you had a 5-dollar bill changed into pennies, how many piles of 8 pennies could you make?

How many extra pennies would be left over?

248

Thinking about division

1. $\frac{1}{7}$ of 56 is __?__
   $\frac{1}{7}$ of 560 is __?__
   $\frac{1}{7}$ of 5600 is __?__

2. $\frac{1}{9}$ of 54 is __?__
   $\frac{1}{9}$ of 540 is __?__
   $\frac{1}{9}$ of 5400 is __?__

3. $\frac{1}{9}$ of 5400 is __?__
   $\frac{1}{9}$ of 5427 is __?__
   $\frac{1}{9}$ of 5391 is __?__

4. $\frac{1}{6}$ of 48 is __?__
   $\frac{1}{6}$ of 480 is __?__
   $\frac{1}{6}$ of 4800 is __?__

5. $\frac{1}{8}$ of 3200 is __?__
   $\frac{1}{8}$ of 3208 is __?__
   $\frac{1}{8}$ of 3192 is __?__

6. $\frac{1}{7}$ of 4900 is __?__
   $\frac{1}{7}$ of 4935 is __?__
   $\frac{1}{7}$ of 4893 is __?__

7. If $\frac{1}{6}$ of 4800 is 800, and if $\frac{1}{6}$ of 24 is 4, then $\frac{1}{6}$ of 4824 is __?__.

8. If $\frac{1}{9}$ of 5400 is 600, and if $\frac{1}{9}$ of 72 is 8, then $\frac{1}{9}$ of 5472 is __?__.

9. $\frac{1}{5}$ of 4500 is 900, so $\frac{1}{5}$ of 4490 is a little __?__ than __?__.

10. $\frac{1}{8}$ of 5600 is __?__, so $\frac{1}{8}$ of 5614 is a little __?__ than __?__.

11. $\frac{1}{7}$ of 6300 is __?__, so $\frac{1}{7}$ of 6290 is a little __?__ than __?__.

12. What is the largest number under 100 that can be divided by 9 without a remainder? by 8? by 7? by 6?

Copy, divide, and check:

	a	b	c	d	e
13.	6)83	7)45	8)58	9)84	7)65
14.	7)91	8)96	6)84	7)94	6)75
15.	8)94	7)88	6)90	6)83	8)90
16.	7)245	9)198	9)135	8)360	9)126
17.	9)205	6)167	7)438	6)279	9)428
18.	7)490	8)248	8)483	7)573	8)600
19.	3)$8.55	4)$7.52	6)$54.24	8)$15.04	7)$21.35
20.	5)$35.35	7)$50.40	4)$39.48	9)$85.50	6)$13.44

Three-place multipliers

1. Tom wanted to find 325×647. This is what he wrote:———————→ He said, "There are really three multiplications in this example." Why did he find 5×647? 20×647? 300×647?

```
                    647
                  × 325
    5 × 647 →     3235
   20 × 647 →    12940
  300 × 647 →  194100
  325 × 647 →  210,275
```

2. How did Tom get the 3235? the 12940? the 194100? the 210,275?

3. Tom's father found 325×647 this way:———————→ How is his way different from Tom's?

```
      647
    × 325
     3235
     1294
    1941
   210,275
```

4. See if you can find 325×647 in the two ways without looking at the boxes.

Study these multiplications. Then see if you can do them without looking at the book.

5.	6.	7.	8.
425	164	321	$5.72
647	289	460	389
2975	1476	19260	5148
1700	1312	1284	4576
2550	328	147,660	1716
274,975	47,396		$2,225.08

Multiply. Check by doing each example again.

	a	b	c	d	e	f
9.	414	298	184	463	624	$2.84
	287	375	536	784	823	289
10.	364	354	263	284	289	$4.10
	230	1200	3500	365	427	183

11. Multiply 741 by 72; by 20; by 240; 375; 130.

12. Multiply 869 by 83; by 40; by 360; 462; 500.

13. Multiply 276 by 47; by 60; by 280; 875; 260.

A PRIZE OF $1.00 to the child who can guess the number of peanuts in this window.
5¢ A GUESS
Money goes to the Playground Fund

Read all about the guessing contest that Mr. Allen set up in his shop window.

1. 297 children guessed the number of peanuts in the window. How much money did Mr. Allen collect for the guesses?

How much did he have left for the Playground Fund after he gave a prize to the winner?

2. Tom guessed 179 bags, with 354 peanuts in a bag. How many peanuts was that?

3. How many peanuts did each of these boys guess were in the window?

Joe: 98 bags, 145 in a bag.
Mike: 145 bags, 98 in a bag.

4. Here are the guesses of some other children. How many peanuts did each guess were in the window?

June: 250 bags, 272 in a bag.
John: 325 bags, 145 in a bag.
Martha: 300 bags, 175 in a bag.
Andrew: 168 bags, 183 in a bag.
Joseph: 194 bags, 98 in a bag.

5. There were 298 bags, with 180 peanuts in each bag. How many peanuts were in the window?

One of the children in Ex. 4 won the prize. Who was it?

6. Martha had $2.36. She won the prize in the Peanut-Guessing Contest. How much money did she have then?

Zero in tens place

1. Sue guessed that there were 206 bags of peanuts in the window, with 154 peanuts in each bag.

To find 206 × 154, she wrote:————→ How did she get the 924? the 30800? the answer 31,724?

```
      Sue        154
                × 206
  6 × 154 →       924
200 × 154 →     30 800
206 × 154 →     31,724
```

2. Now look at Dan's way of finding the answer to 206 × 154. Explain it.

3. Bill said, "Dan didn't need to write the 000. He could write one zero and then write the answer to 2 × 154 on the same line, the way I do. Let me show you."

Look at Bill's multiplication.

What do you think of Bill's idea? Explain each step of his work.

```
     Dan
       154
     × 206
       924
       000
     308
     31,724
```

4. The class voted that Sue's way of finding 206 × 154 was clearest and that Bill's way was shortest. How would you vote?

5. To check Bill's work, multiply 206 by 154. Do you get the same answer that Bill got?

```
     Bill
       154
     × 206
       924
     3080
     31,724
```

These multiplication examples have been done the short way. Copy them without the work. Then do them and see if your answers are correct.

6.		7.		8.		9.	
	876		791		432		865
	207		605		809		403
	6132		3955		3888		2595
	17520		47460		34560		34600
	181,332		478,555		349,488		348,595

10. Check Exs. 6–9 by doing these multiplications:

```
   207          605          809          403
   876          791          432          865
```

Practice in dividing

1. The Lee School Playground Committee wondered whether the lot behind the playground was large enough for a soccer field.

Fred said that he could tell by *stepping off* the distance. What did he mean?

2. Fred said, "My step is about a yard long. A soccer field should be 100 yards long." If the lot is 100 of Fred's steps, or more, will it be long enough?

3. Do you usually step a yard at a time?

4. Fred stepped off the lot. He said, "I made it in just 100 steps, but I think we should measure it with the 100-foot tape." Why?

5. The boys measured the lot. It was about 302 feet long.

Fred said, "We can have our 100-yard soccer field. There are 3 feet in 1 yard; in 302 feet there are as many yards as there are 3's in 302."

Explain each of these ways of dividing 302 by 3. Which way do you like better?

$$\begin{array}{r} 100\ r2 \\ 3\overline{)302} \end{array} \qquad \begin{array}{r} 100\ r2 \\ 3\overline{)302} \\ 300 \\ \hline 2 \end{array}$$

Do the divisions above show that there are exactly 100 yards in 302 feet?

6. 601 feet equals __?__ yards.

7. 306 feet equals __?__ yards.

Estimate, divide and check:

	a	b	c	d	e
8.	$4\overline{)803}$	$2\overline{)601}$	$3\overline{)602}$	$2\overline{)801}$	$3\overline{)902}$
9.	$6\overline{)2404}$	$7\overline{)4205}$	$8\overline{)4806}$	$9\overline{)6304}$	$7\overline{)2803}$
10.	$7\overline{)5697}$	$8\overline{)6432}$	$9\overline{)7563}$	$7\overline{)4903}$	$6\overline{)3722}$
11.	$8\overline{)\$64.05}$	$9\overline{)\$72.05}$	$7\overline{)\$63.91}$	$6\overline{)\$45.00}$	$8\overline{)\$48.02}$

12. A set of 6 books costs $12.05. What is the price of each book?

13. If 8 boys share equally the cost of a radio marked $16.72, how much should each boy pay?

How Far Can You Throw a Baseball?

This Week's Record (in feet)

	Monday	Tuesday	Wednesday	Thursday	Friday
Charlie	27	27	28	31	32
Donald	29	32	34	27	28
Jack	25	28	29	31	32
William	24	27	32	36	36

Records in throwing

1. How far did Charlie throw the baseball on Monday? on Tuesday? on each of the other days?

2. Charlie's average throw for the whole week was __?__ ft.

3. What was Donald's average throw for the whole week? Jack's? William's?

4. Did every boy improve his throwing distance during the week?

5. Was each boy's throwing distance greater on Friday than his average throwing distance?

6. Donald hurt his arm on Thursday. How does the record show this fact?

7. Estimate a distance of 30 feet. Then check your estimate.

8. See if you can throw a ball 30 feet.

9. Nick ran 50 yards in 10 seconds, or an average of __?__ yards a second.

10. If you know the distance you can run in a certain number of seconds, how do you find how far you can run in one second?

11. Prove that this statement is true:

The greater the distance you run in a second, the smaller will be the number of seconds it takes you to run 50 yd.

254

The Stars and Stripes

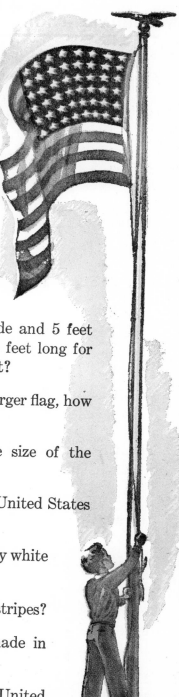

1. The Emerson School can get a flagpole that stands 20 feet above the ground for $17.60. The school can get one that stands 25 feet above the ground for $22.00.

What is the difference in the price of the two poles?

2. Try to think how tall a 20-foot pole would be. Can you name a man who is about 6 feet tall? A 20-foot pole would be more than _?_ times as tall as a 6-foot man.

3. A 25-foot pole would be about _?_ times as tall as a 6-foot man.

4. The school can get a nylon flag 3 feet wide and 5 feet long for $9.50. It can get one 4 feet wide and 6 feet long for $13.25. How much more does the larger flag cost?

5. If the school buys the taller pole and the larger flag, how much will both cost?

6. Draw on the blackboard a rectangle the size of the smaller flag; the larger flag.

7. How many stars are there on the flag of the United States of America? How are they arranged?

8. How many red stripes are there? How many white stripes? How many stripes in all?

9. What do the stars in the flag represent? the stripes?

10. The first flag of the United States was made in 1777. How many years ago was that?

11. A *century* is 100 years. Has the flag of the United States been in use for a century? for 2 centuries?

255

Counting change

When you shop, do you always count your change very carefully? In getting change from a dollar bill after spending 38¢, you should get 2 cents and think "40," get a dime and think "50," get a half dollar and think "one dollar."

Tell what coins you might get and what you would think in getting change after these purchases:

PURCHASE	AMOUNT GIVEN	PURCHASE	AMOUNT GIVEN	PURCHASE	AMOUNT GIVEN
1. $.38	$ .50	$ .84	$1.00	$1.21	$2.00
2. $.38	$1.00	$ .87	$1.00	$1.24	$5.00
3. $.21	$1.00	$1.01	$1.25	$2.53	$5.00
4. $.62	$1.00	$1.13	$1.20	$3.36	$5.00
5. $.71	$1.00	$1.18	$1.50	$3.02	$5.00

6. Name something you can buy in your neighborhood for about $1.00; for about $1.50; for about $5.00; for about $10.00.

7. Are baseball bats always the same price? Explain.

8. In one store croquet sets were marked: $7.95, $4.95, $3.45, $2.45, $1.89. What do you think was the reason for the different prices?

9. Can you tell of some things you bought, the amounts of money you gave the clerk, and the change you received?

10. To pay for a watermelon, Carol gave the clerk a 2-dollar bill. He gave her $1.01 change. How much did Carol pay for the watermelon?

11. To pay for $2.19 worth of groceries, Helen gave the clerk 3 dollar bills. She received 81¢ change. Was that the correct change?

12. If you had a 5-dollar bill changed into dimes, how many dimes would you get?

13. For a 2-dollar bill you could get _?_ nickels.

Some oral practice

1. How many 8's are there in 320? in 3200? in 3216? in 3192?

2. How many 9's are there in 900? in 927? in 945? in 963?

3. What will be the date a week from today?

4. Start at 100 and count backward by 9's; by 8's; by 7's.

5. Tell which is larger:
- four hundred six thousand
- four hundred thousand, six hundred, sixty.

6. James says he will not have a birthday in 1959. How could that be possible?

7. The answer to $30 \div 7$ is between 4 and 5, so the answer to $306 \div 7$ is between __?__ and __?__.

8. The answer to $50 \div 8$ is a little more than 6, so the answer to $500 \div 8$ is a little more than __?__.

9. Turn to page 11. Say the answers to the addition facts. Then think of the examples as multiplications, and say the answers.

10. Say the answers to the subtraction facts on page 21.

11. Say the answers to the division facts on page 168.

Some written practice

1. Add and check:
$18.76 + $27.09 + $6.97 + $76.88

2. $90.00 − __?__ = $27.56

3. Write in figures: seven hundred thousand, seventy.

4. Write the names of the months (abbreviations) in order, and the number of days in each.

5. How much change from a ten-dollar bill should you get when you spend $7.89?

6. Write the names of the days of the week, in order, beginning with Sunday.

7. What is the next number after 630 that can be divided by 9 without a remainder?

8. Write the missing numbers:

$2 \quad 1\frac{2}{3} \quad 1\frac{1}{3} \quad \underline{} \quad \frac{2}{3} \quad \underline{}$

9. Find the average of 72, 86, 94, and 32.

10. Divide 2435 by 7; by 8.

Addition tests

Add and check. Use folded paper in Tests I–IV.

▶ **TEST I**

1.	2 4	2.	4 6	3.	7 1	4.	5 7 9	5.	2 8
	6 0		8		7		3 6		6 4
	5 8		9		3 9		4 5		3 1
	3 9		7 2		1 4 6		6 2 8		5 0 0

▶ **TEST II**

1.	4 2	2.	3 7 6	3.	9 8 4	4.	7 3 2	5.	3 8 2
	1 7		9 0		3 6		1 6 4		7 0 6
	9 4		2 7		4 5		4 5 8		3 4
	3 5		1 3 5		8		1 0 3		5 8
	6 0		2 0 4		3 7 0		5 1 5		6 4 2

▶ **TEST III**

1.	2 0 9	2.	7 4	3.	7 0 3	4.	1 6	5.	3 4 8
	5 7 3		5 0 6		9 2		3 9 2		2 3
	4 1 8		7 3 8		8		5 4		5 6 7
	8 2 5		2 5 1		7		7 0 0		7 5 0
	1 9 0		4 0		3 2 6		8		6 8 4
	7 6 4		6 2		4 1		3 5		4 2 0 9

▶ **TEST IV**

1.	$4 2.7 3	2.	$4 1 5.2 7	3.	$8 6 4.7 2	4.	$7 9 3.8 7
	7 5.0 9		3 4.6 8		3 9.5 0		6 8.4 5
	3 8.6 4		7 2.3 4		7 2.7 5		3 7.5 6
	1 7.5 0		3 0 7.5 2		7 2 5.2 9		3.7 5
	2 6.3 8		6 0.4 0		4 5 3.6 8		9.8 9

▶ **TEST V**   *Copy, add, and check:*

1. $248 + $34.50 + $24.30 + $65.95

2. $32.50 + $79.86 + $85 + $346.82

3. $76.84 + $39.23 + $187.50 + $46.29

4. $78 + $32.50 + $.75

5. $.62 + $28 + $4.35

6. $2.83 + $75 + $12.75

A carpenter uses arithmetic

1. Tom is building a sandbox for his little brother. Look at the picture below. How wide is the sandbox? How long?

2. How many feet of board did Tom need for the 2 long sides together? for the 2 ends? for all 4 sides?

3. How long a board did he need for 1 seat? for 2 seats? How many feet of board did he need all together for sides and seats?

4. At 15¢ a foot, how much did all the boards cost?

5. How much will a half ton of sand cost at $3.50 a ton?

6. Tom's father says he can spend as much as $10.00 for the box and the sand. How much less than that will he spend?

7. Have you ever built anything? What was it? Can you show it to the class?

8. Tell the class about any needs you had for using arithmetic when you were building.

9. Why does a carpenter need to understand fractions?

10. Draw a picture on the board to show how many pegs 2½ inches long a carpenter could cut from a 10-inch strip of wood.

Practice in multiplying

Copy, multiply, and check by going over your work:

	a	b	c	d	e	f
1.	874	736	924	821	675	469
	308	503	704	806	402	107
2.	682	918	346	572	742	871
	507	907	607	708	609	705
3.	608	617	495	645	921	738
	753	901	506	706	308	604

How many of these multiplications can you do in fifteen minutes without a mistake?

4.	408	907	758	604	936	806
	879	634	609	159	704	587
5.	684	795	348	794	836	621
	70	20	40	70	30	50
6.	764	632	791	34	22	68
	90	800	600	4000	9000	8000

No pencils, please!

7. $100 \times 294 = 29,400$
$200 \times 294 = 58,800$ ← Look. Then tell whether 24,100 or 44,100 is a reasonable answer for 150×294.

8. $100 \times 463 = 46,300$
$200 \times 463 = 92,600$ ← Look. Then tell whether 57,875 or 89,675 is a reasonable answer for 125×463.

9. $200 \times 263 = 52,600$
$300 \times 263 = 78,900$ ← Look. Then tell whether 27,325 or 72,325 is a reasonable answer for 275×263.

10. $100 \times 256 = 25,600$
$200 \times 256 = 51,200$ ← Look. Then tell whether 28,840 or 48,640 is a reasonable answer for 190×256.

Put on your thinking cap

▶ Oral review

1. Can you name some things that sell by the foot? by the yard? by the pound? by the ton? by the quart? by the gallon?

2. Multiply each number below by 10; by 100; by 1000.

12   5   0   24   7   10   50

3. What numbers between 79 and 161 can be divided by 8 without a remainder?

4. You know the answer to $38 \div 7$ is between 5 and 6, so you know the answer to $380 \div 7$ is between __?__ and __?__.

5. Six dollars = 5 dollars, 9 dimes, and __?__ pennies.

6. What is the largest remainder you can have when you divide by 6? by 7? by 8? by 9?

7. Name each of these geometric figures:

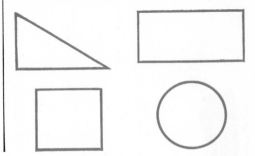

▶ Written review

1. Find the sum of:

689   72   604   46   75   96

2. Find $800 - 641$; $900 - 738$.

3. Multiply 387 by 506.

4. Divide 6329 by 8; by 9.

5. Find the average of:

40   37   28   28   23   30

6. Write these Roman numbers in figures:

XXIX   XIV   XXII   XXVI

7. How many pounds of sand are there in 3 tons?

8. At 5¢ each, how many tops can you buy for $2.25?

9. Dan bought a pair of shorts for $1.57, a sport shirt for $.69, and a pair of sneakers for $2.19. How much did his outfit cost?

10. Six boys are sending an order for swimming trunks at $1.98 a pair. How much will the six pairs cost?

261

Problem Test 7

a perfect score

1. Dan is making 3 bench seats from cedar posts. He needs 4 posts for each seat. At 3 for $2.00, how much will the posts cost?

2. A playground spent $9.49 for balls, $9.75 for bats, and $7.79 for mitts. How much did it spend all together?

3. Sue and Nan made a volleyball net. They used 18 balls of cord at 20¢ a ball. How much did the net cost?

4. The girls (Ex. 3) could have bought a ready-made net for $3.95. How much did they save by making it?

5. Joe spent $37.52 for materials for 4 picnic tables. What was the cost of each table?

6. A recipe calls for $\frac{1}{2}$ cup of sugar, half white, and half brown. How much white sugar is that? How much brown?

7. Joe practiced his music lesson 10 min. on Mon., 30 min. on Tues., 40 min. on Wed., and 40 min. on Thurs. That is an average of _?_ min. a day.

8. Prove that if the driver of this car obeys the speed limit, he cannot get to Greenville in 3 hours.

9. Five girls bought 3 victrola records at $.65 each. What was each girl's share of the cost?

10. How much change will Pete get from $10.00 if he spends $6.47?

Write your score on your Problem Test Record.

SPEED LIMIT
45 MILES AN HOUR

GREENVILLE
143 MILES

A practice page

Divide and check:

	a	b	c	d	e
1.	4)805	9)902	7)4906	8)2409	6)607
2.	7)578	9)567	5)490	8)699	6)517
3.	8)776	6)465	9)695	7)532	4)395
4.	7)$42.49	8)$69.44	6)$8.58	9)$72.36	8)$59.20

Subtract and check:

5.	5000 3786	7123 2894	$60.00 29.99	$68.08 27.39	$49.50 28.76

Multiply, and check by going over your work:

	a	b	c	d	e
6.	129 8	705 8	$4.12 8	$3.07 8	$8.25 8
7.	147 98	809 76	$6.40 67	$8.96 47	$7.69 38
8.	345 206	876 403	893 654	874 369	973 869

Add and check:

9.	789 87 568 97	798 657 586 790	$50.68 7.97 8.78 46.75	$89.67 78.76 96.88 76.97	$429.83 87.69 78.96 907.87
10.	683 29 470 56	864 97 301 194	$ 5.47 18.63 9.24 4.67	$43.24 9.86 2.47 83.25	$ 6.43 .85 29.72 104.50

What you have learned

1. Draw a square. To the right of the square draw a triangle. To the right of the triangle draw a rectangle.

2. What day is it today? What time of day is it now?

3. Billy needs new tires for his bike. How much will they cost at $2.49 each?

4. George bought a fielder's glove for $1.75, a catcher's mitt for $1.98, a mask for $1.85, a bat for $1.49, and a ball for $.79. How much did he spend in all?

5. Find the cost of four basketball goals at $6.60 each.

6. What is the cost of a dozen apples at 3 for 10¢?

7. How many pounds are there in $\frac{1}{4}$ T. of coal?

8. Norman bought 48 three-cent stamps. How much change should he get from two dollars?

9. Alfred wants to chain his boat to the dock. The chain costs 10¢ a foot. What else must he know in order to find the cost of the chain?

10. If you know the cost of six balls, to find the cost of one ball, you __?__.

11. How many six-cent balls can you get for two dollars?

12. Find the average of 85, 93, 84, 76, and 92.

13. Write the Roman numerals from XIX to XXV.

14. Add 3 to each number below; add 5; add 7.

52　　25　　17　　19　　26　　38　　43

15. Tell the missing numbers:

$2\frac{1}{2}$　$2\frac{3}{4}$　3　$3\frac{1}{4}$　__?__　$3\frac{3}{4}$　__?__

16.
- Think of some number.
- Multiply by 2.
- Multiply the result by 3.
- Then divide by 6.

Is your answer the same as the number with which you started? Can you tell why?

17. $8 \times 2 \times 3 \div 6 = $ __?__

18. $132 - 48 + 48 = $ __?__

19. Make an addition problem using the numbers 24 and 6.

20. Make a subtraction problem using the numbers 24 and 6.

Self-Help Test 11

1. 16
    284
    55
    300
    9
    287 (258)

2. $846.35
    278.46
    8.72
    75.86
    897.63
    85.78 (258)

3. $90.87
     − 87.64 (112)

4.   8,674
     − 6,983 (112)

5. Draw a circle. Now draw some lines on the circle to show that $\frac{2}{4} = \frac{1}{2}$. (202)

6. Find the average of 26, 34, and 57. (227)

7. A plane travels 420 miles in 3 hours. What is its average speed per hour? (185)

8. Write in figures: four hundred thousand, four. (208)

Self-Help Test 12

1.   706
    × 47 (223–224)

2.   964
    × 189 (250)

3.   852
    × 509 (252)

4. 56
    × 30 (129)

5.   722
    × 120 (250)

6. 345
    × 200 (222)

7. 10 × 24 (129)

8. 1000 × 30 (222)

9. 6)183 (135)

10. 7)2835 (249)

11. 9)907 (253)

12. 8)$9.76 (166)

13. How many nickels are there in $2.55? (247–248)

14. Find the cost of 2 dozen apples that are selling at 6 for 15¢. (198–199)

15. How much will 36 eight-cent bus tickets cost? (138)

16. Mary Lou made 6 beanbags out of 78 cents' worth of material. Each beanbag cost __?__ ¢. (107–109)

265

Now is the time to test yourself

Copy numbers correctly. Work carefully. Check your answers. Be sure your answers are sensible.

1. At seven cents apiece, how many goldfish can William get for a dollar?

2. It takes $1\frac{1}{4}$ yards of material to make a pair of shorts. Grace has only $\frac{3}{4}$ yard. How much more material does she need? Use this picture to help you, if you need to.

├── 1 YARD ──┤├── 1 YARD ──┤

3. The cost of repairs on four soccer balls was $4.08. What was the average cost of repair for each ball?

4. If there are 144 sheets of paper in each package, how many sheets are there in 104 packages?

5. How many yards are there in 902 feet?

6. Which of the following has the shape of a triangle?

a handkerchief   a dime
a bed sheet   a boat sail

7. Divide 503 by 5.

8. Multiply 288 by 430.

9. Multiply $3.78 by 267.

10. Multiply 624 by 408.

Just for fun

1. Peter says this is a Magic Square. Is it?

Find the sum of the numbers in each row; in each column.

Find the sum of the numbers on the blue arrow; on the orange arrow.

Do you find that all your sums are the same?

2. Can you use three 2's to write a number that has a value of 3?

19	26	3	10	17
25	7	9	16	18
6	8	15	22	24
12	14	21	23	5
13	20	27	4	11

266

Counting and adding fractions
Multiple fractional parts
Multiplying by mixed numbers
Four-place multiplicands

UNIT
39

Counting by fractional parts

1. Count by $\frac{1}{4}$'s from $\frac{1}{4}$ to 4; by $\frac{1}{2}$'s from $\frac{1}{2}$ to 5.

2. Count by $\frac{1}{3}$'s from $\frac{1}{3}$ to 4; by $\frac{1}{8}$'s from $\frac{1}{8}$ to 3.

Tell how the counting you did in Exs. 1–2 helps you add in these problems. Do not use a pencil.

3. Jane has $2\frac{1}{4}$ yd. of lace in one piece and $\frac{1}{4}$ yd. in another. In all, she has __?__ yd. of lace.

4. Bill bought a pound and a half of chocolate cookies and a half pound of vanilla cookies. All together he bought __?__ lb. of cookies.

5. Ann cut each of 2 small pies into 3 equal parts. She and 4 of her friends each ate a piece. In all, they ate __?__ pies.

6. John drew a line $2\frac{1}{2}$ in. long. Then he extended the line $\frac{1}{2}$ in. The line was then __?__ in. long.

7. Alice practiced her music $\frac{3}{4}$ hr. this morning and $\frac{1}{2}$ hr. this afternoon. She practiced __?__ hr. all together.

8. Draw a line $\frac{7}{8}$ in. long. Extend the line $\frac{1}{8}$ in. The line is now __?__ in. long.

9. Count backward by $\frac{1}{4}$'s from 3 to $\frac{1}{4}$.

10. Count backward by $\frac{1}{2}$'s from 5 to $\frac{1}{2}$.

Tell how the counting you did in Exs. 9–10 helps you subtract in these problems. Do not use a pencil.

11. Peter's mother sent him to the store for a pound of cheese. He bought a piece marked $\frac{3}{4}$ lb. The piece he bought weighed __?__ lb. less than the amount of cheese he was told to buy.

12. Mark had 3 cookies. He gave Tom $\frac{1}{2}$ of a cooky. Mark had __?__ cookies left.

13. Fred needs a piece of wire 4 inches long. He has a piece $3\frac{1}{4}$ inches long, but it is __?__ in. too short.

14. Fay is going to the store for $\frac{1}{2}$ lb. of potato chips. The chips come in bags, $\frac{1}{4}$ lb. to a bag. How many bags should she buy?

Tell the missing numbers:

15. 4 $3\frac{3}{4}$ __?__ $3\frac{1}{4}$ __?__ __?__ $2\frac{1}{2}$

16. 4 $3\frac{2}{3}$ $3\frac{1}{3}$ __?__ $2\frac{2}{3}$ __?__ 2

17. 6 $5\frac{1}{2}$ __?__ __?__ 4 __?__ 3

To the Teacher: See Note 5, page 310.

Picking up fractions

1. Cut a sheet of paper into 4 equal parts. Write $\frac{1}{4}$ on each of the parts of paper.

2. Pick up one fourth of the sheet of paper.
Pick up another fourth.
How many fourths have you picked up?

Does 1 fourth + 1 fourth = 2 fourths?
Does $\frac{1}{4} + \frac{1}{4} = \frac{2}{4}$?

3. Pick up another fourth of the paper. How many fourths have you picked up all together?

Does 1 fourth + 1 fourth + 1 fourth = 3 fourths?
Does $\frac{1}{4} + \frac{1}{4} + \frac{1}{4} = \frac{3}{4}$?

4. 2 fourths + 1 fourth = ___?___ fourths. $\frac{2}{4} + \frac{1}{4} = \frac{?}{4}$

5. Pick up another fourth of the paper. How many fourths have you now picked up all together?
Does 3 fourths + 1 fourth = 4 fourths? $\frac{3}{4} + \frac{1}{4} = \frac{?}{4}$

6. Does $\frac{4}{4}$ of the paper equal the whole sheet of paper?

7. Draw a line 3 inches long. Divide the line into 3 equal parts. Write $\frac{1}{3}$ above each part.

8. Show that:
1 third + 1 third = 2 thirds.
$$\frac{1}{3} + \frac{1}{3} = \frac{?}{3}$$

9. Show that:
2 thirds + 1 third = 3 thirds.
$$\frac{2}{3} + \frac{1}{3} = \frac{?}{3}$$

10. Does $\frac{3}{3}$ of the line equal the whole line?

11. Does
1 half + 1 half = 2 halves?
$$\frac{1}{2} + \frac{1}{2} = \frac{?}{2}$$

12. Does $\frac{2}{2}$ of a circle equal a whole circle?

13. Does $\frac{1}{4}$ of a pie + $\frac{3}{4}$ of a pie equal a whole pie?
Make a drawing to prove your answer.

14. Can you make up some examples of your own about adding fractions?

FLAG DAY
JUNE 14

The pupils in a cooking class plan to serve lemonade and cookies to the 200 children in the school at a Flag Day rally.

They plan to make a glass of lemonade for each person. For each glass they will need:

$\frac{1}{2}$ lemon
1 tablespoon sugar
1 glass ice water

1. If $\frac{1}{2}$ lemon is enough for 1 glass of lemonade, then 1 lemon is enough for _?_ glasses.

How many lemons will they need for 200 glasses?

2. How much will 100 lemons cost at 10 for a quarter?

3. There are 16 tablespoons of sugar in a pound. Will 13 pounds of sugar be enough for 200 glasses of lemonade? Look at their recipe above.

4. Find the cost of 13 pounds of sugar at 11¢ a pound.

5. They plan to have 2 cookies for each child. They will need to have _?_ cookies in all.

6. There are 25 cookies in a box. They decided to buy 16 boxes. Will that be enough?

7. Find the cost of 16 boxes of cookies at 20¢ a box.

8. They are buying 200 paper cups at one cent apiece. How much will the cups cost?

9. Can you find the total cost of the cookies, the lemonade, and the cups?

10. Have you ever made plans for a school party? What problems did you have? Tell the class about them.

Fractional parts of numbers

The boys in the Rover Club are learning how to do campfire cooking. They do their own shopping, check the bills, keep a record of how much they spend, and figure each boy's share of the cost.

1. The boys have to know such things as how to find the cost of $\frac{3}{4}$ pound of cottage cheese at 32¢ a pound.

Do you know how to find that? Try to discover a way before reading on.

▶ A pound of cheese costs 32¢.

▶ $\frac{1}{4}$ lb. costs $\frac{1}{4}$ of 32¢, or __?__ ¢.

▶ $\frac{3}{4}$ lb. costs 3 × 8¢, or 24¢.

2. To find the cost of $\frac{3}{4}$ pound of fish at 40¢ a pound, think, "$\frac{1}{4}$ pound will cost $\frac{1}{4}$ of 40¢, or __?__ ¢. $\frac{3}{4}$ pound will cost 3 × 10¢, or __?__ ¢."

3. Here are a dozen eggs divided into 6 equal groups. Each group is what part of a dozen eggs? One sixth of 12 eggs is __?__ eggs.

4. $\frac{1}{6}$ of 12 is 2. $\frac{2}{6}$ of 12 is 2 times 2, or __?__.

5. $\frac{3}{6}$ of 12 is 3 times 2, or __?__.

6. $\frac{4}{6}$ of 12 is __?__; $\frac{5}{6}$ of 12 is __?__.

	a	*b*	*c*
7.	1 yd. = __?__ in.	$\frac{1}{4}$ yd. = __?__ in.	$\frac{3}{4}$ yd. = __?__ in.
8.	1 hr. = __?__ min.	$\frac{1}{4}$ hr. = __?__ min.	$\frac{3}{4}$ hr. = __?__ min.
9.	1 lb. = __?__ oz.	$\frac{1}{4}$ lb. = __?__ oz.	$\frac{3}{4}$ lb. = __?__ oz.
10.	1 lb. = __?__ oz.	$\frac{1}{8}$ lb. = __?__ oz.	$\frac{3}{8}$ lb. = __?__ oz.
11.	1 ft. = __?__ in.	$\frac{1}{3}$ ft. = __?__ in.	$\frac{2}{3}$ ft. = __?__ in.
12.	1 ft. = __?__ in.	$\frac{1}{4}$ ft. = __?__ in.	$\frac{3}{4}$ ft. = __?__ in.
13.	1 doz. = __?__ things	$\frac{1}{3}$ doz. = __?__	$\frac{2}{3}$ doz. = __?__
14.	1 gal. = __?__ qt.	$\frac{1}{4}$ gal. = __?__ qt.	$\frac{3}{4}$ gal. = __?__ qt.
15.	1 dollar = __?__ ¢	$\frac{1}{4}$ dollar = __?__ ¢	$\frac{3}{4}$ dollar = __?__ ¢

Some oral practice

Tell these answers. Do all of Ex. 1. Then do all of Ex. 2, and so on.

	a	b	c	d
1.	$\frac{1}{5}$ of 45	$\frac{2}{5}$ of 45	$\frac{3}{5}$ of 45	$\frac{4}{5}$ of 45
2.	$\frac{1}{7}$ of 35	$\frac{3}{7}$ of 35	$\frac{5}{7}$ of 35	$\frac{6}{7}$ of 35
3.	$\frac{1}{8}$ of 48	$\frac{2}{8}$ of 48	$\frac{3}{8}$ of 48	$\frac{4}{8}$ of 48
4.	$\frac{5}{8}$ of 48	$\frac{6}{8}$ of 48	$\frac{7}{8}$ of 48	$\frac{8}{8}$ of 48
5.	$\frac{1}{6}$ of 42	$\frac{3}{6}$ of 42	$\frac{5}{6}$ of 42	$\frac{4}{6}$ of 42
6.	$\frac{1}{4}$ of 36	$\frac{2}{4}$ of 36	$\frac{3}{4}$ of 36	$\frac{4}{4}$ of 36
7.	$\frac{1}{9}$ of 72	$\frac{4}{9}$ of 72	$\frac{5}{9}$ of 72	$\frac{7}{9}$ of 72
8.	$\frac{1}{7}$ of 56	$\frac{5}{7}$ of 56	$\frac{3}{7}$ of 56	$\frac{2}{7}$ of 56
9.	$\frac{1}{10}$ of 100	$\frac{3}{10}$ of 100	$\frac{5}{10}$ of 100	$\frac{7}{10}$ of 100
10.	$\frac{6}{10}$ of 100	$\frac{4}{10}$ of 100	$\frac{8}{10}$ of 100	$\frac{9}{10}$ of 100

Some written practice

1. Find the cost of:

$\frac{2}{3}$ doz. eggs at 60¢ a doz. $\frac{7}{8}$ lb. candy at 80¢ a lb.

$\frac{3}{4}$ lb. meat at 72¢ a lb. $\frac{2}{3}$ yd. lace at 30¢ a yd.

	a	b	c
2.	$\frac{3}{4}$ yd. = __?__ in.	$\frac{7}{8}$ lb. = __?__ oz.	$\frac{2}{3}$ ft. = __?__ in.
3.	$\frac{3}{4}$ gal. = __?__ qt.	$\frac{3}{4}$ hr. = __?__ min.	$\frac{5}{6}$ yd. = __?__ in.

	a	b	c	d
4.	$\frac{7}{8}$ of 64	$\frac{5}{8}$ of 24	$\frac{2}{3}$ of 18	$\frac{3}{4}$ of 32
5.	$\frac{2}{3}$ of 12	$\frac{6}{8}$ of 40	$\frac{3}{4}$ of 40	$\frac{2}{3}$ of 27
6.	$\frac{3}{8}$ of 32	$\frac{3}{5}$ of 45	$\frac{2}{4}$ of 12	$\frac{7}{10}$ of 70

271

Problems in shopping

The boys in the Rover Club plan to bake beans in their campfire. They will need $2\frac{1}{2}$ pounds of beans. At 10¢ a pound, how much will the beans cost? Try to find out before reading further.

At 10¢ a pound, how much will 2 lb. of beans cost?
At 10¢ a pound, how much will $\frac{1}{2}$ lb. of beans cost?
Then how much will $2\frac{1}{2}$ lb. of beans cost?

1. At 10¢ a pound, how much would $3\frac{1}{2}$ lb. of beans cost? $4\frac{1}{2}$ lb.? $5\frac{1}{2}$ lb.? $6\frac{1}{2}$ lb.?

2. How much would $2\frac{3}{4}$ lb. of fish cost at 28¢ a pound? Try to find out without reading further.

$$2 \times 28¢ = 56¢$$
$$\tfrac{3}{4} \text{ of } 28¢ = 21¢$$
$$77¢$$

▶ At 28¢ a pound, the 2 pounds of fish will cost 2 times 28¢, or 56¢.

▶ At 28¢ a pound, $\frac{3}{4}$ pound will cost $\frac{3}{4}$ of 28¢, or 21¢.

▶ So $2\frac{3}{4}$ lb. will cost 56¢ + 21¢, or 77¢. Do you agree?

Find the cost of:

	a	b
3.	$1\frac{1}{4}$ lb. cookies at 40¢ a lb.	$2\frac{1}{2}$ yd. ribbon at 20¢ a yd.
4.	$2\frac{1}{2}$ lb. prunes at 24¢ a lb.	$8\frac{1}{4}$ ft. wire at 4¢ a ft.
5.	$3\frac{1}{4}$ lb. fish at 36¢ a lb.	$3\frac{5}{8}$ yd. muslin at 48¢ a yd.
6.	$2\frac{1}{2}$ lb. green peas at 20¢ a lb.	$4\frac{3}{8}$ yd. lace at 16¢ a yd.
7.	$2\frac{3}{8}$ lb. cheese at 32¢ a lb.	$3\frac{3}{4}$ gal. syrup at $1.20 a gal.
8.	$4\frac{3}{4}$ lb. bananas at 16¢ a lb.	$2\frac{7}{8}$ yd. rayon at 80¢ a yd.
9.	$1\frac{3}{4}$ lb. meat at 72¢ a lb.	$2\frac{3}{4}$ lb. meat at 72¢ a lb.
10.	$2\frac{7}{8}$ lb. cheese at 64¢ a lb.	$3\frac{1}{8}$ lb. cheese at 64¢ a lb.
11.	$3\frac{1}{4}$ yd. lace at 20¢ a yd.	$2\frac{3}{4}$ yd. lace at 20¢ a yd.

Checking grocery bills

Do you ever shop for groceries?   Appoint a committee to find out the prices of these things at your local grocery store:

A pound of butter   A pound of cheese   A dozen eggs
A pound of hot dogs   A quart of milk   A pound of apples

Use the committee's prices and find the cost of these groceries:

a	b	c
1. $\frac{1}{2}$ lb. butter	$\frac{1}{4}$ lb. cheese	$\frac{3}{4}$ doz. eggs
2. $1\frac{1}{2}$ lb. hot dogs	4 qt. milk	$2\frac{1}{2}$ lb. apples

3. If you gave a dollar for each of the things in Exs. 1 and 2, what coins should you get in change?   Tell how to count your change.

Find the cost of the following orders at your local grocery store:

a	b	c
4. 2 lb. cheese 2 qt. milk	1 lb. cheese $\frac{1}{2}$ lb. butter	$1\frac{1}{2}$ doz. eggs 3 lb. apples
5. 1 doz. eggs 1 qt. milk	$1\frac{1}{2}$ lb. butter $2\frac{1}{2}$ lb. hot dogs	5 lb. apples $\frac{1}{2}$ lb. butter
6. 2 lb. hot dogs $3\frac{1}{2}$ lb. apples $\frac{1}{2}$ lb. butter	$\frac{1}{4}$ lb. butter 2 qt. milk 4 lb. apples	$\frac{1}{4}$ lb. cheese 3 lb. apples $\frac{1}{2}$ lb. butter

7. At the Serve-Yourself Store where Carolyn shops, the clerk adds on a machine to find the total cost of the things bought.   Here are some of Carolyn's bills.   Check them.   A star marks the total cost.

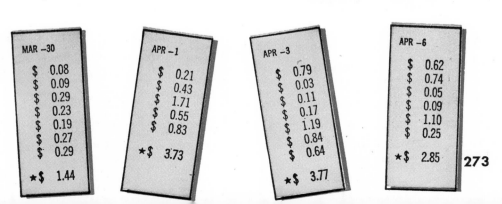

```
MAR —30        APR —1          APR —3          APR —6
$  0.08        $   0.21        $   0.79        $   0.62
$  0.09        $   0.43        $   0.03        $   0.74
$  0.29        $   1.71        $   0.11        $   0.05
$  0.23        $   0.55        $   0.17        $   0.09
$  0.19        $   0.83        $   1.19        $   1.10
$  0.27                        $   0.84        $   0.25
$  0.29       *$   3.73        $   0.64
                                              *$   2.85
*$   1.44                     *$   3.77
```

273

Campfire cooking

1. You can see the measuring cup the boys use for cooking. Tom said, "When we bake beans, we'll need $\frac{5}{8}$ cup of molasses." How could they measure $\frac{5}{8}$ of a cup?

Is $\frac{5}{8}$ more than $\frac{1}{2}$? $\frac{1}{2} = \frac{?}{8}$

Is $\frac{5}{8}$ less than $\frac{3}{4}$? $\frac{3}{4} = \frac{?}{8}$

How could they measure $\frac{3}{8}$ of a cup? $\frac{7}{8}$ of a cup?

2. The boys want to broil half a tomato for each boy.

How many tomatoes should they order for 2 boys? 4 boys? 8 boys? 10 boys? 20? 24?

Can you make a rule for finding how many tomatoes they should order for any number of boys?

3. They buy $\frac{1}{4}$ lb. of meat for each boy when they make meat balls.

How many pounds of meat should they order for 4 boys? for 8 boys? 12 boys? 16 boys? 20 boys? 21 boys? 22? 23? 24?

4. If the boys need $\frac{1}{2}$ pound of butter for pancakes and have only $\frac{1}{4}$ pound, how much more should they buy?

5. Paul got 3 one-dollar bills changed into quarters. How many quarters did he get?

6. If it takes $\frac{1}{2}$ hour to mix a pudding and $\frac{3}{4}$ hour to bake it, how long does it take in all? Use a clock to prove your answer.

7. If $\frac{1}{4}$ lb. of potato chips costs 18 cents, $\frac{1}{2}$ lb. costs __?__ cents.

274

Choosing correct answers

Four answers are given to each of the following questions. Only one answer is correct. Which one is it? No pencils!

1. What is the average of 12, 24, 18, and 30?   32   13   21   29

2. How many inches are there in $\frac{3}{4}$ yard?   18   9   12   27

3. Is the temperature in your room now about 60°, 90°, 70°, or 32°?

4. How many ounces are there in $\frac{1}{2}$ pound?   16   24   8   4

5. How many months have 31 days each?   8   4   7   1

6. $10 is worth how many dimes?   10   100   1,000   10,000

7. Which of these fractions equals $\frac{1}{2}$? $\frac{7}{8}$ $\frac{2}{4}$ $\frac{5}{6}$ $\frac{1}{3}$

8. What do you do to find the cost of several different things?
    add   subtract   multiply   divide

9. Would you estimate the length of this arithmetic book in inches, feet, yards, or miles?

10. What is the answer to this example? $8\overline{)7209}$
    91 r1   901 r1   910 r1   9001 r1

11. What is the change from a 5-dollar bill after a purchase of $3.77?
    $1.33 $2.33 $1.23 $2.23

12. How many minutes are there in 3 hours?   180   195   325   225

13. Jane's grandfather's farm is 2 hours away from her home by automobile. Which distance below tells about how far away in miles that is?
    16 miles   24 miles   74 miles   200 miles

14. Jim is 9 years old. Which of these probably shows his height?
    33 inches   4 feet 2 inches   72 inches   1 yard 1 inch

15. Which of these shows the number of inches in 3 feet?
    $12 + 3$ $12 \div 3$ $12 - 3$ 3×12

Multiplying a 4-place number

The Adams School wants to buy two of these sets of horizontal bars for its playground. Why are the bars at different heights?

$$\begin{array}{r} \$26.25 \\ \times\ 2 \\ \hline \$52.50 \end{array}$$

1. A set like this costs $26.25. How much would two sets cost? Can you find out without looking at the box?

2. Find the cost of two sets of horizontal bars at $24.75 a set; at $25.94 a set; at $27.49 a set.

3. Will 4 playground slides at $28.39 each cost more than $50? How much more?

Estimate and multiply. Check by going over your work.

	a	b	c	d
4.	3 × $24.93	6 × $30.05	5 × $15.96	6 × 1968
5.	4 × $65.82	7 × $19.58	8 × $28.48	7 × 3847
6.	7 × $12.09	8 × $47.37	8 × $67.26	8 × 9059
7.	9 × $18.47	9 × $29.58	6 × $30.47	6 × 4990

276

Making horizontal bars

John and his father thought they might save some money by buying the materials and making a set of horizontal bars for their back yard.

1. John found the lowest bar should be $4\frac{1}{2}$ ft. above the ground, the tallest bar 7 feet above the ground, and the other bar $5\frac{1}{2}$ feet above the ground. How is this shown in the diagram below?

2. He also found the uprights (the posts standing up) should be set into concrete 3 ft. below the ground. How is this shown in the diagram?

John says he needs $7\frac{1}{2}$ ft. of pipe for the shortest upright. Do you agree?

3. How many feet of pipe does he need for one of the tallest uprights? for the 2 tallest uprights?

4. How many feet of pipe are needed for the fourth upright? How many feet for all 4 uprights?

5. The three horizontal bars are each 4 feet long. How many feet of pipe are needed for the three horizontal bars? for the bars and the uprights together?

6. At $.28 a foot, find the cost of 48 feet of pipe.

7. The plumber is charging $10.00 to cut the pipe and connect it. How much will the pipe and the plumber's charge amount to?

If a ready-built set costs $26.25, how much will John save by making his own set for $23.44?

8. What information would you need to find how much it would cost to build horizontal bars in your back yard?

Learning how to shop

In shopping with her mother, Julia learned that many groceries come in different size packages at different prices.

In one store Julia and her mother saw these prices:

COCOA	SALAD DRESSING	BAKING POWDER
8-oz. box 25¢	$\frac{1}{2}$-pt. jar 27¢	4-oz. box 16¢
1-lb. box 47¢	1-pt. jar 50¢	8-oz. box 31¢
2-lb. box 89¢	1-qt. jar 94¢	1-lb. box 59¢

1. How much would they save by buying a 2-lb. box of cocoa instead of two 1-lb. boxes?

2. How much would they save by buying a 1-lb. box of cocoa instead of buying 1 lb. in 8-oz. boxes?

3. Julia's father said, "It is never cheaper to buy more of anything than you need, if it will spoil before you can use it." Will cocoa spoil if it stands around a long time?

4. How much would they save by buying a quart jar of salad dressing instead of buying a quart in pint jars?

5. Julia's brother, Larry, said they should not buy the quart jar because they did not need that much then.

Julia said they should buy the quart jar because they would need the salad dressing later.

With whom do you agree?

6. How much could they save by buying a 1-lb. box of baking powder instead of buying a pound in 4-oz. boxes?

7. Find ways to save money when shopping. Tell the class about them.

8. Find out whether it is cheaper where you live to buy milk by the pint or by the quart.

9. At the grocery store, what do you buy that comes in packages of different sizes?

What two things do you have to know about each package to figure out which package is the best buy?

10. Your class might like to find out the prices of the different size packages or bags of corn meal. Then you could figure out which size is the best buy.

How much would be saved by getting the best buy?

Multiplying mentally
Problems in grouping
Oral and written practice
Problems without numbers

UNIT
40

Mental arithmetic

1. Both Joe and his sister want bicycles. The kind they want costs $49.90.

To find the cost of the 2 bicycles, Joe thought, "2 × $50 is $100. But that is $.20 too much." How could he tell that? The answer is $100.00 − $.20, or __?__ .

2. To find 3 × $14.75, Joe thought, "3 × $15 is $_?_. But that is 3 × $.25, or __?__, too much." The answer is __?__.

3. To find 5 × $10.15, Joe thought, "5 × $10 is $_?_. But that is 5 × $.15, or __?__, too little." The answer is __?__.

4. Would you estimate the cost of 3 tennis nets at $6.98 each to be $21.06 or $20.94? Why?

5. Would you estimate the cost of 6 camp chairs at $4.90 each to be $29.40 or $30.60? Why?

6. Would you estimate the cost of 8 songbooks at $1.05 each to be $7.60 or $8.40? Why?

7. Would you estimate the cost of 5 records at $1.12 each to be $4.40 or $5.60? Why?

8. Joe figured in his head the cost of 4 pairs of shoes at $3.95 a pair. Can you?

Use Joe's method to find the answers to these multiplications:

	a	b	c	d
9.	3 × $9.98	3 × $29.95	3 × $49.75	6 × $99.25
10.	4 × $5.15	4 × $25.12	4 × $50.50	5 × $10.98
11.	5 × $19.10	5 × $20.25	5 × $498.00	8 × $3.25
12.	6 × $3.95	6 × $9.80	6 × $24.95	7 × $4.95
13.	7 × $2.98	7 × $99.98	7 × $998.00	8 × $24.95
14.	8 × $7.05	8 × $6.95	6 × $101.50	8 × $3.75
15.	9 × $1.98	9 × $2.04	7 × $200.15	9 × $2.98
16.	7 × $49.90	8 × $8.98	9 × $100.20	9 × $9.98

279

BUY YOUR TICKETS HERE

	EACH	
Merry-Go-Round	10¢	3 for 25¢
Roller Coaster	15¢	4 for 50¢
Whip	10¢	4 for 30¢
Shooting Gallery	20¢	3 for 50¢
The Old Mill	10¢	3 for 25¢
Skating Rink	25¢	3 for 70¢
Swimming Pool { Adults	40¢	
Children	25¢	

At the park

1. How much can you save by buying 3 Merry-Go-Round tickets at one time, instead of buying 3 tickets one at a time?

2. How much can you save by buying the other kinds of tickets in groups, instead of one at a time?

3. Harold bought 4 tickets for the Whip and 1 for the Old Mill. How much did he spend?

4. Mr. and Mrs. Stone bought swimming-pool tickets for themselves and their 3 children. How much did the tickets cost?

5. If you had 50¢ to spend for tickets, what kind of tickets would you buy?

6. What kind of tickets would you buy if you had a dollar to spend?

7. Tom bought 3 Merry-Go-Round tickets. Jerry bought 4 tickets for the Whip.

Tom traded one of his Merry-Go-Round tickets for one of Jerry's Whip tickets. Was that an even trade?

8. How many tickets for the Old Mill can Joy get for 50¢?

9. Ann, Marie, June, and Sally wanted to go to the skating rink.

Ann bought the 4 tickets. She spent __?__ ¢.

How much does each of the other girls owe Ann for a ticket?

10. Did the girls (Ex. 9) save anything by having Ann buy all the tickets at once? How much?

11. Miss Baldwin took the 24 children in her class to the park.

How much did it cost for all the children to ride on the Merry-Go-Round?

12. How much would it cost for all the children (Ex. 11) to ride on the Roller Coaster? on the Whip?

13. How much would it cost for all the children in Miss Baldwin's class to go to the shooting gallery? to go to The Old Mill? to go skating? to go swimming?

14. Miss Baldwin bought a dollar's worth of Roller Coaster tickets. How many tickets did she get?

15. Ted bought 6 tickets to the shooting gallery. Then he sold them for 20¢ each. How much did he earn?

16. Fred bought 4 tickets for Whip rides. He used one and sold the others for 10¢ each. Did he get a free ride?

281

Review practice

Tell the missing numbers:

	a	b	c
1.	16 qt. = __?__ gal.	½ T. = __?__ lb.	½ hr. = __?__ min.
2.	36 in. = __?__ yd.	¾ yd. = __?__ in.	⅜ lb. = __?__ oz.

Add. Tell the missing examples in each row.

3.
$$\begin{array}{cccccc} 14 & 24 & 34 & ? & 54 & ? \\ 3 & 3 & 3 & \cdot & 3 & \cdot \end{array}$$

4.
$$\begin{array}{cccccc} 27 & 37 & ? & 57 & ? & 77 \\ 5 & 5 & \cdot & 5 & \cdot & 5 \end{array}$$

Multiply, and check by going over your work:

	a	b	c	d	e
5.	923 70	462 80	593 60	714 90	685 40
6.	397 268	634 197	850 543	709 678	507 814
7.	943 206	768 407	594 508	638 903	827 104

Copy, add, and check:

8.	346 927 405 783 142	935 89 47 9 603	69 42 3 28 536	302 984 75 427 108	784 236 47 3 457

Copy, divide, and check:

9. $6\overline{)603}$ $9\overline{)8109}$ $8\overline{)753}$ $7\overline{)684}$ $5\overline{)395}$

10. $8\overline{)504}$ $7\overline{)329}$ $6\overline{)475}$ $9\overline{)684}$ $6\overline{)530}$

No pencils, please!

1. Name the days of the week in order.

2. Name the months of the year in order and tell the number of days in each month.

3. When the mercury in a thermometer rises, is it getting warmer or colder?

4. Name three things you can buy by the quart; by the pound.

5. $\frac{1}{4}$ of any thing is one of the _?_ equal parts into which the thing is divided.

6. Marshmallows are put up in $\frac{1}{4}$-pound packages.
How many packages are needed to make a pound?   to make $\frac{1}{2}$ lb.? to make $\frac{3}{4}$ lb.?

7. Find the cost of $\frac{1}{2}$ doz. cupcakes at 48¢ a dozen.

8. How many inches are there in $1\frac{1}{4}$ yd.?

9. Sam practices on his violin each day from 5:50 to 6:20. How many minutes does he practice each day?

10. Estimate the cost of 4 quarts of berries at 49¢ a quart.

11. Multiply each of these numbers by 2; by 10:

36   40   19   52   71

12. $7 + 8 + 3 + 4 + $ _?_ $ = 30$

13. Your change from two dollars after spending $1.63 might be _?_ pennies, _?_ dime, _?_ quarter.

14. The school bus is due at school at 8:30 A.M. each day. Today it arrived at 8:45. How many minutes late was it?

15. Begin with 4, multiply by 3, subtract 7, divide by 5. The answer is _?_.

16. Begin with 8, add 7, multiply by 3, divide by 9. The answer is _?_.

17. Is $\frac{1}{3} + \frac{1}{3}$ more than $\frac{1}{2}$?

18. Does $\frac{1}{4}$ of 24 equal the same number as $\frac{2}{8}$ of 24?   Why?

19. Which of these mean the same as $3\frac{1}{2}$?

$\frac{3}{2}$ $3.50 $\frac{5}{2}$ $3\frac{2}{4}$ $3\frac{4}{8}$

20. $7 \times 9 + $ _?_ $ = 70$

21. What number $\times 10 = 100$?

22. $5 \times$ what number $= 40$?

283

Some oral practice

Tell the missing numbers:

	a	b	c
1.	3 wk. = _?_ days	3 lb. = _?_ oz.	$\frac{1}{4}$ yd. = _?_ in.
2.	5 min. = _?_ sec.	1 mi. = _?_ ft.	$\frac{3}{4}$ hr. = _?_ min.
3.	4 yr. = _?_ mo.	$\frac{1}{2}$ yr. = _?_ mo.	$\frac{1}{2}$ gal. = _?_ qt.

	a	b	c	d	e
4.	$\frac{1}{4}$ of 36	$\frac{1}{3}$ of 48	$\frac{3}{8}$ of 16	$\frac{1}{5}$ of 60	$\frac{3}{4}$ of 24
5.	$\frac{3}{4}$ of 36	$\frac{1}{2}$ of 24	$\frac{3}{4}$ of 16	$\frac{1}{4}$ of 48	$\frac{4}{5}$ of 20
6.	$\frac{1}{9}$ of 72	$\frac{1}{6}$ of 72	$\frac{2}{5}$ of 40	$\frac{5}{6}$ of 18	$\frac{3}{4}$ of 48
7.	$\frac{5}{8}$ of 24	$\frac{1}{6}$ of 54	$\frac{3}{4}$ of 28	$\frac{4}{5}$ of 10	$\frac{2}{3}$ of 36
8.	$\frac{1}{5}$ of 45	$\frac{7}{8}$ of 40	$\frac{1}{2}$ of 30	$\frac{1}{4}$ of 36	$\frac{4}{5}$ of 40
9.	$\frac{2}{5}$ of 35	$\frac{5}{6}$ of 24	$\frac{3}{8}$ of 32	$\frac{3}{5}$ of 40	$\frac{5}{8}$ of 32

Some written practice

Copy, subtract, and check:

	a	b	c	d	e
1.	8743 4579	7930 7392	9400 8831	6395 925	7346 7292
2.	$46.50 39.90	$50.00 23.73	$69.09 35.89	$75.25 49.00	$84.49 19.25

Copy, divide, and check:

3. 6)3624	7)3598	8)6960	9)5603	7)3723
4. 4)3795	9)2487	8)6035	7)5715	9)8763
5. 8)6457	4)3367	7)2809	9)5402	5)4375
6. 2)$14.30	7)$25.69	7)$46.34	6)$45.30	3)2386

284

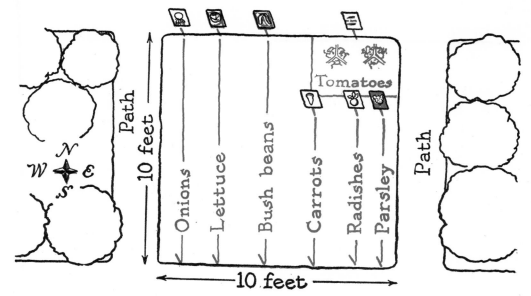

Garden plans

1. Above is the plan of Walter's garden. How long is it? How wide? What shape is it?

2. Walter knew he should lay out his garden with the rows running from north to south. How does his plan show that?

3. Walter paid 10¢ for the beans he planted and 10¢ for the onions. His two tomato plants cost 5¢ each.

He bought one package of each of the other seeds at 5¢ a package. Find the total cost of the things he planted.

4. Have you ever planted a garden? Tell the class how you did it. Make a drawing to show the plan of your garden.

5. Walter paid 5¢ for a package of radish seed.

He sold 6 bunches of radishes at 10¢ a bunch. How much did he make on his radishes?

6. Walter paid 5¢ for a package of carrot seed.

He sold 4 bunches of carrots at 14¢ a bunch. How much did he make on his carrots?

7. Walter sold also 5 bunches of parsley at 5¢ a bunch. Since his parsley seed cost 5¢, he made __?__ on the parsley.

8. Using your answers to Exs. 5–7, figure out how much Walter made in all on his radishes, carrots, and parsley.

Problems without numbers

1. James knows how much a tennis racket, a ball, tennis shoes, and a tennis net each cost.

To find the cost of all these things, he should __?__. (Add, subtract, multiply, or divide?)

2. Molly knows how many players are needed for a softball team. She knows how many children there are to play.

To find how many teams they can form, she should __?__.

3. Rose knows she lost some money on her way to school. She knows how much money she had when she left home. She knows how much money she had when she reached the school.

To find how much she lost, she should __?__.

4. Ethel knows how much money she has. She knows how much a bathing suit costs. To find how much more she needs to buy the suit, she should __?__.

5. Jack knows how many benches there are at the baseball lot. He knows how many persons can sit on each bench.

To find how many persons in all can be seated on benches, he should __?__.

6. Donna knows how many cakes were bought for a party. She knows what each cake cost. To find the cost of all the cakes, she should __?__.

7. Leon knows how much a box of doughnuts costs. He knows how many doughnuts are in the box. To find the cost of each doughnut, he should __?__.

8. Myrtle knows how many doughnuts she needs for a party. She knows how many doughnuts come in a box. To find how many boxes to buy, she should __?__.

9. Jim knows how many cards there are in a game. He knows how many boys are playing. To find how many cards to deal to each boy, he should __?__.

10. Jeff knows how many rooms there are in Franklin School. He saw a list showing how many pupils are in each room.

To find the total number of children in the school, do you think he should add or multiply? Why?

11. Ross knows how much the camp fee is for a week. To find how much it would cost to stay for 3 weeks, he should __?__.

Making up problems
Analyzing some number
relationships. Review
practice

UNIT
41

Problems about going to camp

1. Charlotte and Ellen are going to Camp Hiawatha for 8 weeks. They go to camp on July 1st.

On what date will camp be over? You may need to look at a calendar to find out.

2. The camp fee is $184 for the 8 weeks. How much is that per week? (*Per* week means by the week.) Is $23 per week more than $3 per day?

3. Here are some of the things Charlotte wants for camp. She has found out the prices and written them down. How much would all these things cost?

Flashlight bulbs	$ .40
Rubber cap	.50
Bathing slippers	.75
Swimming suit	2.98
Tennis shoes	2.29
Flashlight	1.19

4. Here are some of the clothes Ellen needs for camp. How much would all these things cost?

2 pairs shorts at $1.25 a pair
3 shirts at $.49 each
1 pair blue jeans at $1.49 a pair
1 pair saddle shoes at $3.95 a pair
1 sweater at $4.98

5. To pass their beginner's swimming test, the girls must be able to swim the length of the pool and back 3 times.

The pool is 36 feet long. How far do they have to swim to pass their beginner's test?

6. The girls get an honor badge for knowing 50 trees, 50 wild flowers, and 25 birds.

Charlotte knows 27 trees, 19 wild flowers, and 16 birds. How many more of each must she learn to win her badge?

287

True or false?

*Tell which of these answers are **true** and which are **false**:*

1. $10 \times 328 = 3280$ **7.** 2 lb. = 24 oz.   **13.** 1 yr. = 52 wk.

2. 60 sec. = 1 hr.   **8.** A.M. = afternoon   **14.** $43 - 19 = 24$

3. $\frac{1}{2}$ yr. = 6 mo.   **9.** $\frac{3}{4}$ of 32 = 27   **15.** $\frac{1}{2}$ doz. = 6

4. $1\frac{1}{2}$ ft. = 18 in.   **10.** $\frac{1}{3}$ is smaller than $\frac{1}{4}$ **16.** $1\frac{1}{2}$ yd. = 1 yd. 18 in.

5. 2000 lb. = 1 T.   **11.** $\frac{3}{4}$ hr. = 45 min.   **17.** 8 dimes = 1 dollar

6. 3 pt. = $1\frac{1}{2}$ qt.   **12.** $9 \times 8 = 72$ **18.** $\frac{1}{4}$ lb. = 16 oz.

How well can you figure?

In these examples be sure to check all your work.

1. $403 + 729 + 84 + 682 + 1,386$

2. $\$6.98 + \$15.50 + \$8.05 + \$105.10 + \$38.89$

	a	*b*	*c*	*d*
3.	6×9327	60×284	$38 \times \$.57$	$9 \times \$58.72$
4.	748×301	$63 \times 5¢$	$7 \times \$16.08$	$84 \times 15¢$

	a	*b*	*c*
5.	$\$60.00 - \$3.67$	$2,876 - 984$	$7,050 - 792$
6.	$4,392 - 1,839$	$9,000 - 824$	$5,768 - 2,009$

	a	*b*	*c*	*d*	*e*
7.	6)504	8)2432	6)3564	8)6480	7)3851
8.	7)413	9)3456	7)5328	4)3632	5)3870
9.	6)425	8)2782	6)2781	6)3795	8)3684

Some oral practice

What words or numbers belong in the blank spaces?

1. $97 - 25 = $ _?_

2. 803,602 is read _?_

3. $45 + 33 = $ _?_

4. $7 + 9 + 6 = $ _?_

5. $\frac{1}{7}$ of $42 = $ _?_

6. $\frac{3}{8}$ of $24 = $ _?_

7. 9:35 is _?_ min. of _?_

8. $1\frac{1}{2}$ lb. $= $ _?_ oz.

9. 3 ft. $= $ _?_ in.

10. $\frac{1}{2}$ yd. $= $ _?_ in.

11. 3 ft. 6 in. $= $ _?_ in.

12. $100 \times 42 = $ _?_

13. 2 gal. $= $ _?_ qt.

14. 1 day $= $ _?_ hr.

Some written practice

1.	2.	3.
248	925	892
753	74	326
80	589	45
906	56	84
79	131	7
826	207	830

4. Multiply 764 by 708.

5. Multiply 5646 by 9; by 7.

6. Divide 7564 by 9; by 8.

7. Divide 6432 by 8; by 7.

8. Subtract 746 from 5000.

9. From 9790 take 8904.

10. If a car goes at the rate of 35 miles an hour, how many miles does it go in 4 hours?

11. Find the cost of $2\frac{1}{2}$ doz. lemons at 50¢ a doz. and a pound of sugar at 11¢ a pound.

12. What will 3 dozen rubber balls at 10¢ each cost?

13. At 3 for a nickel, what will 12 balloons cost?

14. Find the cost of 25 six-cent pinwheels.

15. Find the average of 35, 38, 49, and 62.

16. Write the number that comes next after 49,599.

17. Draw a picture to show that $\frac{3}{6} = \frac{1}{2}$.

Making up problems

Complete each of the following sentences. Then make up an easy problem that shows what each sentence means. The problem for the first exercise is made up for you.

1. If you know the cost of two different dresses and want to know how much less one dress costs than the other, you should ___?___.

If a silk party dress costs $7.98 and a velvet party dress costs $8.50, how much less does the silk dress cost than the velvet dress?

2. To find the cost of any number of sections of track for an electric train when you know the cost of one section, you should ___?___.

3. To find the number of feet in a certain number of yards, you should ___?___.

4. To find the number of yards in a certain number of feet, you should ___?___.

5. Your share of the expense of a party depends upon the total party expense and the ___?___ of persons giving the party.

To find your share of the expense, you should ___?___.

6. If you know how much one movie ticket costs, to find the cost of 6 tickets you should ___?___.

7. If you know how much money you have and you wish to find how much more you need in order to buy a pair of skates, you should ___?___.

8. You know the cost of one pound of bananas. To find how many pounds you can buy for $1.00, you should ___?___.

9. You wish to share a number of peanuts equally with a certain number of boys. To find how many to give to each boy, you should ___?___.

10. If you know how many pretzels you had and how many are left now, to find how many you ate, you should ___?___.

11. To change any number of feet to inches, you should ___?___.

12. To change any number of inches to feet, you should ___?___.

13. To change any number of gallons to quarts, you should ___?___.

14. To change any number of pints to quarts, you should ___?___.

Interesting number ideas

1. Here are two interesting studies of the multiplication facts of nines. Can you explain why Table A works out the way it does?

What interesting relationships do you discover in Table B? What is the sum of the figures in each answer? How do the two answers joined by any one of the red lines differ?

A
$9 \times 1 = 10 - 1$
$9 \times 2 = 20 - 2$
$9 \times 3 = 30 - 3$
$9 \times 4 = 40 - 4$
$9 \times 5 = 50 - 5$
$9 \times 6 = 60 - 6$
$9 \times 7 = 70 - 7$
$9 \times 8 = 80 - 8$
$9 \times 9 = 90 - 9$
$9 \times 10 = 100 - 10$

B
$9 \times 1 = 9$
$9 \times 2 = 18$
$9 \times 3 = 27$
$9 \times 4 = 36$
$9 \times 5 = 45$
$9 \times 6 = 54$
$9 \times 7 = 63$
$9 \times 8 = 72$
$9 \times 9 = 81$
$9 \times 10 = 90$

2. Miss Allison gave her pupils the long addition example shown in the box at the right. Can you figure out how Mary found the sum? how Bill found the sum? Did they both get the same answer?

Mary	Bill	
463	463	
289	289	
743	743	1495
824	824	
962	962	
407	407	2193
28		3688
26		
34		
3688		

3. In the addition examples below, add as you usually do and check your answers by the method you usually use. Then check your answers by using either Mary's way of adding or Bill's way.

Be sure you understand both ways. Whose way do you like better?

a	b	c	d	e
275	563	608	285	67
438	284	974	956	764
653	706	315	93	98
409	983	880	697	931
750	975	639	475	502

291

Put on your thinking cap

▶ Oral review

1. What does A.M. mean? P.M.?

2. A sign at the bus station says that the 6:35 P.M. bus for Ardmore will be 15 minutes late in leaving. At what time will the bus leave?

3. How many hours are there between 8:00 A.M. and 1:00 P.M.? between 2:30 P.M. and 7:30 P.M.? between 3:45 P.M. and 6:00 P.M.? between 6:15 A.M. and 9:00 A.M.? between 7:00 A.M. and 7:00 P.M.? between 8:00 P.M. and 8:00 A.M.?

4. At what time do you go to bed? get up?
How many hours are you in bed each night?

Read these numbers. In each row tell which is the largest number; the smallest.

5. 723,967   500,460   303,303

6. 398,374   800,008   540,600

7. Add 7 to each of these numbers; add 8; add 9:

86   35   59   63   48   72

8. Multiply each of the numbers in Ex. 7 by 10; by 100.

9. $7 + 9 + 6 + 5 + 3 =$ _?_

10. $5 + 3 + 9 + 8 + 4 =$ _?_

11. $5 + 7 + 8 + 4 + 6 =$ _?_

12. $9 + 5 + 7 + 4 + 6 =$ _?_

13. Find $\frac{1}{8}$ of:

64   48   72   56   40   24   32

14. How much should you pay for a pound and a half of candy at 60¢ a pound? for $\frac{3}{4}$ lb. of nuts at 80¢ a pound?

15. Last week Jean weighed $58\frac{3}{4}$ lb. This week she weighs 59 lb. She has gained _?_ lb.

Estimate the answers to these examples:

16. $2 \times \$6.89$ $\$6.00 - \$4.75$

17. $2 \times \$3.78$ $\$12.00 - \$5.15$

18. Begin with 6, add 8, multiply by 4, divide by 2.

19. Find $\frac{3}{4}$ of:

12   16   24   28   36   32   40

20. Does $2814 \div 7 = 402$, or 42, or 420?

292

Put on your thinking cap

▶ Written review

Add and check:

1. 67	2. 447	3. 846	4. 7309	5. 270
93	271	73	463	3009
48	605	420	728	21
65	431	69	92	427
80	180	55	4526	994
84	725	327	830	716

6. Find the sum of $17.90, $7.49, $18.05, and $46.12.

7. Find the difference between $7.74 and $50.00.

8. How much more is $50.49 than $29.95?

Subtract and check:

9. 5634	10. 8302	11. 6070	12. 9003	13. 8526
2987	3438	93	125	39

Multiply. Check by going over your work.

14. 520	15. 652	16. 708	17. 4786	18. 748
57	94	706	4	64

Divide and check:

19. 9)7203   20. 8)6427   21. 7)5978   22. 6)4907

23. Bert helps his grandmother sell cookies. How much should he charge for one and one-half dozen large cookies at 50¢ a dozen?

24. Find the cost of $\frac{3}{4}$ yd. of calico at 48¢ a yard, and a 15-cent zipper.

25. Andrew saved 138 pennies. If he lays them on his desk in piles of 5, he will have __?__ piles of 5 pennies each and __?__ extra pennies.

26. If plums are selling at 8 for 25¢, will a dozen plums cost as much as 50¢?

Can you solve all of these?

1. Find the total of:

$7.89 $53.95 $.79 $204

2. How much larger is the population in a town of 4,000 people than in a town of 3,780 people?

3. For $2.25 you can get __?__ three-cent stamps.

4. Find the cost of $2\frac{1}{2}$ qt. of ice cream at 80¢ a qt., and a 45-cent cake.

5. Multiply 469 by 608.

6. Multiply 3842 by 8.

7. Find $\frac{1}{8}$ of 3240.

8. Find $\frac{5}{6}$ of 60.

9. At 2 for 5¢, how many balloons can you get for 25¢?

10. For a picnic lunch, some Girl Scouts bought 3 qt. of milk at 22¢ a qt. How much did they spend for the milk?

11. Write the date for a week from today; the date for two weeks from today.

12. Arrange these Roman numbers in order from the smallest to the largest:

XI   XXI   XIX   XXIV   IX

13. What should a clerk charge for $1\frac{1}{2}$ doz. eggs at 64¢ a doz. and a lb. of butter at 52¢ a lb.?

14. How many inches are there in $2\frac{1}{4}$ yards?

15. Martha received $10 for her birthday. She bought two new tires for her bicycle at $2.39 each. How much money did she have left?

16. Find the average of 86, 23, 62, 51, 48.

17. Oliver left the playground at 3:25 P.M. and reached home at 3:40. How long did it take him to walk home?

18. Draw a line $3\frac{3}{4}$ in. long.

19. Find the cost of 6 lassos at 39¢ each.

20. At 3 for 5¢, 9 popcorn balls will cost __?__.

21. Lucy had a pound of margarine. She used $\frac{1}{4}$ lb. for a chocolate cake and $\frac{1}{4}$ lb. for a corn pudding. How much margarine was left?

22. $\frac{3}{4}$ yd. of lace at 36¢ a yard will cost __?__ ¢.

Review of addition,
subtraction, multiplication,
and division. Problem
solving. Maintenance

UNIT

42

Fish Bait for Sale

FISHWORMS 10¢ doz.
SMALL FROGS 40¢ doz.
GRASSHOPPERS 15¢ doz.
MINNOWS 20¢ doz

Selling fish bait

Stanley and his chum sold fish bait last summer. Look at the sign on their roadside stand.

1. What kind of bait was cheapest? most expensive? How do you account for the difference in prices?

2. One day last summer they sold the following:

14 doz. worms   6 doz. minnows
2 doz. frogs   3 doz. grasshoppers

How much money did they take in that day?

3. Another day they sold:

2 doz. worms   9 doz. minnows
5 doz. frogs   8 doz. grasshoppers

How much money did they take in that day?

4. How much money did they get for $2\frac{1}{2}$ doz. frogs?

5. One day they had an order for $1\frac{1}{2}$ doz. worms and 2 doz. frogs. How much did they get for that order?

6. Sometimes the boys could have sold more bait than they had; so they decided to buy some bait from other boys. They paid:

8¢ a dozen for worms
30¢ a dozen for frogs
10¢ a dozen for grasshoppers
14¢ a dozen for minnows

Find how much profit they would make if they bought and sold the following:

1 doz. worms   1 doz. minnows
1 doz. frogs   1 doz. grasshoppers

7. Have you ever sold anything at a roadside stand? If so, tell the class about your sales.

Addition practice

Take the test on addition facts on page 11 today.

▶ PRACTICE SET I

1. Add 6 to each of these numbers: 29   36   43   55   67

2. Add 7 to each of these numbers: 84   93   78   65   56

3. Add 8 to each of these numbers: 87   76   58   49   60

4. Add 9 to each of these numbers: 22   76   39   64   88

5. Add 20 to each of these numbers: 32   45   56   60   73

6. Add 30 to each of these numbers: 16   28   35   63   82

7. Add 40 to each of these numbers: 13   35   47   53   69

▶ PRACTICE SET II

	a	b	c	d	e	f	g	h	i
1.	6	8	9	8	7	6	8	9	3
	7	5	7	9	8	9	6	5	8
	9	4	3	5	9	4	2	7	7
	3	2	6	7	3	8	9	4	9
2.	9	9	4	7	5	8	3	9	7
	9	4	8	3	9	7	8	7	8
	3	7	5	8	7	5	9	4	5
	7	5	6	4	2	0	6	6	9
	2	1	3	6	3	4	5	2	4
3.	7	9	8	6	4	5	3	6	8
	6	6	5	7	9	7	9	9	8
	4	3	2	3	6	9	0	3	5
	8	4	6	2	3	4	8	7	7
	3	7	4	8	7	6	4	5	4
	4	2	1	3	4	5	1	2	3

Addition practice

a	b	c	d	e	f
1. 94	58	79	324	736	892
37	72	20	609	94	300
56	43	35	783	62	76
40	69	48	265	428	8
85	51	54	832	507	47

a	b	c	d	e
2. 627	738	$14.50	$ 4.15	$302.65
491	274	7.23	23.10	47.49
373	165	10.67	9.89	25.23
846	507	8.08	7.50	400.50
538	320	.79	12.49	70.37
254	482	.25	3.01	63.82

a	b	c	d	e
3. 573	524	$15.60	$ 2.89	$802.75
289	36	2.80	12.76	28.63
463	289	3.98	5.37	29.84
276	74	.46	8.63	9.64
304	63	27.33	.75	543.20
768	987	.75	79.12	75.00

▶ PRACTICE SET IV   *Copy in columns, add, and check:*

1. $38 + 7 + 45 + 6$

2. $125 + 74 + 32 + 12$

3. $$1.54 + $.75 + $.32$

4. $$6.45 + $4.00 + $.38$

5. $$.75 + $6.24 + 4

6. $$2.38 + $.08 + 5.07

7. $79 + 268 + 75 + 483 + 72$

8. $56 + 79 + 286 + 9 + 463 + 75$

9. $$2.43 + $.43 + $5 + $3.47 + 6.25

10. $$10 + $2.75 + $.57 + $.83 + 5

11. $$.24 + $4 + $7.05 + $6.23 + $.27$

12. $$.75 + $2.49 + $6 + $8.74 + $.95$

Subtraction practice

Take the test on subtraction facts on page 21 today.

▶ PRACTICE SET I

	a	b	c	d	e	f
1.	447	937	703	928	718	953
	327	530	602	102	310	201
2.	1032	1648	1749	1347	1279	1712
	101	818	940	501	519	801
3.	1359	1286	1882	1079	1487	1678
	457	352	932	743	912	952

▶ PRACTICE SET II

1. From 700 subtract 374; subtract 285; 138; 463; 542.

2. From 934 subtract 468; subtract 579; 385; 697; 246.

3. From 8741 subtract 1692; subtract 5973; 4767; 7086.

▶ PRACTICE SET III

	a	b	c	d	e	f
1.	9734	8645	7346	6401	8560	7300
	4826	7589	6182	2379	3893	4812
2.	8672	9364	8936	7003	9400	7362
	8498	8896	7972	3905	8894	4859
3.	7630	8329	7635	6247	9984	8421
	6697	7290	7097	4009	8998	3652

▶ PRACTICE SET IV

1. From $5 subtract $1.89; subtract $2.45; $3.70; $4.04.

2. From $20 subtract $3.50; subtract $17.23; $8.05; $19.47.

Multiplication practice

Do all the examples on page 11 as multiplication facts.

▶ **PRACTICE SET I**

	a	b	c	d	e	f	g
1.	23 2	21 4	14 2	20 3	31 3	34 2	24 2
2.	71 2	50 7	92 4	83 3	61 5	31 7	60 8

▶ **PRACTICE SET II**

	a	b	c	d	e	f	g
1.	42 5	59 2	35 4	13 6	24 7	36 8	76 7
2.	12 9	85 5	63 7	54 8	86 4	45 3	98 9

▶ **PRACTICE SET III**

	a	b	c	d	e	f	g
1.	127 8	495 6	704 9	178 7	807 6	370 5	460 8
2.	470 4	627 6	796 3	639 9	809 8	860 2	750 6

▶ **PRACTICE SET IV**

	a	b	c	d	e	f	g
1.	40 61	85 19	18 41	39 57	64 83	72 26	53 67
2.	263 701	720 346	651 809	943 256	478 701	609 507	509 608

▶ **PRACTICE SET V**

1. Multiply $3.75 by 6; 7; 8; 9.   **2.** Multiply $18.50 by 7; 9; 8; 6.

Division practice

Take the test on division facts on page 168.

▶ PRACTICE SET I

	a	*b*	*c*	*d*	*e*
1.	7)150	4)144	3)197	8)270	6)195
2.	4)197	8)328	7)280	9)362	7)569
3.	6)439	7)632	8)563	6)102	9)819

▶ PRACTICE SET II

1.	4)850	3)736	2)593	5)855	6)936
2.	8)1837	7)2341	6)3742	9)5632	7)6642
3.	6)2756	8)3944	7)5031	8)2736	9)4962

▶ PRACTICE SET III

1.	7)4935	6)2940	8)3248	4)2836	5)3950
2.	3)2940	4)3212	7)4903	8)7440	6)4218
3.	4)1602	8)2563	9)5436	7)3714	8)4005

▶ PRACTICE SET IV

1. Divide $9.18 by 6; by 4; 3; 8; 7.
2. Divide $36.88 by 5; by 7; 9; 2; 6.
3. Divide $107.35 by 3; by 4; 5; 9; 6.

▶ PRACTICE SET V

1. $\frac{28}{5} = 28 \div 5 = \underline{\ ?\ }$
2. $\frac{37}{9} = 37 \div 9 = \underline{\ ?\ }$
3. $\frac{49}{6} = 49 \div 6 = \underline{\ ?\ }$

▶ PRACTICE SET VI

1. Find $\frac{1}{9}$ of: 78   89   116   204   684
2. Find $\frac{1}{7}$ of: 67   93   104   356   767
3. Find $\frac{1}{8}$ of: 79   84   157   346   467

▶ PRACTICE SET VII

1. $9 \times \underline{\ ?\ } = 279$
2. $\underline{\ ?\ } \times 8 = 456$
3. $7 \times \underline{\ ?\ } = 315$

300

Problem Test 8

1. Sammy wants to rope off a rectangle 8 ft. long and 6 ft. wide for a marble contest. How many feet of rope will he need? Draw a diagram.

2. Find the cost of $2\frac{3}{4}$ lb. of meat at 80¢ a pound.

3. How many weeks are there in 98 days?

4. A season ticket to a swimming pool costs $20. The season lasts 10 weeks. The ticket costs __?__ a week.

5. Grover says he earns an average of $1.25 a week. Could it be true that Grover sometimes earns in a week more than $1.25, sometimes less than $1.25, sometimes exactly $1.25?

6. Mary Lee weighed 57 lb. when she went to camp and 63 lb. when she came home. How much did she gain?

7. Al went fishing from 10 A.M. until noon and from 2 P.M. to 5 P.M. Look at the picture. How much did he pay for the boat?

Boats for Hire
25¢ an Hour

8. Find the cost of sixteen 3-dollar capes for the school band.

9. Jeff is going to Pineville for the day. The bus fare is 45¢ each way. How much money does he need for fare?

10. Which would be cheaper: strawberry plants at 8¢ each, or at $1.00 a dozen?

Write your score on your Problem Test Record.

Some fourth-grade problems

1. Mr. Norton gave Ted the money to buy circus tickets for the four members of the Norton family you see in the picture. How much money did Ted need?

2. David can add and check 3 addition examples in 5 min. How many can he do in 20 min.?

3. If popcorn sells for 56¢ a pound, what will $\frac{1}{4}$ pound cost?

4. How much change will Sam get from $2.00 when he buys $1\frac{1}{2}$ lb. of hamburger at 64¢ a lb.?

5. Six boys went camping for a week. Their expenses were $38.40, which they shared equally. What was each one's share?

6. How many feet of guard rail will be needed around a deep pool 10 ft. long and 8 ft. wide?

7. Helen bought a beach ball for $1.59 and gave the clerk a five-dollar bill. How much change should she have received?

8. Find the cost of two pairs of blue jeans marked $1.98 a pair.

9. If your classroom temperature is 70° and the temperature outside is 56°, how much warmer is it inside?

10. If the Newton fire engine travels at a rate of 60 miles an hour, can it reach Granville, which is 29 miles away, in about 15 min. or 30 min.?

Self-Help Test 13

1. Find the sum of $346 + 209 + 425 + 830 + 763.$ (187)

2. Find the sum of $\$12.49 + \$23.50 + \$70.25 + \$50.$ (187)

3. Find the difference between 769 and 830. (18)

4. How much more is 900 than 374? (18)

5. How much smaller is 3189 than 4062? (112)

6. $\begin{array}{r} 345 \\ \times\ 6 \end{array}$ (44)

7. $\begin{array}{r} 907 \\ \times\ 8 \end{array}$ (44)

8. $\begin{array}{r} 640 \\ \times\ 9 \end{array}$ (44)

9. $\begin{array}{r} \$53.05 \\ \times\ 7 \end{array}$ (276)

10. $\begin{array}{r} \$.25 \\ \times\ 78 \end{array}$ (130–131)

11. $\begin{array}{r} 436 \\ \times\ 392 \end{array}$ (250)

12. $\begin{array}{r} 582 \\ \times\ 706 \end{array}$ (252)

13. $\begin{array}{r} \$.87 \\ \times\ 200 \end{array}$ (222)

14. $\begin{array}{r} 475 \\ \times\ 67 \end{array}$ (223–224)

Self-Help Test 14

1. $8\overline{)99}$ (151)

2. $7\overline{)234}$ (127)

3. $9\overline{)279}$ (135)

4. $8\overline{)\$1.04}$ (133)

5. $6\overline{)\$8.50}$ (166)

6. $7\overline{)\$49.49}$ (167)

7. $7\overline{)362}$ (127)

8. $7\overline{)423}$ (135)

9. $4\overline{)1602}$ (249)

10. Find the average of 24, 32, 45, 53, and 61. (227)

11. Write these in Roman numerals: 8, 19, 23. (230–231)

12. Write in figures: two hundred thousand, four hundred thirty. (208)

13. Draw a square, a triangle, and a rectangle. (240)

14. Will next year be leap year? (178–179)

15. How many pounds are there in a ton? (192)

Now is the time to test yourself

Copy the numbers correctly. Work carefully. Check your answers. Be sure every answer is sensible.

1. $784 + 72 + 306 + 57 + 400$

2. $9)\overline{7634}$

3. 9632
  $- 897$

4.   840
  $\times 607$

5.   362
  $\times 40$

6. Find the cost of $\frac{3}{4}$ lb. of meat at 60¢ a pound, a 12-cent package of rolls, and an 18-cent can of tomato juice.

7. Write the next four numbers after 86,998.

8. How much will Joe have to pay for a dozen oranges if they are marked to sell at 4 for 10¢?

9. Traveling at the rate of 90 miles an hour, how far will a small passenger plane travel in $2\frac{1}{2}$ hours?

10. The lady who lives next door to Donald went away for the month of August.

She paid Donald 15¢ a day for taking care of her dog while she was gone. How much did she pay him in all?

Just for fun

Can you find 5 things wrong in this picture?

APPLES
10¢ A LB.
3 LB. FOR 35¢

FLOUR
$119
A BAG

45¢
A DOZ.

EGGS ONE DOZEN

APPLE JUICE
60¢ A GALL.

MILK
20¢ A PT.
11¢ A QT.

Making Help-Yourself Cards

You will find Help-Yourself Cards very useful in learning the number facts that you do not know.

(Front)

Suppose that one fact you need to learn is that 8 and 9 are 17. On the front of a card write the example, and on the back of the card write the example with the answer, as shown here. In the same way make a card for each other fact that you need to learn. The number facts are given on pages 306–309.

$$\begin{array}{r} 8 \\ 9 \\ \hline \end{array}$$

(Back)

To use the cards, look at the front of each card and try to say the answer quickly. If you cannot think of the right answer quickly, turn the card over, look at the answer, and try to remember it. If you did say the answer, turn the card over and see whether or not you said the right answer.

$$\begin{array}{r} 8 \\ 9 \\ \hline 17 \end{array}$$

Study the cards till you can go through the pack three times without a mistake.

To save copying examples

This picture shows you how to write your answers on folded paper, so as to save your copying the examples.

$$\textbf{1.}\quad \begin{array}{r} 5 \\ 6 \\ \hline \end{array} \qquad \begin{array}{r} 3 \\ 8 \\ \hline \end{array} \qquad \begin{array}{r} 7 \\ 5 \\ \hline \end{array} \qquad \begin{array}{r} 4 \\ 9 \\ \hline \end{array}$$

$$\textbf{2.}\quad \begin{array}{r} 7 \\ 3 \\ \hline \end{array} \qquad \begin{array}{r} 1 \\ 9 \\ \hline \end{array} \qquad \begin{array}{r} 4 \\ 5 \\ \hline \end{array} \qquad \begin{array}{r} 4 \\ 4 \\ \hline \end{array}$$

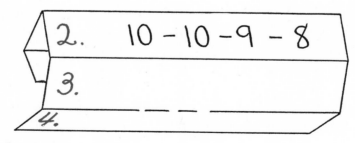

To the Teacher: See Note 6 on page 310.

The addition facts with answers

1 1 — 2	2 1 — 3	3 1 — 4	4 1 — 5	5 1 — 6	6 1 — 7	7 1 — 8	8 1 — 9	9 1 — 10
1 2 — 3	2 2 — 4	3 2 — 5	4 2 — 6	5 2 — 7	6 2 — 8	7 2 — 9	8 2 — 10	9 2 — 11
1 3 — 4	2 3 — 5	3 3 — 6	4 3 — 7	5 3 — 8	6 3 — 9	7 3 — 10	8 3 — 11	9 3 — 12
1 4 — 5	2 4 — 6	3 4 — 7	4 4 — 8	5 4 — 9	6 4 — 10	7 4 — 11	8 4 — 12	9 4 — 13
1 5 — 6	2 5 — 7	3 5 — 8	4 5 — 9	5 5 — 10	6 5 — 11	7 5 — 12	8 5 — 13	9 5 — 14
1 6 — 7	2 6 — 8	3 6 — 9	4 6 — 10	5 6 — 11	6 6 — 12	7 6 — 13	8 6 — 14	9 6 — 15
1 7 — 8	2 7 — 9	3 7 — 10	4 7 — 11	5 7 — 12	6 7 — 13	7 7 — 14	8 7 — 15	9 7 — 16
1 8 — 9	2 8 — 10	3 8 — 11	4 8 — 12	5 8 — 13	6 8 — 14	7 8 — 15	8 8 — 16	9 8 — 17
1 9 — 10	2 9 — 11	3 9 — 12	4 9 — 13	5 9 — 14	6 9 — 15	7 9 — 16	8 9 — 17	9 9 — 18

The subtraction facts with answers

2	3	4	5	6	7	8	9	10
1	1	1	1	1	1	1	1	1
1	2	3	4	5	6	7	8	9

3	4	5	6	7	8	9	10	11
2	2	2	2	2	2	2	2	2
1	2	3	4	5	6	7	8	9

4	5	6	7	8	9	10	11	12
3	3	3	3	3	3	3	3	3
1	2	3	4	5	6	7	8	9

5	6	7	8	9	10	11	12	13
4	4	4	4	4	4	4	4	4
1	2	3	4	5	6	7	8	9

6	7	8	9	10	11	12	13	14
5	5	5	5	5	5	5	5	5
1	2	3	4	5	6	7	8	9

7	8	9	10	11	12	13	14	15
6	6	6	6	6	6	6	6	6
1	2	3	4	5	6	7	8	9

8	9	10	11	12	13	14	15	16
7	7	7	7	7	7	7	7	7
1	2	3	4	5	6	7	8	9

9	10	11	12	13	14	15	16	17
8	8	8	8	8	8	8	8	8
1	2	3	4	5	6	7	8	9

10	11	12	13	14	15	16	17	18
9	9	9	9	9	9	9	9	9
1	2	3	4	5	6	7	8	9

The multiplication facts with answers

1	2	3	4	5	6	7	8	9
$\frac{1}{1}$	$\frac{1}{2}$	$\frac{1}{3}$	$\frac{1}{4}$	$\frac{1}{5}$	$\frac{1}{6}$	$\frac{1}{7}$	$\frac{1}{8}$	$\frac{1}{9}$

1	2	3	4	5	6	7	8	9
$\frac{2}{2}$	$\frac{2}{4}$	$\frac{2}{6}$	$\frac{2}{8}$	$\frac{2}{10}$	$\frac{2}{12}$	$\frac{2}{14}$	$\frac{2}{16}$	$\frac{2}{18}$

1	2	3	4	5	6	7	8	9
$\frac{3}{3}$	$\frac{3}{6}$	$\frac{3}{9}$	$\frac{3}{12}$	$\frac{3}{15}$	$\frac{3}{18}$	$\frac{3}{21}$	$\frac{3}{24}$	$\frac{3}{27}$

1	2	3	4	5	6	7	8	9
$\frac{4}{4}$	$\frac{4}{8}$	$\frac{4}{12}$	$\frac{4}{16}$	$\frac{4}{20}$	$\frac{4}{24}$	$\frac{4}{28}$	$\frac{4}{32}$	$\frac{4}{36}$

1	2	3	4	5	6	7	8	9
$\frac{5}{5}$	$\frac{5}{10}$	$\frac{5}{15}$	$\frac{5}{20}$	$\frac{5}{25}$	$\frac{5}{30}$	$\frac{5}{35}$	$\frac{5}{40}$	$\frac{5}{45}$

1	2	3	4	5	6	7	8	9
$\frac{6}{6}$	$\frac{6}{12}$	$\frac{6}{18}$	$\frac{6}{24}$	$\frac{6}{30}$	$\frac{6}{36}$	$\frac{6}{42}$	$\frac{6}{48}$	$\frac{6}{54}$

1	2	3	4	5	6	7	8	9
$\frac{7}{7}$	$\frac{7}{14}$	$\frac{7}{21}$	$\frac{7}{28}$	$\frac{7}{35}$	$\frac{7}{42}$	$\frac{7}{49}$	$\frac{7}{56}$	$\frac{7}{63}$

1	2	3	4	5	6	7	8	9
$\frac{8}{8}$	$\frac{8}{16}$	$\frac{8}{24}$	$\frac{8}{32}$	$\frac{8}{40}$	$\frac{8}{48}$	$\frac{8}{56}$	$\frac{8}{64}$	$\frac{8}{72}$

1	2	3	4	5	6	7	8	9
$\frac{9}{9}$	$\frac{9}{18}$	$\frac{9}{27}$	$\frac{9}{36}$	$\frac{9}{45}$	$\frac{9}{54}$	$\frac{9}{63}$	$\frac{9}{72}$	$\frac{9}{81}$

The division facts with answers

$1 \over 1)\overline{1}$	$2 \over 1)\overline{2}$	$3 \over 1)\overline{3}$	$4 \over 1)\overline{4}$	$5 \over 1)\overline{5}$	$6 \over 1)\overline{6}$	$7 \over 1)\overline{7}$	$8 \over 1)\overline{8}$	$9 \over 1)\overline{9}$
$1 \over 2)\overline{2}$	$2 \over 2)\overline{4}$	$3 \over 2)\overline{6}$	$4 \over 2)\overline{8}$	$5 \over 2)\overline{10}$	$6 \over 2)\overline{12}$	$7 \over 2)\overline{14}$	$8 \over 2)\overline{16}$	$9 \over 2)\overline{18}$
$1 \over 3)\overline{3}$	$2 \over 3)\overline{6}$	$3 \over 3)\overline{9}$	$4 \over 3)\overline{12}$	$5 \over 3)\overline{15}$	$6 \over 3)\overline{18}$	$7 \over 3)\overline{21}$	$8 \over 3)\overline{24}$	$9 \over 3)\overline{27}$
$1 \over 4)\overline{4}$	$2 \over 4)\overline{8}$	$3 \over 4)\overline{12}$	$4 \over 4)\overline{16}$	$5 \over 4)\overline{20}$	$6 \over 4)\overline{24}$	$7 \over 4)\overline{28}$	$8 \over 4)\overline{32}$	$9 \over 4)\overline{36}$
$1 \over 5)\overline{5}$	$2 \over 5)\overline{10}$	$3 \over 5)\overline{15}$	$4 \over 5)\overline{20}$	$5 \over 5)\overline{25}$	$6 \over 5)\overline{30}$	$7 \over 5)\overline{35}$	$8 \over 5)\overline{40}$	$9 \over 5)\overline{45}$
$1 \over 6)\overline{6}$	$2 \over 6)\overline{12}$	$3 \over 6)\overline{18}$	$4 \over 6)\overline{24}$	$5 \over 6)\overline{30}$	$6 \over 6)\overline{36}$	$7 \over 6)\overline{42}$	$8 \over 6)\overline{48}$	$9 \over 6)\overline{54}$
$1 \over 7)\overline{7}$	$2 \over 7)\overline{14}$	$3 \over 7)\overline{21}$	$4 \over 7)\overline{28}$	$5 \over 7)\overline{35}$	$6 \over 7)\overline{42}$	$7 \over 7)\overline{49}$	$8 \over 7)\overline{56}$	$9 \over 7)\overline{63}$
$1 \over 8)\overline{8}$	$2 \over 8)\overline{16}$	$3 \over 8)\overline{24}$	$4 \over 8)\overline{32}$	$5 \over 8)\overline{40}$	$6 \over 8)\overline{48}$	$7 \over 8)\overline{56}$	$8 \over 8)\overline{64}$	$9 \over 8)\overline{72}$
$1 \over 9)\overline{9}$	$2 \over 9)\overline{18}$	$3 \over 9)\overline{27}$	$4 \over 9)\overline{36}$	$5 \over 9)\overline{45}$	$6 \over 9)\overline{54}$	$7 \over 9)\overline{63}$	$8 \over 9)\overline{72}$	$9 \over 9)\overline{81}$

To the Teacher

This series is planned to develop progressively the important concepts, relationships, and computational skills needed in arithmetic. In doing this, the books of the series organize the learning into a meaningful system of related ideas; they make maximum use of children's needs for number; and they provide the practice, self-diagnosis, and remedial work required to make learning permanent. Most careful attention has been given to the problem of reading for understanding. The books are the outcome of years of research and classroom experience.

For the textbook for each grade there is available a *Teacher's Guide*. The *Guide* contains concrete suggestions for making the learning of arithmetic meaningful and interesting. It provides helps for utilizing the textbook material most effectively. It also gives a concise statement of the authors' philosophy and psychology of teaching the subject.

NOTE 1 (*Page 67*). On pages 67, 153, and 220, entitled "Be your own teacher," are exercises designed to help children realize that they can without teacher or book guidance think out for themselves solutions to arithmetic situations that are new to them. Pupils will of course use a great variety of methods of solving the problems. Seldom will they use conventional methods. These pages will be welcomed by the teacher who wishes to challenge her more able pupils to do independent, creative, quantitative thinking. The solutions offered should be compared and evaluated by the participating pupils. Do not attempt to teach conventional methods.

NOTE 2 (*Page 75*). When pupils are using small divisors (5 or less) in divisions which do not require carrying, teachers have found that the *short* form of division is preferable to the *long* form. See beginning of use of long form on page 98.

NOTE 3 (*Page 102*). Pages 102–108 present a meaningful, sensible method of dividing by one-place divisors. Proceed slowly and thoughtfully through these pages, encouraging the pupils to think through each division rather than to follow a set pattern of computation. These pages give drill in thinking. On page 109 the conventional method of dividing is introduced. When the pupils arrive at this point they will have the necessary background for understanding and performing divisions of this type. You may wish to have the pupils occasionally review pages 102–108, in order to keep their work in division meaningful and sensible.

NOTE 4 (*Page 117*). In these Just for Fun exercises the operations are to be performed in the order of appearance of the signs. In later grades pupils will learn that the order of operations accepted by mathematicians requires that multiplications and divisions should be performed before additions and subtractions, but fourth-grade pupils need not be concerned with that convention.

NOTE 5 (*Page 267*). Do not introduce at this time conventional forms for adding and subtracting fractions.

NOTE 6 (*Page 305*). Sets of Help-Yourself Cards in the four fundamentals, called *Modern-School Individual Number Cards*, may be purchased from World Book Company.

IN APPRECIATION

The authors are indebted to Mrs. John R. Clark, Miss Ruth Baldwin, and Miss Monica Hoye, as well as to numerous teachers and elementary school pupils.

310

Tables of measurement

Length

12 inches (in.) = **1 foot (ft.)**
3 feet = **36 inches** = **1 yard (yd.)**
$5\frac{1}{2}$ **yards** = $16\frac{1}{2}$ **feet** = **1 rod (rd.)**
320 rods = **5280 feet** = **1 mile (mi.)**

Weight

16 ounces (oz.) = **1 pound (lb.)**
100 pounds = **1 hundredweight (cwt.)**
2000 pounds = **1 ton (T.)**

Time

60 seconds (sec.) = **1 minute (min.)**
60 minutes = **1 hour (hr.)**
24 hours = **1 day (da.)**
7 days = **1 week (wk.)**
30 days = **1 month (mo.)**
12 months = **1 year (yr.)**
52 weeks = **1 year**
365 days = **1 year**
366 days = **1 leap year**
100 years = **1 century**

Liquid Measure

2 cups = **1 pint (pt.)**
2 pints (pt.) = **1 quart (qt.)**
4 quarts = **1 gallon (gal.)**

Index